Praise for

DOMINION

Named a Best Book of the Year by *The Globe and Mail*,
History Today and *The Hill Times*

"This model popular history offers Canadians a coherent but unillusioned narrative about how their state came to be, which emphasizes the ruthlessness as well as the ambition of its architects."

—*History Today*

"The development of the railway has been celebrated for decades, but it's essential to note that while many people gained because of it, many others lost. This reckoning is overdue. Bown's work will ensure that the birth of the CPR will be seen in a new light."

—*Victoria Times Colonist*

"In *Dominion*, Bown ... [gives] readers an expanded social context for the period as well as other new revelations. . . . While there were gains which must be acknowledged, the losses fell on those least able to bear them."

—*Winnipeg Free Press*

"With impeccable detail and captivating narrative, Bown tells of the technological advances and the dark deals that were instrumental in the CPR's construction, as well as the famine and disease that traveled across the country as the rails were laid."

—Tony Chapman, host of *Chatter that Matters*

Praise for

STEPHEN R. BOWN

"*The Company* is compelling, both as a lively narrative about a corporation that helped shape North American development and as a thoughtful exploration of the complex Indigenous cultures that once dominated the continent."　　　　　—Charlotte Gray, *The Wall Street Journal*

"Bown is a meticulous researcher and a gripping storyteller."
　　　　　　　　　　　　　　　　—*Canadian Geographic* on *Scurvy*

"Fascinating.... As a depiction of an explorer's life it is intelligent and often thrilling."　　　　　—*The Sunday Times* on *The Last Viking*

"[A] thrilling must-be-read-at-one-sitting page-turner."
　　　　　　　　—*The Washington Times* on *A Most Damnable Invention*

"Magnificent."　　—*Publishers Weekly* on *Merchant Kings*, starred review

STEPHEN R. BOWN

DOMINION

THE RAILWAY
AND THE RISE OF CANADA

ANCHOR
CANADA

Library and Archives Canada Cataloguing in Publication
Title: Dominion : the railway and the rise of Canada / Stephen Bown.
Names: Bown, Stephen R., author.
Description: Previously published in 2023. | Includes bibliographical references and index.
Identifiers: Canadiana 20230207537 | ISBN 9780385698740 (softcover)
Subjects: LCSH: Canadian Pacific Railway Company—History—19th century. | LCSH: Railroads—Canada—Design and construction—History—19th century. | LCSH: Railroads—Canada—History—19th century. | LCSH: Canada—History—1867-1914.
Classification: LCC HE2810.C2 B69 2024 | DDC 385.0971—dc23

Cover design by Andrew Roberts
Cover image: *The Fraser Canyon, Cascade Mountain range, British Columbia. View from the Canadian Pacific Railway.* 1892. Wallace B. Chung and Madeline H. Chung Collection, Rare Books and Special Collections, University of British Columbia Library, CC-OS-00176.
Maps by Andrew Roberts
Map on page vii referenced from *The National Dream: The Great Railway 1871–1881* by Pierre Berton, copyright © 1970, 2001 by Pierre Berton Enterprises Ltd. Published by Anchor Canada, a division of Penguin Random House Canada Limited.
Maps on pages viii, ix, xi, and xii referenced from *The Last Spike: The Great Railway 1881–1885* by Pierre Berton, copyright © 1971, 2001 by Pierre Berton Enterprises Ltd. Published by Anchor Canada, a division of Penguin Random House Canada Limited.
Map on page x based on *Map of Numbered Treaties of Canada*, courtesy of Wikimedia Commons.
Typeset by Terra Page

Printed in Canada

Published in Canada by Anchor Canada,
a division of Penguin Random House Canada Limited,
a Penguin Random House Company

www.penguinrandomhouse.ca

10 9 8 7 6 5 4 3 2 1

Penguin
Random House
ANCHOR CANADA

CONTENTS

———

PART THREE: **THE REALITY**

PART FOUR:
THE CONSTRUCTION

Canada Before the C.P.R. (1871)

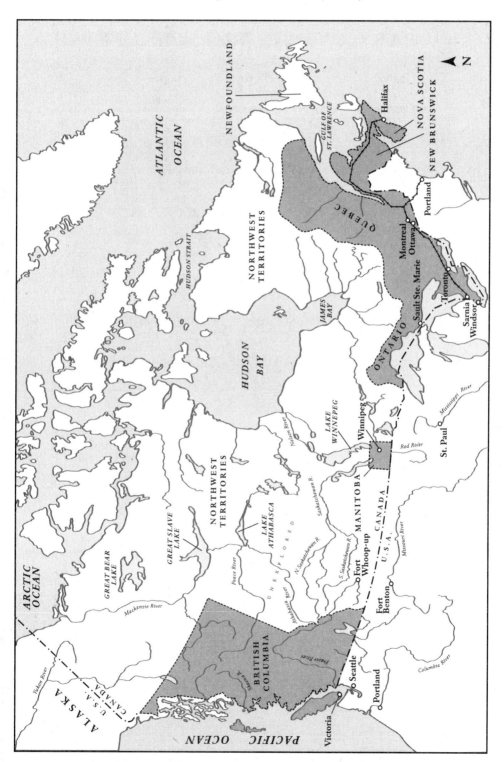

Sandford Fleming's 1872 Survey and the 1881 Change of Route

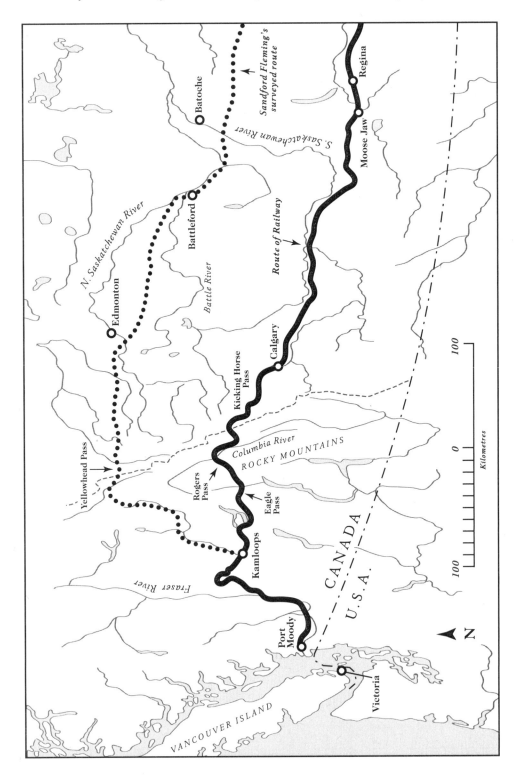

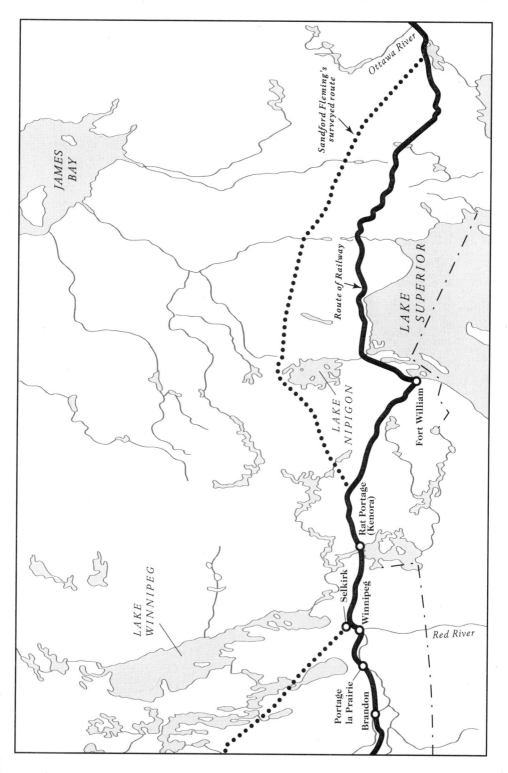

The Numbered Treaties

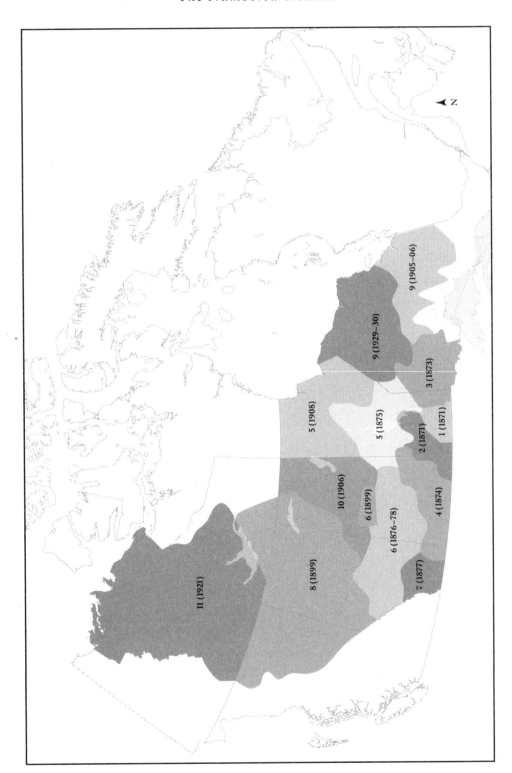

The Onderdonk Contracts and the Fraser Canyon

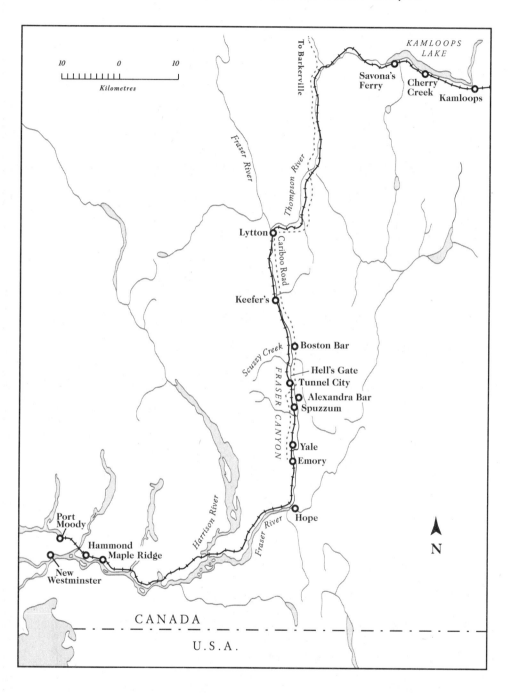

Kilometres

10   0   10

KAMLOOPS LAKE

To Barkerville

Savona's Ferry

Cherry Creek

Kamloops

Fraser River

Thompson River

Lytton

Cariboo Road

Keefer's

Scuzzy Creek

Boston Bar

Hell's Gate

Tunnel City

Alexandra Bar

Spuzzum

FRASER CANYON

Yale

Emory

Hope

Port Moody

Hammond

Maple Ridge

New Westminster

Harrison River

Fraser River

N

CANADA

U.S.A.

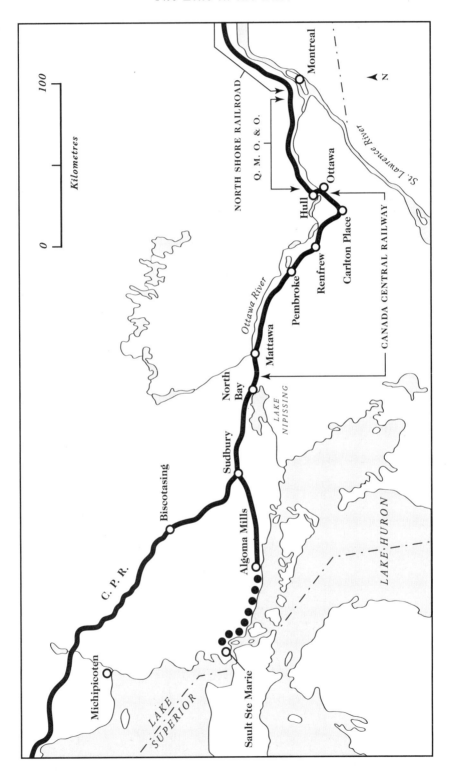

THE RISE OF THE CANADIAN EMPIRE

———

The Canadian Pacific Railway was Canada's first and greatest megaproject, a political and engineering feat of staggering dimension, with over four thousand kilometres of track, much of it driven through terrain unsuitable for railways. At the time, it was the longest and most difficult railway ever built. The CPR was a great triumph of imagination, vision, politics and engineering, as well as a horrible environmental and social tragedy. The railway presaged a soaring immigrant population and titanic economic expansion and stymied the U.S. dominance of North America by enabling Canada's consolidation. But it also enabled the often-cruel repression of the land's original inhabitants and the exploitation of thousands of labourers. To understand the CPR, one must keep that dichotomy in mind.

By the late nineteenth century, the fur trade was in decline. After two centuries adorning the pinnacle of high society, the exalted beaver hat was toppled from its pre-eminence and replaced with something equally frivolous—the silk hat. Beavers from North America were out and silkworms from China were in. This could have spelled economic disaster for the venerable Hudson's Bay Company, which had managed the economy of Rupert's Land and the Pacific slope from its headquarters in London and Montreal for two hundred years, but new opportunities presented themselves.

Long antagonistic toward settlement to preserve the fur business, the company now saw its future in actively supporting and encouraging settlers, and, as the only commercial outlet with entrenched forts and trading outposts on all the major river systems that were then the only transportation routes, it was uniquely positioned to take advantage of the new and evolving situation. The company began running steam-powered paddlewheelers on parts of the Red and Saskatchewan Rivers. But a major logistical problem hindered its activities: there was no practical route from the eastern Canadas to the new settlements developing along these rivers. Lake Superior was turbulent and difficult to navigate, and the land route north of it was nearly impassable to anything other than canoes and porters on portages. The rugged rocks of the lake's north shore made it nearly impossible to build a road there. The new region of commercial enterprise along the Red River was being serviced by paddlewheelers from the American territory of Minnesota, even after the entirety of the HBC's old haunts became part of the new country of Canada in 1870. It was clear this territory wouldn't long remain under Canada's control without a means for the eastern settlements along the St. Lawrence River to reach it without having to travel through the United States.

To the west of the Rocky Mountains lay the British colony of British Columbia. An idea emerged in political and business circles in Ottawa and Montreal to connect the disparate British colonies in North America into a single entity that would stretch from the Atlantic to the Pacific, much as the United States had done a generation earlier. To many, the idea of connecting the British Pacific colonies to Canada and creating a new dominion, while keeping the capital in Ottawa, would be a brilliant and profitable undertaking. It would create an economic hinterland that could provide a ready-made source of consumers to bolster the output from the moribund factories of the East. The former Rupert's Land could be settled with immigrants, who would provide a captive market for eastern manufactured goods. But creating a true empire would require a connection between the political jurisdictions to enable travel and economic development and a shared political culture with mutually beneficial objectives.

The mid- to late nineteenth century was the era of the railway: in Europe, where the technology was developed, and then in the U.S., where tens of thousands of kilometres of tracks were rapidly laid, including the first transcontinental railway, completed in 1869. In our era, it is the digital economy that gets all the attention, but in the late nineteenth century a railway was the vital infrastructure needed to create a broader web of economic activity and bind it to a nation to improve livelihoods and prosperity through the efficient transport and exchange of goods. In 1867, a sickly Swedish chemist named Alfred Nobel announced his incredible new invention that he called dynamite, a substance that had more than ten times the blasting capacity of gunpowder and would pave the way for the industrial megaprojects that made the modern world—harbours could be blasted and cleared for larger ships; canals such as the Erie could be carved for barges to haul heavy bulk commodities; land could be levelled for roads and railways; and tunnels could be dug through mountainsides. With dynamite, the industrial revolution fuelled an economic and political revolution.

For some people, railways served political objectives and were the physical manifestation of things more imaginary, such as the idea of a nation, while others just wanted to make money. Capitalism was the original crowdsourcing, a means to pool resources to undertake projects grander and more complex than any individual could afford, and to spread the risk of failure among a greater number. A transcontinental railway was the very definition of mission-oriented capitalism. Railways were the symbolic and psychological glue to bind an empire, as well as the practical means to rule it. With a transcontinental railway, Canada could aspire to become a less populated version of the United States.

John A. Macdonald was the progenitor of this dream. He observed the prosperity generated by the increasing number of railways along the St. Lawrence and imagined a new dominion extending from the Atlantic to the Pacific. But the political, logistical, financial and technical hurdles for such an ambitious project were daunting. Not the least was convincing the colony of British Columbia to join with Canada, instead of remaining independent or becoming annexed to the United States. Most of British Columbia's commerce was with San Francisco, and the U.S. had purchased Alaska from Russia in 1867, thereby sandwiching B.C. between American territories with no access to any other political jurisdiction except by travel through the U.S.

In 1871, B.C. agreed to join eastern Canada with the condition that Canada would build a transcontinental railway "at the earliest possible date." Surveys would begin immediately, and hopefully the project would be completed within a decade. Naturally there were delays. The scouting and surveying of the route was itself a monumental undertaking, subject to revision for political priorities. There were cost overruns, political opposition, two uprisings led by Louis Riel and the initial refusal of the Niisitapi (Blackfoot) to allow the railway through their territory. In the 1870s, disease, primarily smallpox, was ravaging the West and American whiskey traders were encroaching from the south, while a severe decline in the bison (commonly known as buffalo) population, upon which the Métis and Indigenous peoples depended, brought starvation.

The construction of the Canadian Pacific Railway was the defining event of its era, around which most other events orbited—a catalyst for the powerful global forces that were pushing the land toward something new. Its story is a sweeping tale, with technological, political, economic, geographical and social components. It involves the dreams of politicians in Ottawa, Toronto and Montreal; the financing genius and manipulative shenanigans of railway promoters to devise a business plan that would justify the expense; the feats of engineers to push a railway through the rock and bog around Lake Superior and through the rugged mountains of British Columbia; the adventures and hardships of explorers and surveyors; the occasional resistance of Indigenous peoples; and the terrific and horrific work of the labourers who poured their lives into it. More than twelve thousand labourers toiled on the railway at any given time, and many thousands of horses and oxen. Pay was poor, the work back-breaking, dirty and dangerous, and there were many deaths among the predominantly European immigrant construction crews. Conditions were even worse for the Chinese workers, who were often assigned the most dangerous jobs, those involving dynamite blasting and tunnelling.

Yet the railway lay the foundation not just for Canada as it is today, a country that spans the continent from coast to coast, but also for the European-style settlement of the West and the creation of Canada's national park system. The last spike, fully connecting eastern Canada to Vancouver, wasn't driven until November 7, 1885, nearly two decades after the idea began percolating in the minds of ambitious politicians.

The era was marked by greed, hubris, blatant empire building, oppression, corruption and theft. These times were good for some, hard for most, disastrous for others, yet they persevered nevertheless. They passed their days, perhaps had families, contributed to building their communities and hoped for better times and a future for their children despite enduring what are, from our vantage point, incomprehensible hardships and uncertainties. The CPR's conceptualization and construction made possible a new country, but it came at a terrible price for some.

In recent years Canadian history has been given a rude and long overdue awakening from the slumber of certainty, like when the sun in
spring melts the snow to reveal a land bedraggled and muddy, but ready
for new growth. Ready, perhaps, to approach a more accurate appreciation of the many forces, often competing and contradictory, that have
led to the world we now find ourselves in. Humans are the only species
that lives in two worlds: the tangible physical one, and the other based
on imaginary narrative, narrative that can be used to inspire and motivate
toward common goals or to justify mocking and denigrating dissenting
opinions, cultures and choices. Previous histories of the Canadian Pacific
Railway have been focused too keenly on a single strand of the story. In
Dominion, I have endeavoured to broaden the picture, in an effort to more
honestly portray the powerful forces that were moulding the world in the
late nineteenth century and the lives of the people caught up in this flood
of change, which ultimately laid the foundation for the development of
Canada as an independent state.

PART ONE

—

THE DREAM

CHAPTER ONE

A FATEFUL CHOICE

———

I n the summer of 1870, the colonial government of British Columbia
in Victoria dispatched three representatives far to the east, to a
chaotic frontier town that had recently been named the capital of
a new nation: the city of Ottawa, located at the swampy confluence
of the Rideau and Ottawa Rivers. There was no easy way to travel across
the vast hinterland between these two isolated settlements, hemmed
in to the north of a recently formalized border with the United States.
The three dignitaries strode the gangplank onto their steamship in
Victoria and chuffed their way south to San Francisco, where they
boarded a sleeper car of the Union Pacific Railroad and rumbled for
many days east to Chicago, connected to other American railways farther east to get north to Toronto, and thence on to Ottawa after a week
or so. Had they decided to remain within territory claimed by the
British Empire, they would have spent many months of hard travel on
foot and by horse-drawn coach, canoe, screeching Red River cart, York

boat and even dogsled. They would have arrived exhausted, and in need of a haircut and a good tailor.

The purpose of their journey was to negotiate the terms by which their tiny outpost on the Pacific might join in a political union with the newly formed country of Canada along the St. Lawrence. Perhaps they appreciated the irony of having to travel almost entirely through one foreign country to discuss their union with a different foreign country. Surely they must have seen the industry and activity in the U.S., which, at the time, made anything north of the border compare unfavourably.

In 1866, Vancouver Island and the mainland colony of British Columbia were merged at the demand of a British government eager to cut costs for the distant outpost. A year later, in 1867, the United States purchased Alaska from Russia, and it was noted in the legislative council of British Columbia in 1870 that the colony was now sandwiched between United States territories to the north and to the south. The colony was also isolated from the other British colonies in North America by the imposing rampart of the Rocky Mountains— the north-to-south international boundary, though mostly theoretical at that point, cut across the natural lines of communication. By this time, Victoria had grown into a respectable and stable seaport capital with a population of almost six thousand. The city was partly paved, had gaslit streets with stately homes, banks, hotels, churches, schools, parks and government buildings. Its growing economy was based on lumbering, fishing and shipping. Yet it had become obvious that the small, isolated colony, with a shrinking population outside Victoria and diminishing returns from the Cariboo mines after the receding tide of the gold rush, could not long remain an isolated British colony.

The Colony of British Columbia itself was nearly an accident of history. It morphed from the Hudson's Bay Company fur trading outpost Fort Victoria, which had been founded in 1841 by James Douglas, in anticipation of the company being ousted from Old Oregon, which indeed happened in 1846, when Britain and the United States agreed to an international border along the 49th parallel. The commandeering and somewhat dictatorial Douglas, son of a Scottish sugar trader and a "coloured free" woman from Guiana, became the colony's first governor in 1858, during the Fraser River gold rush.

Victoria was no longer a fur outpost in a distant land governed by a patchwork of independent cultures whose only connection to global industrialization and urbanization was the trading posts of the Hudson's Bay Company. Yet nor was it an independent society based upon British government traditions. It was a land in transition, and central authority or standardized laws and customs were still a dream (or a nightmare, depending on your point of view). And the people who arrived en masse, beginning in 1858 and continuing throughout the 1860s, had no experience in the fur trade, which was founded upon mutual exchange between peoples, cultural and ceremonial relationships and in many cases marriage into local Indigenous societies.

While the Hudson's Bay Company had been operating in the region since the end of the eighteenth century, it was generally welcomed and prospered only insofar as it catered to the interests of local peoples. Gold mining, however, was a much more intrusive activity that involved foreigners damming and dredging waterways, tramping all over the land and building roads and towns. There was also the simmering issue of fishing rights for salmon along the rivers, where newly arrived prospectors began competing with Indigenous fishers.

The newcomers had no knowledge of any Indigenous customs or languages and had no economic, social or family connection to those cultures. To them, the Indigenous peoples were foreign and unfamiliar, and they viewed the young city and the other settlements that were developing as their own ethnic enclaves, bulwarks against the wilderness and the original inhabitants who lived there. These new settler communities were not glorified fur trade forts where social and genetic blending created a unique culture that bridged the gap between the Indigenous peoples and the primarily Scottish, French, Métis or Canadian fur traders. They were something entirely new and different. To the Indigenous peoples, the newcomers established closed societies: there could only be conflict with the rising tide of gold seekers over land and resources.

Some gold seekers may also have been infused with the then fashionable idea that Indigenous peoples were a disappearing race. Certainly, tangible evidence of the population decline was starkly apparent, as diseases had reduced the population along the coast, where the people had been most numerous and settled, as well as in the Interior, to barely a quarter of what it had been a century earlier. Whole regions that were once dotted with villages had returned to a state of near wilderness, giving newly arriving people a false perception of Indigenous culture and the impression that the land had never been used and was now being underused and that therefore pre-existing peoples' rights didn't exist. The sheer numbers of miners flooding the region completely swamped Indigenous populations and threatened their customs and economy. Sawmills whined, carpenters hammered, boats were constantly navigating the Fraser River, and miners were scrambling up streams searching for gold.

Establishing some sort of political order from the chaos of the gold rush and its waves of shiftless roustabouts from California was the defining accomplishment of James Douglas's political career—that and resisting the move to an elected, or responsible, legislature. The greatest fear for Douglas, the former HBC boss turned political boss of the fledgling colony, was increasing violence between the various independent Indigenous tribes and the unruly mobs of footloose prospectors, which included Chinese, Germans, Norwegians, Jews, Americans, Irish, Latin Americans, French, Belgians and Canadians. There were also many Indigenous miners, who naturally felt that most of the gold belonged to them and who were angered by displaced salmon weirs, overrun communities and molested women. Trying to somehow manage the influx of tens of thousands of miners and prevent bloodshed between them and the Indigenous peoples was no small task.

Throughout this time, the government in Victoria, small, underfunded and not representative, was responding rather than initiating. It had no control over the international border and knew there would inevitably be violence and unresolvable conflict. In the American territories to the south there had already been slaughter and bloodshed. Douglas and his officials were searching for the least bad option, as they saw it. According to one early observer, "A rush to newly discovered gold fields brings in view every trait of human character. The more vicious standing out in bold relief, and stamping their impress upon the locality. This phase and most primitive situation can be accounted for partly by the cupidity of mankind, but mainly that the first arrivals are chiefly adventurers." Someone had to wrestle this swarm of unruly vagabonds into a semblance of order before they caused enormous damage.

British authorities had sent out Judge Matthew Baillie Begbie. The flamboyant Begbie cut quite a figure when he descended the gangplank at Victoria under a pallid sky in November 1858. The new judge was as tall as the imposing Douglas, with a prodigious waxed moustache and stylish pointy Vandyke, and typically dressed in a sort of toned-down Wild West style. Colonial Secretary Edward Bulwer-Lytton had professed that the ideal candidate for B.C.'s new circuit judge should be a man "who could, if necessary, truss a murderer up and hang him from the nearest tree," and in Begbie he came close to realizing this vision. An indifferent law student at Cambridge, Begbie much preferred the more prosaic pursuits of cards, rowing, tennis, boxing, singing and acting, and had been reduced to the lowly position of court reporter for the *Law Times* when news of the adventurous but ill-defined job on the lawless frontier came up. With some legal knowledge and a lofty disdain for protocol, lawyers and law books, Begbie, it turned out by chance, was perfectly suited for the job of sole judge in a vast wilderness precinct.

The thirty-nine-year-old had just the commanding presence, rough-and-ready attitude and bold conviction to impose order in the mining camps, where many of the miners were accustomed to the vigilante frontier justice of the California gold rush. Aware of the importance of appearances, Begbie carried himself with unquestionable dignity and always had with him his dark judicial robes and a scraggly white wig—and donned these accoutrements of justice whether presiding over court in a dirt-floored tent, in the local saloon or on horseback on a hillside. He heard disputes over mining claims, thefts and murders and was often judge, prosecutor and defence all in one. He was known to quote law to the gathered witnesses and juries from a tattered copy of the legal code of California, before rendering "British" justice. His sentences were most often severe, but he didn't ever earn his epithet "the Hanging Judge." (When accosted by an American prospector and accused of hanging many of the man's countrymen, Begbie replied to the effect that he didn't hang anyone, he just established order in the court and instructed juries on the law.) Punishment, he believed, was the best deterrent, especially in the mining shanties, where he was the only authority among throngs of unruly transients. Responding to Douglas about a complaint from a man whom he had ordered whipped, Begbie replied: "My idea is that if a man insists on behaving like a brute, after a fair warning, and won't quit the Colony; treat him like a brute and flog him."

Because of his hardline tactics and harsh punishments, Begbie earned the enmity of quite a few along his lonely circuit of backwoods B.C. On one occasion, he was lounging on his hotel balcony when he overheard a group of men on the street below plotting to ambush him as he rode out of town. He slipped into his room, returned to the balcony with his chamber pot and casually emptied it onto the heads of his erstwhile assassins. His prevailing attitude seems to have been that humanity's natural barbarism was barely contained by fear of priests, hangmen and humiliation in front of one's peers. But Begbie was steeped in the values of the Scottish Enlightenment and egalitarianism between peoples. He learned a number of Indigenous dialects and even conducted trials in those languages without the use of an interpreter. He formed great friendships with a number of chiefs and he was sympathetic to the potential for injustice when imposing colonial law on Indigenous people. On one occasion early in his tenure, he found a white California miner guilty of assault against an Indigenous man, based solely on the testimony of Indigenous witnesses, something never before done. He allowed Indigenous witnesses to swear their oaths of truth upon objects sacred to them rather than on the Bible.

Begbie's sense of justice transcended his era. In 1886, he overturned a law that levied unusually high licence fees on laundry businesses in Victoria, finding that it discriminated against Chinese people even though the bylaw didn't mention them specifically, because at the time laundries were overwhelmingly run by Chinese. Years later, when he became the chief justice of the Supreme Court of the new province of British Columbia, Begbie overturned the conviction of an Indigenous man accused of holding a potlatch, which had been declared illegal under the Indian Act.

After his early years of living rough and rambling among the backwoods mining communities, he maintained a spacious apartment in New Westminster and then in Victoria. He never married, despite the attentions of women, but was a highly social host of parties and tennis competitions and a sought-after dinner guest. When he died in Victoria in 1894, his tombstone was engraved with the words "Lord, be merciful to me a sinner." In some ways Begbie was a simple man, and his simple law, frequently invented in his own head, was readily understood by the majority of people in the regions he patrolled. He did more as an individual, with his attention to ceremony, honesty and gravitas, and with his sense of fairness, to bring order to the mining camps than an army could ever hope to have done.

DESPITE BEGBIE'S ENERGETIC QUEST for order and justice, at the rough and rude miners' camps there was the predictable call for the Stars and Stripes to protect the rights of the predominantly American miners. Unlike in Old Oregon decades earlier, when American settlers organized themselves and voted to become American citizens, most American miners in British Columbia had little interest in land, government or manifest destiny (the professed desire to absorb the entire continent); they just wanted their gold. But the fear of an American takeover was strong. That an aggressive American government would follow the miners into the territory and commandeer it for the United States is a theme that pervades Canada's early history.

One incident that had the potential to erupt into something larger was a bloodless little confrontation called McGowan's War. In 1858 a Black barber named Isaac "Ikey" Dixon, who later became a respected and popular writer for the *Cariboo Sentinel* in Barkerville, was assaulted at a Christmas dance by some Californians who took issue with his race. The unprovoked act against an innocent man sparked a conflict over jurisdiction and procedure between the two magistrates in the nearby settlements of Hill's Bar and Yale. Of course there was more to it: the settlements were dominated by different violent political factions that had their origins in San Francisco, the Law and Order Party and the Committee of Vigilance, which dominated Hill's Bar and Yale respectively. Yale's justice of the peace, Peter Brunton Whannell, placed Dixon in protective custody during the investigation. George Perrier, the magistrate for Hill's Bar, eventually sent a posse headed by the notorious Ned McGowan from San Francisco, who was friends with the two suspects in Dixon's assault, and kidnapped his rival magistrate from Yale, dragged Whannell back to Hill's Bar and held him in prison on charges of contempt of court. It presaged a larger conflict: McGowan flew the Stars and Stripes from one of his boats during the foray, and Whannell had penned a note to Governor Douglas claiming the region was descending into anarchy and that he feared for his life. It was exactly what Douglas most feared: miners taking the law into their own hands and imposing unwanted cultural attitudes upon their fellows. Spontaneous incidents like this, Douglas knew, could easily take on a life of their own.

Begbie immediately set out for Hill's Bar with twenty-two armed Royal Engineers and their leader, Colonel Richard Clement Moody, a short, scrawny man with a sunken chest, a droopy moustache and a furious nest of whiskers jutting down from his jaw, oddly exposing a bare nubbin of a chin. But appearances to the contrary, as soon as their sternwheeler docked at Yale, Moody boldly strode down the gangplank toward the boisterous gang of armed and perhaps intemperate prospectors and cowed them into submission. He later described the scene in his inimitable style: "The notorious Ned McGowan, of Californian celebrity at the head of a band of Yankee Rowdies defying the law! Every peaceable citizen frightened out of his wits!—Summons & warrants laughed to scorn! A Magistrate seized while on the Bench, & brought to the Rebel's camp, tried, condemned, & heavily fined! A man shot dead shortly before! Such a tale to welcome me at the close of a day of great enjoyment."

McGowan was apparently deflated in the face of Moody's bravado— the presence of armed troops no doubt played a part—and he immediately surrendered and order was restored. Afterward, the milling mob celebrated Moody with "a Salute, firing off their loaded Revolvers over my head—Pleasant—Balls whistling over one's head! as a compliment! Suppose a hand had dropped by accident! I stood up, & raised my cap & thanked them in the Queen's name for their loyal reception of me."

The crowd dispersed and McGowan was quietly tried by Begbie, who decided to be lenient and only fined him, since most of the man's crimes were more in the realm of possibility than actuality. He then dismissed both quarrelling justices of the peace from their posts.

VICTORIA MAY HAVE BEEN the pre-eminent city in British Columbia in 1870, but economically it was part of San Francisco's hinterland— virtually all of Victoria's trade was with that city, as was virtually all of its communication and shipping with the rest of the world. Even the mail had to be sent through the United States using American stamps. In 1869, San Francisco was the terminus of the only cross-continental railway, the Union Pacific, which, although just completed, was already hauling two thousand people each month. Transportation from Vancouver Island was virtually monopolized by San Francisco companies, and the new telegraph lines were also based out of the southern city. San Francisco boasted a population of sixty thousand in the late 1860s, ten times the size of Victoria's.

The colony was smothering under the debt that had been accumulated during the gold rush. Governor Douglas had commissioned the first government buildings in Victoria, nicknamed the Birdcages for their distinctive design, and the first major road system of the Interior, the Cariboo Road, which ran up the Fraser Canyon and hundreds of kilometres north and east to the heart of the gold territory at Barkerville. Douglas had also thwarted the development of commercial and transportation routes along the natural geographical north–south paths to the U.S., thereby forming the kernel of overarching political control over the vast territory.

But all of this world-building had been expensive, and the British colonial office was not overly pleased to be saddled with the cost of infrastructure—such as roads, bridges and ferries, not to mention courthouses, schools and a police force—capable of providing a bulwark against

American manifest destiny and to spur the development of an independent economy. The colony was facing a bleak economic future with the mines petering out and many Americans drifting south once again, lured by the new prosperity in the wake of the completion of the Union Pacific. There was some subtle and some not-so-subtle urging from Britain for the colony to hurry up and gain some form of self-sufficiency.

By 1870, the newly functioning legislature of the unified colony was faced with the greatest of possible dilemmas—its own political future. There were three options open to the beleaguered colony: remain an independent entity linked to Britain (financially improbable); join the new country of Canada as a province; or become another star on the American flag, since all the natural lines of political and economic concourse lay with the United States.

CHAPTER TWO

THE OVERLANDERS

———

Since the days of David Thompson two generations earlier, fur traders had been crossing the formidable barrier of the Rocky Mountains from the prairies. There were also numerous well-established trade routes in many regions that predated the fur traders. Athabasca Pass was the most famous, a treacherous fifty-kilometre land portage connecting the Whirlpool River of the Athabasca River system to the Columbia River system. But by the 1860s it was no longer maintained or regularly traversed—the territory of Old Oregon through which the lower Columbia flowed was now part of the United States, and the old routes long trodden by the fur traders were no longer in regular use. When the news of gold along the Pacific slope eventually trickled east in 1862, however, a group of two hundred Canadians and immigrants, calling themselves the Overlanders, decided upon a grand adventure. Led by Thomas McMicking of Welland County, Canada West, they wended their way by railway, steamboat and horse cart to Fort Garry (now Winnipeg), where they pooled their resources and purchased about one hundred Red River carts, with their famously screeching wheels. In these they crossed the dusty tracks of the prairie 1,600 kilometres to Fort Edmonton, one of the oldest and most prominent fur trading outposts, which was, by then, developing into a small community. About 125 of these adventurous nomads hired a Métis guide, André Cardinal, and continued west through the Rockies, plodding with their herds of cattle and horses along what would later be considered one of the prime routes for a railway. Their journey proved far more arduous and dangerous than they had expected. There was but one woman among them, Catherine O'Hare Schubert, the wife of one of the trekkers, Francis Augustus Schubert. The couple had three young children, ages five, three and one, and Catherine was concealing a secret: she was already four months pregnant when they left Fort Garry.

A black-and-white photo from later in Catherine's life shows a handsome woman with an intelligent countenance and a thoughtful gaze. But her life had not been an easy one. Born into poverty in Ireland, at sixteen she had crossed the Atlantic in steerage on a rickety sailing ship to escape the potato famine and a typhus epidemic.

THE GREAT HUNGER, AS IT WAS CALLED, saw more than a million Irish perish miserably from disease and starvation in the mid-nineteenth century, reducing the nation's population by nearly a quarter. The problem began with an infestation of potato blight that rotted potato plants before they could be harvested, and the natural disaster was compounded by political indifference and incompetence. By 1855, over two million people had fled the country in one of the great mass exoduses of history. The main destinations for these impoverished and starving emigrants, mostly young, single men and women, were England, Australia and across the Atlantic to the United States and the Canadas.

The brokers who booked their sea passage often lied about the inhumane shipboard conditions and poor provisions in order to receive up-front payment, such that when the emigrants reached their destination they were in wretched condition. Historians estimate that, illegally crammed into dilapidated and overcrowded "coffin ships," upwards of 100,000 steerage-class passengers died during the voyage and were unceremoniously tossed overboard. Measles, diphtheria, diarrhea, tuberculosis, whooping cough, intestinal parasites, cholera, smallpox, influenza, typhus and typhoid fever were the main culprits. The passengers were particularly susceptible because they were already malnourished and generally in poor health. Scurvy was rampant, blending with the toxic mélange of ailments and afflictions that preyed upon the defenceless emigrants.

During the 1847 sailing season alone, more than twenty thousand mostly Irish died en route or soon after disembarking at Grosse-Île, a quarantine depot near Quebec City. When the ships disgorged them onto the docks, feverish and cadaverous, squinting in the seldom-seen sun, they were herded into clumps, denied basic humanitarian aid and fresh water as they huddled, awaiting their fate, staring glassy-eyed at the stiff bodies of their less lucky compatriots, who were hoisted on hooks from the putrid bowels of the ships and stacked on the docks like firewood, soon to become smothered in a seething horde of feasting rats.

According to Robert Whyte, a Protestant clergyman voyaging as a passenger aboard one of these ships, the conditions were so horrible he could hardly express himself: "frightful" and "horrid" and "appalling," he sputtered. He related how, during the mandated quarantine before disembarking, the passengers had stood in the hold "up to their ankles in filth. The wretched emigrants crowded together like cattle and corpses remain long unburied." Once they made it ashore, there was scant improvement. There were "hundreds . . . literally flung on the beach, left amid the mud and stones to crawl on the dry land how they could." Even those discharged as healthy soon succumbed as they staggered off, shivering, eyes burning from fever, children crying for their lost or dead mothers. Some just lay out in the open, while others were able to struggle to sheds or tents to await processing by officials. "After a voyage of two months' duration we were to be left still enveloped by reeking pestilence, the sick without medicine, medical skill, nourishment or so much as a drop of pure water—for the river . . . was polluted by the most disgusting objects thrown overboard from the several vessels. In short, it was a floating mass of filthy straw, the refuse of foul beds, barrels containing the vilest matter, old rags and tattered clothes, etc." Whyte's shocked outrage prompted him to write a small book about what he had seen. "Untutored, degraded, famished and plagu-estricken, as they were," he concluded, "I assert that there was more true heroism, more faith, more forgiveness to their enemies and submission to the Divine Will exemplified in these victims, than could be found in ten times the number of their oppressors."

Hundreds of thousands of immigrants with similar stories washed up in Boston, New York, Quebec and Montreal, many wandering farther west to take low-paying jobs as domestic servants and labourers, some enduring horrible abuses and exploitation. Many famously worked upon the railways.

AFTER SHE HAD RECOVERED from the ordeal of her Atlantic crossing, Catherine O'Hare went to work as a maid in Springfield, Massachusetts, before marrying her German husband three years later and moving north to St. Paul, along the Mississippi. The couple pressed on north to Fort Garry, where they opened a store and began a small farm in the growing community along the Red River, which was populated primarily by Métis with economic and cultural links to the fur trade. But disaster struck. In the spring of 1862, a flood destroyed their farm and their general store folded, dashing their dream of prosperity. When they spied the animals and carts of the Overlanders preparing to set off on an epic journey into the unknown Far West, they signed on, having nothing to lose.

The Overlanders' cavalcade consisted of 97 carts, 110 animals and approximately 150 people. They made good time and had grand adventures crossing the open grasslands, generally roaming from one fur trade outpost to the next. Catherine carried their youngest child on her back and Francis hoisted the older two, or stashed them in pouches on horses. Catherine and the three children lent the Overlanders a less warlike and more domestic air that likely prevented violence from the many Cree, Saulteaux and Nakoda (Assiniboine) people the group met on the prairies. Instead of a war party, the Plains riders saw unarmed migrants and typically offered assistance with hunting and guiding. Each night the Overlanders pulled the carts close, lit a big fire and camped out under the stars on the vast grassy expanse, feasting on roasted bison and ducks and handfuls of tiny sweet strawberries, dreaming of the future.

One evening after a parched eleven-hour slog on a burning hot day, their thirst was nearly unbearable. They suffered, Thomas McMicking wrote, "in silence, every one bearing his trouble like a Briton, when suddenly, above the creaking of our carts, the shrill notes of the sweetest music rang out on the midnight air. It was the sound of the bull-frog, that had borrowed its melody from the fact that indicated our approach to water. . . . And though our party were generally considered temperate at home, we might without slander be accused of hard drinking on that occasion." On another day they came across great boneyards of bleached bison remains, half-buried in dust, and mosquitoes "in such dense clouds as to almost darken the air and inflicting such torment, in some instances even positive torture, as to drive the more sensitive individuals, and animals, to distraction."

Throughout the long summer days they drove the animals forward, fording them across the numerous rivers and creeks that webbed the landscape. The land was achingly beautiful, "an attractive country, pleasantly diversified by hills and valleys, wood and prairie land, draped in a rich mantle of living green, thickly studded with small lakes and gaily decked and enlivened with beds of wild flowers of great variety and boundless extent." One lonely Irishman burst into song:

> *Where the wild rose, and pea in abundance*
> *Does bud and bloom and fade away unseen*
> *And waste their beauty and fragrance far away*
> *Upon a lonely western Prairie green.*

They reached Fort Edmonton on July 23 and sent a contingent to the fort to trade their carts for horses. Nearby were encamped many Niisitapi (Blackfoot) and people of mixed heritage who were attached to the fort, giving it a very lively and festive atmosphere. One of the young men wrote back to his brother in the East, "It is a nice place. I think I could live here contented if I could get provision but they do not raise enough for themselves. They live most of the time on pemmican and potatoes. . . . There are some pretty [Niisitapi] girls here, some of the boys say, as they have ever seen." Within days the troop had hired a guide to take them as far as Tête Jaune Pass, an open grassy clearing near the Fraser River a hundred kilometres west of Jasper, many weeks' travel to the west through the mountains. The pass was named after Pierre Bostonais, a Métis-Haudenosaunee (Iroquois) fur trader with the Hudson's Bay Company who was distinguished by his blond hair. After crossing the pass, they would likely find Secwépemc (Shuswap) to guide them farther.

As they travelled west from Fort Edmonton, the prairie soon gave way to thick, hilly forests where carts would have been useless. The cattle struggled through the soft ground of "nasty low wet country," plodding ever higher toward the mountains. It was a special day when they finally spied "lofty snow-clad peaks, standing out in bold relief against the blue sky beyond, and glistening in the sunlight [which] gave them the appearance of fleecy clouds floating in the distance . . . sublimely grand and overpowering."

Then the hardship began, as they searched for the elusive route of the Tête Jaune, or Yellowhead, Pass, which was reputedly frequented by Secwépemc. Perhaps one of these intrepid wanderers noted that, despite the congested deadfall and overgrown forest, the level ground would make an ideal place to situate a road or railway.

They pressed on west of Jasper House and on to the headwaters of the Fraser River. Horses fell off treacherous paths and died; they were scratched and bruised from scrambling over rocky outcroppings and were nearly lost in dense underbrush before the party reached a large river. One of the men, Alexander Fortune, wrote of Catherine and her children: "Great sympathy was manifested for the brave and devoted mother of those three children. Her presence in the company helped cultivate a kindly and more manly treatment of man to man." It was here that they tasted a culinary delight "so delicate and rare that it might have tempted the palate of Epicurus himself." It was a roasted skunk, "which our guide prepared and served up to us in true Indian style . . . we wondered that we had not discovered its good qualities sooner, and unanimously resolved, that his skunkship had been a slandered and much abused individual."

The Overlanders decided to split up at Tête Jaune Cache. The larger group would try their luck rafting the Fraser River downstream to Fort George (now Prince George), despite the river's frightening reputation. Four men drowned in the frothy waters of the Fraser's canyons, with many rafts smashed against rocks and most of their goods and provisions lost, before they reached the outpost.

The smaller contingent, numbering around thirty-six, with one hundred cattle and some horses, included Catherine and her family. By now she was heavily pregnant and there was some concern about what would happen if they didn't reach a settlement soon. The band opted to travel south down a broad forested valley to the North Thompson River and raft it south to Fort Kamloops. Soon after they had split from the other group, they met a group of Secwépemc on a fishing excursion who supplied them with many enormous freshly caught salmon, which they roasted over an open fire, no doubt a tasty complement to the meagre portions of skunk. It was now early September, and the people were having a terrible time hacking a route through the brush to get their animals through. Finally, on September 22, on the bank of the North Thompson, they slaughtered the cattle, abandoned most of the horses and built a flotilla of rafts and canoes to take them south.

Only two men drowned during the six-week rapid-riddled float down the North Thompson River. It was a terrifying ordeal. Most of their food was lost when rafts overturned and they were soon in the early stages of starvation. After they killed and ate their few remaining horses (which had not fared well on the rafts), whenever they pulled ashore they scavenged for wild rosehips and squirrels to sustain their waning lives. Thomas McMicking recalled that it was a journey that "few *men* would have the courage to undertake. By her unceasing care for her children, by her unremitting and devoted attention to their every want, and by her never-failing solicitude about their welfare, [Catherine] exemplified the nature and power of that maternal affection which prompts a mother to neglect her own comfort for the well-being of her child, by which she rises superior to every difficulty, and which only glows with a brighter intensity as dangers deepen around her offspring." Certainly the situation was a dire predicament for anyone, let alone a pregnant mother of young children worrying about what lay ahead for her family.

Catherine went into labour as the raft neared Fort Kamloops in October 1862. They pulled the raft ashore at the Secwépemc village that lay at the convergence of the North Thompson and Thompson

Rivers, and upon seeing her state, a cluster of women rushed her inside one of the dwellings and ministered to her while she gave birth. An unnamed Secwépemc woman soon emerged into the sun and held up a baby girl, calling out, "It's Kumloops, Kumloops!" The couple debated naming their daughter Kamloops but then decided on the more prosaic Rose, after the rosehips that had sustained them on the journey. Rose has been credited as the first "white" baby born in the B.C. Interior, a distinction of dubious significance. By this time there were many hundreds of mixed-heritage children throughout the territory, since most of the Hudson's Bay Company employees had Indigenous wives and families—including the governor of the colony, James Douglas, who had met his wife, Amelia Connolly, the daughter of a Scottish fur trader and his Cree wife, farther north, at Fort St. James, decades earlier.

Catherine and her husband never did strike it rich, as almost no one does in a gold rush. They worked for the Hudson's Bay Company at Fort Kamloops for a season, where some form of fur trading outpost had been operating since 1812, although by the 1860s it was known more as a horse pasture for travellers and prospectors venturing inland from the coast. It wasn't much to behold, consisting of several log buildings surrounded by a small palisade and thriving vegetable gardens. The couple soon moved west along the Fraser River and opened an inn and restaurant in Lillooet; Francis prospected in the summers, mostly unsuccessfully, and Catherine ran the humble waystation. They had two more children before moving to the Okanagan to farm in 1881. They built a schoolhouse on their farm and in 1885 persuaded the provincial government to send a teacher for the local families. Catherine lived until 1918, a decade after her husband had died from falling off a ladder.

THE REGION NOW CALLED British Columbia was on the cusp of great change in the 1860s. Indigenous peoples had been perishing in astonishing numbers for several generations. The Indigenous population had declined from around ninety thousand in the mid-eighteenth century to sixty thousand by the mid-nineteenth century, and to a mere twenty-five thousand twenty years later, in 1870. When the Overlanders rafted down the North Thompson and Fraser Rivers in 1862, they beheld deserted villages littered with dead bodies, victims of the smallpox epidemic then raging uncontrolled throughout the land. One morning one of the travellers awoke to discover to his horror that the rushes he had slept upon were covering a fresh mass grave for smallpox victims. There appeared to be plenty of open terrain ready for farms to service the influx of gold prospectors, and soon there were other immigrants. None of these newcomers, mostly illiterate and irrevocably dislocated from their own worlds, knew that the local population had recently been four times larger or that the land that seemed so sparsely inhabited had teemed with much greater numbers in the not too distant past. Inured to suffering and death, the newcomers desperately sought security and stability, a place to raise a family and make their way in the world.

The hardships, challenges and adventures of the Overlanders illustrate the magnitude of the geographical challenge faced by those who sought to link the disparate lands of what is now Canada with a stable and reliable transportation route, and why the Victoria delegates opted to travel east to Ottawa through the United States rather than through the ostensibly "British" territory.

Around the same time the Overlanders were crossing the continent from east to west, a dispute over a wagon road, and a possible future railway route, occurred in the newly self-proclaimed jurisdiction of British Columbia. In an era without a framework for dispute resolution that crossed cultural boundaries and was acceptable to all, conflict was often bloody.

CHAPTER THREE

A ROAD FROM
THE PACIFIC

———

A n enigmatic moon-faced English gentleman with narrow eyes and a stubborn set to his jaw, Alfred Waddington had made a small fortune in California before moving north to Victoria in 1858. He became involved in local politics, agitating against the more restrictive and disenfranchising tendencies of the old family-company compact and in support of small government, open acceptance of different religions and some political rights for women. He could afford these altruistic dalliances since he was independently wealthy. In 1860, at sixty years of age, Waddington became obsessed with establishing a new town north along the coast, deep in Bute Inlet, from which he dreamed of building a road and later a railway inland along the Homathko River and over the Chilcotin Plateau near the Quesnel River, to intersect with the Cariboo Road near Barkerville, the better to remove gold from the region.

Waddington abruptly devoted all his attention and his personal finances to this quixotic project that would consume the remainder of his life and his fortune. His proposed road would shave perhaps three hundred kilometres, and nearly two weeks of travel time, for freight packed to the gold fields along the Cariboo Road, which followed the Fraser River and its treacherous canyons.

Waddington's plan was a satisfactory engineering solution, but it wasn't a satisfactory political one—at least not to the people who lived along the proposed route and who hadn't been consulted. The same situation bedevils governments today—how to balance the rights of citizens with dreams of increased efficiency and prosperity who live in distant cities, seeking practical solutions to economic problems, with the rights of people who live lives at least partially independent of those concerns and who felt or feel aggrieved at the intrusion, particularly with the lack of consultation or an accounting of the benefits to themselves.

Waddington began his lobbying and survey work just as the 1862 smallpox epidemic began its terrifying rampage along the B.C. coast. Over the next two years it killed more than half the Indigenous population. Amidst this frightening and mysterious plague, Waddington's workers, who included many Indigenous Tsilhqot'in (Chilcotin) men, began clearing the route in 1863. The conditions were not ideal, owing to the remote location of the route and the tangled verdant growth and tortuous topography of the region, which was riddled with canyons and creeks requiring bridges, and steep grades that needed switchbacks. It was back-breaking and slow work for meagre pay.

These unfavourable conditions and the region's unsuitability for a road were being reported in the newspapers in Victoria and New Westminster. The *British Columbian* was dismissive of the entire enterprise in a June 1, 1864, editorial, also noting the poor quality of the harbour. The trail was "utterly unworthy of the name"; the bridges were "inadequate and trumpery crossings, constructed in the most unworkmanlike and temporary manner, and even now falling into ruin"; and the grade of the trail was "too steep even for a mule trail." The conclusion was that Waddington's obsession and boasting "can only be accounted for on the ground of monomania; and we would feel disposed to spare the old gentleman's feelings as at the present moment were there not too much system perceptible in his madness."

The road crew also laboured without sufficient provisions, especially the Tsilhqot'in workers: Waddington "so stinted in their provisions that they were led to starve the Indians employed in packing for them"—who were already in distress and mourning over losing hundreds of their people to disease, and perhaps wondering if the plague hadn't been deliberately introduced. After all, they had never experienced anything so terrifying and destructive before and its arrival correlated with the coming of survey crews. The smallpox epidemic had so far killed nearly half of their 1,500-strong population.

This ill treatment of the Indigenous workers, with foreigners flooding their land and building roads, was a humiliating indignity, and came with the realization that they could no longer defend their territory from encroachment. In the spring of 1864, a steamer arrived from Victoria bearing more survey and construction crews. Either to sow fear or perhaps to engage in a cruel prank, one of Waddington's workers went about asking for the names of the gathered Tsilhqot'in and wrote them down in a book. He then proclaimed that since he had their names recorded, they would soon die of smallpox. This was naturally a horrifying prospect for people who had just endured the mysterious death of many of their family members and countrymen, and an idea took hold that to rid the land of the source of the disease they would have to expel the invaders.

Klatsassin was one of the most respected warriors and leaders among the Tsilhqot'in at the time. He was in his late thirties or early forties and had two wives, one of whom was a young girl recently captured in a raid against the nearby Dakelh (Carrier) settlement, and five children ranging in age from a teenaged son to an infant daughter. R.C. Lundin Brown, a missionary who later met Klatsassin in prison, described him:

"There was no mistaking him. . . . His strong frame, piercing dark blue eyes, aquiline nose, and very powerful under-jaw, proclaimed the man of intelligence, ambition, strong force of will." Brown then digressed into a pseudo-scientific denigration of the man based on phrenology, the determination of personality traits based on skull shape that was then popular. He pronounced Klatsassin to have the "dark complexion," "narrow forehead" and "high cheekbones" that were apparently "characteristics of the North American savage."

Klatsassin and his son had been working with the road crews hoping to earn some food—the salmon harvest the previous fall had been disrupted by the smallpox epidemic and the oolichan run was late. Hunger was widespread throughout the region. Many of the Tsilhqot'in were barely subsisting even while the road crews had a surplus of supplies. Jobs for two dozen packers didn't provide enough food for hungry families. On April 28, 1864, Klatsassin led a band of twenty-four to the rudimentary ferry station about fifty kilometres east from the coast along the inlet and demanded provisions from the ferry operator. When the man refused, they shot him, threw his body in the river and plundered the food.

Klatsassin then led his band farther east toward where the main road crew of twelve was working. They painted themselves and danced in preparation for a morning assault. At dawn they attacked and killed nine men while three escaped. Over the next few days Klatsassin led his war band on several more raids, including attacking a pack train, bringing the total deaths to twenty-one. Soon volunteer posses of mostly Americans set off to scour the wild land and apprehend Klatsassin and his followers. They bungled about aimlessly for months trying to capture the warriors, but the territory was vast and rugged and unknown to them, while the Tsilhqot'in eluded capture until hunger drove them to seek a negotiation. The gold commissioner, William Cox, agreed to meet them to discuss the future. On August 15, Klatsassin and seven followers entered Cox's camp, situated near the abandoned Hudson's Bay Company fort along the Chilko River, expecting to negotiate terms of peace, but instead they were promptly arrested and taken to Quesnelmouth (now Quesnel) and incarcerated in a log cabin. Klatsassin claimed that he had been promised immunity during the parley, but Cox denied that he had promised anything. This raises a question: Why, then, would Klatsassin have come to the meeting, knowing he would be captured and incarcerated?

A trial was arranged for September 28 and 29, to be presided over by Judge Begbie in his most challenging case, while the land teetered on the precipice of anarchy and violence. The U.S. was then in the midst of a deadly civil war that saw the death of 620,000 and temporarily stemmed the rushing tide of migrants from the south. In the 1850s, Washington Territory, directly south of British Columbia, had been riven with war between the various Indigenous tribes and government soldiers after gold was discovered; this was followed by an uneasy truce and treaties that recognized U.S. sovereignty in the region and the creation of several reservations for the Yakima and Cayuse and others. It was the recent memory of this bloodshed in the adjacent territory and the desire to avoid it that were always on the minds of colonial authorities in Victoria and New Westminster in the 1860s, despite, or perhaps because of, their limited ability to project power into the Interior.

At the trial, Begbie organized a jury of seven in a primitive encampment. He spoke to the accused in their own language and recorded the testimony from all sides in his detailed report. Klatsassin claimed that they were at war with the invaders, and that it was the threat and fear of smallpox that drove their actions. Nevertheless, the jury found him and his party guilty. Begbie interviewed Klatsassin extensively and was impressed with his intelligence, insights and honesty. He wrote to Governor Frederick Seymour: "The Indians have I believe been most injudiciously treated and if a sound discretion had been exercised

towards them I believe this outrage would not have been perpetrated."
He also wrote, "I do not envy you your task of coming to a decision" on
granting clemency. Begbie's job was to preside over the trial and the
jury's was to determine guilt, while the punishment was foreordained
and mandatory for capital offences: hanging. It was up to the governor
to decide on clemency or a pardon.

The idea that the attacks were an unprovoked "massacre" was never
a universal sentiment at the time, and the outcome has remained con-
troversial since. "Depend on it," wrote John Robson, editor of the
New Westminster Columbian, once news of the attacks reached the
coast weeks later, "for every acre of land we obtain by improper means
we will have to pay for dearly in the end, and every wrong committed
upon those poor people will be visited on our heads." While both
Judge Begbie and Governor Seymour recognized the complexity of
the case and the ambiguous facts, the deaths of twenty-one people
couldn't go without some form of public retribution or punishment.
Klatsassin and the four others found to be guilty were, in accordance
with the law, hanged on October 26, and one other man the following
year. Certainly, on the facts, and the testimony of several non-
Tsilhqot'in Indigenous witnesses from the surrounding regions,
themselves victims of Tsilhqot'in aggression, these men were guilty of
a great many violent crimes. But the question of jurisdiction is what
has hung over the event for 160 years.

Was it murder or war? Was it an uprising against the invasion of territory without consent or a murderous criminal gang on a rampage?
These have been the questions asked by the people involved, and in the
press, since 1864. There has never been any unanimity on the matter, but
today it seems that most would lean toward declaring the "massacre" to
be an act of war against invaders. The Tsilhqot'in were an aggressive or
even warlike people in the estimation of their neighbours, and their
raiding and capturing of others for slaves was a common complaint.

Attacking unarmed sleeping civilians doesn't seem very noble or brave, but dawn raids upon camps were a common warfare tactic in that era and must be considered within that context. In the minds of Klatsassin and his band, they were at war and the attacks were an expression of that; that was how they defended their territory. The language of dissent was violence, just as the response from the colonial government was violence, albeit with a veneer of due process to ensure it followed certain accepted customs. In an era with a weak and distant central authority without resources, and a land filled with armed and trigger-happy roustabouts with a penchant for vigilante justice, perhaps it was not the worst of possible outcomes.

The government should have done something, some said at the time and which has been reiterated since. But what government? It was more imaginary than real, an idea of authority that had yet to manifest beyond a few settlements. The government consisted of a handful of people in Victoria (barely a few years after the fur trading outpost had morphed into a larger settlement) with grand dreams and proclamations, who waited weeks between communications from the Interior and further weeks to get a response to their decisions. The self-proclaimed government could not project any actual power so far from its base in Victoria. It had no real ability to enforce order over the land it claimed, other than the reputation of Judge Begbie. The political jurisdiction was imaginary. Furthermore, the people whom the colonial officials arrested and tried had no knowledge of the consequences of the process—indeed, they were following their own rules.

This placed Victoria officials in a real quandary: admit that they had no actual moral or legal authority or physical capability to police the vast territory, and perhaps watch the region spiral into chaos and violence, as had recently happened south of the border, or accept that they were going to convict and hang people who were not aware of the punishment for their actions and did not acknowledge Victoria's authority.

The Tsilhqot'in were an aggressive and feared people, and many in the region welcomed the stabilizing presence of an overarching authority and a set of laws, even while wishing to preserve their own customs.

The government expenses accumulated during the sordid affair—the cost of all the posses marching through the bush trying fruitlessly to apprehend the Tsilhqot'in in their own vast and rugged territories, and the bills from the trial and justice apparatus—saddled the neophyte colony with, for the era, a staggering debt of $80,000 that the imperial government in London declined to pay. Even before, with declining economic activity, the colony had been approaching insolvency, but now that was a looming spectre—yet a further inducement to join the Canadas, if only to have someone else pay off the debt. In a sense, Klatsassin was responsible for pushing the colony of British Columbia into confederation with Canada. Perhaps he should be afforded the posthumous honour, however dubious he would have considered it, of being recognized as one of the founders of the nation.

Klatsassin and his followers have since been exonerated by the provincial government of B.C. and by the Canadian government.

ASTONISHINGLY, WADDINGTON WAS NOT DETERRED by Klatsassin's uprising. That there was opposition to his road and railway scheme from the people who lived on the land didn't appear to bother him. Waddington even had the audacity to ask for compensation from the colonial government for the "massacre" and overstated his progress on the road. He surged ahead with his scheme, selling development plots in the new town he envisioned, to be named Port Waddington, naturally. His actions also hinted at his duplicity. He had been paying his workers in "Bute Road scrip" rather than cash. On a steamer returning to Victoria, he heard several men complaining and disparaging the work and progress of the undertaking. He hastily gathered them together for a little speech he had prepared: "You hold as payment for work," he announced, "a large amount of road scrip. Every word you say in disparagement of the road will tend to depreciate the value of that scrip. You are, therefore, pursuing a most suicidal course in speaking as you are doing. Your best policy on arriving at Victoria is to speak in the highest terms as to the quality and practicability of the Bute Inlet route, as by that course you will be enabled to dispose of the paper you hold at a good price." He then treated the weary workers to liberal quantities of brandy to liven their spirits. When the ship docked, the men cheered Waddington and his road project and the local press echoed and amplified the optimistic demeanour of the men toward the great new route into the Interior that was sure to bring prosperity in its wake.

From the safe distance of nearly 160 years, a reader might enjoy a wry smirk: Was it the hubris of having a town named after him that fuelled Waddington's obsession? It couldn't have been money, given his age and comparative lack of time to enjoy it. Perhaps it was a failure to appreciate that his own life had a best-before date, and that for his era he was fast approaching it. Nevertheless, he marched onward, dissipating most of his fortune before being drawn into eastern politics. Despite his project remaining mostly a fantasy of blazed trees and survey markers, he sailed to London to promote what he was now calling his railway, delivering prepared remarks to possible promoters and investors, as well as to the Royal Geographical Society and select government agencies. Alas, there proved to be little interest beyond polite queries. Nor was he any more successful in Montreal or Ottawa after Confederation in 1867.

During his time in Canada, Waddington had become acquainted with the ever optimistic (or deluded) William Kersteman, the enthusiastic promoter of a railway between Pembina in northern Minnesota and Winnipeg, which would then cross the prairies northwest to Yellowhead Pass in today's Jasper National Park. Waddington envisioned Kersteman's railway continuing west, on a path that ran counter to geographical or economic sense, connecting to his beloved Port Waddington on the Pacific—incredibly, given the recent events, blazing through Tsilhqot'in territory to get there.

Waddington and Kersteman pressed their grandiose scheme fruitlessly. Despite political and economic setbacks, they did not despond, and continued their boasting and speechifying. Both were convinced that if a railway was to be successful it would have to be designed and built not by ditherers and obfuscators but by Americans, people who knew how to get things done. They courted American capitalists to take up the mantle of their dream, the conduit by which John A. Macdonald became involved, to his later chagrin, with one George W. McMullen, an Ontario-born Chicago business operative who had recently developed a fashionable interest in railways. The two men met in Ottawa when McMullen was in town on other business and soon had assembled a cabal of American capitalists, some associated with the recently completed Northern Pacific Railway in the U.S., who were eager to make a quick buck on a project sure to be a magnet for government subsidies.

But the shenanigans of these schemers would transpire in the future, without "poor Waddington," as he was called in his obituary. He died in Ottawa in 1872, in no small irony of smallpox, eight years after the "Chilcotin War" had disrupted his first attempts to push a road from the Pacific.

CHAPTER FOUR

IDEA OF EMPIRE

———

The city of Ottawa, home to around seventeen thousand, was a muddy backwater of seemingly endless construction in 1867. Throughout the 1860s, it was undergoing a frenzy of building to fulfill its new role as the national capital of the country of Canada. Early photographs show the city as a giant work site. Streets, banks, churches, houses and hotels were sprouting like mushrooms after a rainstorm, sandstone edifices and surveyor blocks marking out their boundaries. The streets remained little more than unpaved tracks between the rows of buildings. The rutted mud thoroughfares thronged with farmers bringing their produce to market; canals were crowded with barges laden with goods, riding the system of locks that connected to the St. Lawrence; steam locomotives on steel tracks linked the strip of farms and towns that stretched from Quebec City to Toronto. Canal workers, lumberjacks, stonemasons, bricklayers, textile mill workers and carpenters flooded into the city looking for employment. Irish and Gaelic melded with German, French, the burr of Scottish and likely some Haudenosaunee and Algonquin.

Astringent gusts of tobacco and coal smoke competed with the scent of horses, pigs and perfume and the sweet odour of wood pulp. Sinkholes threatened unwary pedestrians, and broken and slippery planks on boardwalks tilted to topple them into the mud. Lot prices were rising faster than wages, and overcrowding disrupted the ordered life that many in this government town pined for. A new breed of speculators and real estate pumpers boasted of the increasing plenitude of businesses like clothiers and milliners and furniture makers, who would be catering to the rising influx of a more refined cohort, the elected officials and the attendant civil service. These more respectable members of society would promenade the boardwalks in their finery, women in their heavy dresses dangling parasols and men in suits and top hats, with cigars protruding from their mouths.

One newspaper editorial from the 1860s boasted that respectable citizens were only occasionally disturbed by a drunkard staggering into the street from one of the many taverns and pubs, and rarely accosted by beggars. "Few cities in the province have been more free from professional beggars than has this hitherto, with the exception of one or two old fellows who were fond of a drop and who solicited a charity to obtain it," pronounced the *Ottawa Citizen* on March 12, 1867. But this didn't entirely blunt local criticism of Town Hall. "The Corporation and the Police ought to be ashamed of themselves to treat a man that pays his taxes as I do, in the shameful way I have been used," wrote one disgruntled dandy on April 9. "I am, sir, a married man, a man of family. I carry a neat cane to assist me when I walk abroad. A day or two ago I was walking along Sussex street and my cane went through a knot hole in the sidewalk, and in addition to falling and soiling my clothes, my cane—a cane sir for which I paid one dollar and fifty-seven cents—was broken in two. Is this the treatment for a British subject in the Capital of the country? Is this the way the Corporation looks after the comforts of the public? What are our police for if it is not their duty to see that there are no small holes in the sidewalk, laid as traps to break valuable canes in the hands of staid and sober citizens? I trust this matter will receive that attention at the hands of the authorities which its importance deserves." And no doubt it did, without delay. But knotholes in the wooden sidewalks were only one of many civic problems the boom town faced, perhaps not even the most important: that same spring, "the late change in the weather" produced an "obnoxious effluvia arising from a large quantity of night soil recently deposited on the summit of the hill (on the foot-path) [which] is most disgusting, as well as deleterious to the health of the surrounding neighbourhood."

The city was well known for hot, sweaty summers where the air could be cut with a knife; the wheels of carts and carriages were rimmed brown with mud, horseshit and splatter, and gutters overflowed with rotting refuse, periodically washed away in torrential rainstorms. The market stank of dead fish, offal from the meat mongers, decaying vegetables and sewage. But the damp, freezing winters were far worse. Travel by horse sled was the only way to get around, other than clambering over the impressive mounds of dirty ice and snow, and the streets were "covered with a coating of frozen manure, which makes them almost impassable," as one letter to the *Ottawa Citizen* put it on March 25, 1867.

Although transportation sometimes posed problems, overall industry hummed. It was the era of the lumber barons, and mighty sawmills populated the banks of the Ottawa River, which was clogged with logs and rotting bark. Barges used canals to deliver bulk commodities like stones, bricks and steel. The daytime hours were filled with the screeching of water-powered sawmills and woollen mills, machine shops and foundries and the manufacturing of other cutting-edge technology, from carriages, sleighs and boots to bricks, britches and furniture.

Back then, everything in Ottawa seemed half-finished rather than half-started. This included the new and grand collection of stately wonders being built on a slight promontory overlooking the Ottawa River from the south. Construction of the new Parliament Buildings and governor general's residence had begun in late 1859. Piles of busted sandstone blocks, scaffolding and heaps of lumber littered the site, which was animated by a tableau of horses, carts and scuttling workers: carpenters, masons, blacksmiths and stonecutters and a host of other, lower-skilled tradesmen totalling perhaps five hundred. This sudden influx of people was the main reason that rents had become exorbitant. The distinctive Gothic revival buildings were a contrast to the neoclassical style of the American capital. It was a mighty undertaking for a sparsely populated, rugged colonial outpost, even if it had grander ambitions. The seat of government was not fully completed until 1876 and was, not surprisingly, massively over budget.

Ottawa, named for the Algonquin word *adawe*, "to trade," was situated at a scenic spot at the confluence of the Rideau and Ottawa Rivers. It had been a travel route for generations of Algonquian-speaking people who inhabited the region, primarily around Lake Huron and Georgian Bay, and who used the river to travel to Montreal to trade. After the defeat of the French and their Indigenous allies during the Seven Years' War in 1763, many immigrants from Britain began flooding into Montreal and then farther west, including the location that would become Ottawa, which began as a tiny village in the early nineteenth century, little more than a farm and a small lumber operation. The tide of British immigration increased following the American Declaration of Independence in 1776 and kept growing in subsequent years. The two independent jurisdictions of Upper Canada (Loyalist, Protestant, English-speaking) and Lower Canada (predominantly Catholic and French-speaking) were created by the British government in 1791.

A more permanent population had begun to congregate in the region by the later 1820s, when it was plotted out by Lieutenant Colonel John By, an officer of the British Royal Engineers tasked with surveying and constructing the Rideau Canal to provide a quicker military transport route between the naval bases at Kingston and Montreal. Construction of the canal began in 1826 and was mostly complete by 1832. Nearly a thousand Irish and French labourers died of malaria from the swarms of mosquitoes in the swampy sections during the summer seasons.

In 1841, both the Canadas had been amalgamated into the Province of Canada, an attempt to dilute the French vote in the more populated Lower Canada by giving each region the same number of votes in the new combined government. It was hoped that the amalgamation would enable a more unified transportation system to integrate the regions into a common economy that could become self-sufficient and move toward responsible government. The capital of the new entity roved between Montreal, Kingston, Toronto and Quebec until Queen Victoria chose to permanently situate it in Ottawa, once a railway was complete. In 1854, the Bytown and Prescott Railway connected Bytown (later renamed Ottawa) to Prescott on the St. Lawrence. As with most railways, the cost greatly exceeded the allocated budget and resulted in a massive financial burden on the local government. But the railway and the canal made Ottawa ideal for a centrally located capital, on the border between the two provinces of Canada.

IT WAS FROM THE BOOM TOWN of Ottawa that John Alexander Macdonald, the country's first prime minister, could survey his new domain and plot for its expansion. While the Parliament Buildings were slowly taking shape in the 1860s, the social architecture for a new and expanded nation that included the Maritimes and land farther west likewise progressed apace.

The perennial topics of conversation throughout Canada, as it then existed, were the speed of new railway construction, American politics, the end of the Civil War, and Americans generally and their dastardly opposition to a British consolidation that would limit their ability to absorb Canada. "They understand that the union of the Provinces is synonymous with the consolidation of British interests in America," observed an editorial in the *Ottawa Citizen* on March 13, 1867. "So long as the Provinces were politically, commercially and almost geographically isolated our neighbours saw some chance of the Provinces falling into the Union one by one, and they were contented to wait patiently the working of time." Opinions in London and New York echoed this sentiment, although sometimes with opposing views on whether union of the provinces would be a good thing or not. Britain was in favour, of course, to strengthen itself against the seemingly untenable pressure to join the U.S. and to stop the drain on the British Treasury for administration and defence.

Elected to the Legislative Assembly under the Conservative banner, Macdonald went on to become the premier of Canada in 1857. During this era governance of the Province of Canada was untenable, deadlocked between the interests and demands of Canada East and Canada West. Governments were endlessly squabbling, frequently falling, losing their majority, and generally accomplishing far less than the land needed. Even more so than today, there was no cultural cohesion, shared history, naturally linked economic interests or mutual future dreams. The roads were mean, rutted tracks barely fit for an ox cart, railway construction was just barely getting under way, and cities were small and poorly planned and lacking in urban amenities (except for Montreal, which had a much older and distinct history). The weather alternated between freezing cold and unwholesome humid heat, complete with multitudes of flies and mosquitoes. The Maritimes had a stronger cultural and economic affiliation with the New England states than to Canada West (Upper Canada), and most of Quebec outside Montreal spoke French and had a different religion, culture and colonial history. The Canadas competed with each other instead of with outsiders. The country was sparsely populated, at barely 3.5 million, and the distance between settlements made travel and profitable commerce a challenge, while impenetrable forests covered the land, with farm settlements hacked out of the raw bush.

The Indigenous cultures, though rich and complex, had been shattered by disease and warfare. From an estimated population of 500,000 in the early seventeenth century, before contact with French explorers, travellers and traders, the Indigenous population in Canada had declined to 102,358, according to the 1871 census—a loss of nearly 400,000 people, or 80 per cent of the population. This was caused primarily by exposure to infectious diseases that came in waves from east to west across the continent with increased travel, economic activity and settlement. Of course, these figures don't account for the many thousands of people from the earliest days who were of mixed heritage, whether Métis or other cultural and genetic blends from the fur trade, many of whom joined the larger population and were unrecorded.

The population of European origin, on the other hand, had steadily increased from continued immigration and high birth rates. Between 60,000 and 80,000 United Empire Loyalists fled north after the American Revolution and settled in what was then being called British North America: Nova Scotia, New Brunswick and Upper Canada. Perhaps 30,000 more late Loyalists also came to Upper Canada in the following decades. By the 1830s, Lower Canada's population was more than 500,000 and Upper Canada's numbered 237,000, while the Maritime colonies combined also exceeded 500,000 non-Indigenous people. And in the 1850s, the Irish potato famine dramatically increased Irish immigration to the Canadas.

The Canadian economy was primarily rural; what few roads there were were crude; cities, apart from Montreal, were messy works in progress; and economic activity was locked up by a handful of politically connected families and vested interests that were resistant to innovation. Opportunities were limited in this managed and stultified economy. Many arrived, observed the state of the country and promptly fled south to the U.S., including many thousands of the Irish immigrants who had survived the coffin ships. The border with the United States, so close and alluring, was more imaginary than physical—in most places it wasn't demarcated, let alone patrolled or guarded. Anyone could just ride their horse over it, the untamed forests offering more challenge than officialdom.

The skeletal stone shell of the Parliament Buildings and the chaotic detritus that littered the site—mere bones of the final organism— mirrored the state of the land: incomplete yet hinting at possibility. To anyone used to London or New York, or any more developed city, Ottawa was a sleepy provincial backwater of mud streets, poor water and leaking sewage pipes, a place best avoided. The consensus in Britain and the U.S. was that it was only a matter of time before the entire erratic ragtag patchwork of towns and farms that made up the Canadas would inexorably slide into the American orbit and thereby improve itself. And this would hopefully prevent Britain from being drawn into a pricey conflict with the U.S. Yet, despite the reality of the land in the late nineteenth century, nearly all the political actions that drove Macdonald's career can be seen as passionate opposition to American expansion.

FROM A POLITICIAN'S STANDPOINT things are always going to get better, or they were better in the past. No politician ever rose to power by telling people that things are just fine as they are, that no changes are needed. It's difficult to make a passionate argument for what you already have, but proposed alternatives, free as they are from collisions with reality, can exude an untempered vitality. When Macdonald dreamed, he dreamed big. The union of the disparate independent jurisdictions of British North America—Upper and Lower Canada, Nova Scotia and New Brunswick—was his first nation-building objective. It would make things better, he claimed.

Macdonald began to envision a larger, stronger union that would include the Maritime colonies and would have a different structure and division of powers between the central government and the regions. In 1864, at a great meeting and conference in Charlottetown, all the delegates accepted that a union would be beneficial if the terms could be agreed upon. This was followed by the Quebec City Conference, where the delegates worked specifically on the seventy-two resolutions that were the basis of the Canadian constitution. The next several years were devoted to pushing the votes to create the new country through the various legislative assemblies, and dealing with the British government, whose consent was needed to allow the colonies to unite—always with an eye to maintaining ties to Britain and avoid being subsumed in the magnetic vortex of the American Empire, becoming a mere historical footnote in that nation's manifest destiny.

The division of powers in the new Confederation gives some insight into the relative importance of technology and services at the time. It probably would be structured differently if drafted today, but back then the things that were important from a nation-building perspective were canals, ports and railways. These were the keys to building and running a cohesive nineteenth-century economy and transporting goods and people so that it would be possible to build a self-sustaining web of commerce and community. As such, authority over these areas was assigned to the federal government. Merely minor or non-existent things like roads, hospitals and public education were left to the provinces to regulate, as befitted their regional or secondary status in the family tree of responsibility. Most roads were merely mud paths anyway, and travel along them was by ox cart, horseback or foot—anything of larger bulk, speed or importance travelled by canal barge or railway. Most people died young from conditions for which there was no medical solution: diphtheria and smallpox, typhus and typhoid fever winnowed the high birth rate. Few could afford for their children to be in school rather than working and generating income or contributing to the farm. About half the population was illiterate.

In the Canadian territory, the main exports were grain and raw timber, and fish in the Maritimes. There were no large manufacturing enterprises that employed more than ten to twenty workers. There was only a handful of small cities, but they were notable for their filth and lack of amenities. Most of the population were farmers dwelling in rustic cabins who earned their bread with endless back-breaking labour, churning rocky soil and clearing stumps with horses and oxen. Agricultural fairs and barn raisings were the main social events other than church, and public executions always drew a crowd, with boisterous imbibing and perhaps some fighting.

Canadians were not generally a refined people and not inclined to philosophical distinctions but rather were inured to the hardscrabble daily grind of survival, with clannish loyalty based on some mix of ethnicity, religion and partisan politics. As a people, Canadians were not inclined to dream of big geographical or political ambitions or the betterment of society—most had barely any idea of their place in the world and could read the newspapers only with difficulty. They could scarcely entertain a more nuanced empathy toward the plight and possible rights of others. The twin pillars of society seemed to be the church and the tavern, and public drunkenness wasn't limited to special occasions—an election was prime time to drink and shout and perhaps fight in the dirt.

Elections were jolly, boisterous and occasionally violent events. Only men of property, not uncommon in a land of small farmers, held the right to vote. Still, this represented less than a quarter of the population.

The idea of general male voting, let alone universal voting, was a hard-won right and in many ways a radical concept in history. Women wouldn't be allowed to vote until the early twentieth century, and Indigenous people could vote only if they renounced their treaty status as "Indian" and then met the property requirement. (Macdonald controversially pushed through the franchise for some Indigenous people, but this was rescinded by the Liberal government of Prime Minister Wilfrid Laurier in the 1890s; Indigenous people didn't regain the right to vote until 1960.) Universal enfranchisement was inconceivable at the time and was opposed on the basis that it could create a form of mob rule. People needed protection from democracy, and it was believed that only those with a financial stake in society should be given the right to choose how it was run.

Corruption was endemic and vote buying was common in any contested riding—voting was held on different days, so that efforts to subvert the outcome were more effective and so that key candidates might be elected in more than one riding. (Laurier, for example, once represented three different constituencies in the House of Commons at the same time, and Macdonald was elected in Victoria, a place he had never been.) Sometimes the vote happened outside a tavern, and candidates or their attendants bought rounds of booze to lubricate loyalty and bolster the assertiveness and bravery perhaps needed to stand and be counted publicly, for there was no secret ballot until 1874, the third election after Confederation. A man would be publicly shamed if he had taken the bribe and then refused to proclaim as he had promised.

As the nineteenth century progressed, Victorianism ushered in a form of social restriction absent in previous generations. It was now important to keep up the appearance of everything being prim and proper: a tidy house, punctual church attendance and adherence to social conventions—what would later be called political correctness, where challenging accepted attitudes and thoughts was frowned upon.

The pious beliefs of the age were to be the cause of many conventions that are considered unjust today, such as the respective roles of men and women, the rights of Indigenous people within society and the legitimacy of their culture, the harsh and violent punishment for certain crimes, and later, the indoctrination of Indigenous children in residential schools for their so-called greater good. The moral certainties of any age, including our own, will lead to similar problems for future people who view the world differently.

People's decisions, and the moral makeup of a society in general, aren't just random bursts of oppression or power; they are often determined by the technology, economic prosperity and education of the era: ideas on how to structure a society, from rights to the roles of men and women, leadership and hierarchy, evolve out of a society's lifeway, not the inverse. The sanctimony and the belief in the rigid rule of law and religion that were the hallmarks of Victorianism were born of the need to regulate a disparate group of people, to bring order and structure to a society rapidly changing under the power of the Industrial Revolution, expanding global geographic knowledge and a surging population. Rigid conventions were something to hold on to amidst the storm, rules to mould the chaos and provide an anchor for their lives, boundaries within which to conduct themselves and provide meaning to lives that were often harsh and riddled with disappointments and tragedies. There was no centralized network of social support systems—the technology didn't allow for it—and health care, education and charity were merely local matters.

Nonetheless, it's hard to escape the conclusion that the Canadians of the 1860s and 1870s were a small and petty people, content to wallow in an unearned sense of superiority, sneering at the Americans with their thriving economy and growing prosperity while professing some peculiar sense of moral elevation or a greater sense of decorum. The literate classes, at least those that hadn't departed south, turned up their noses at republicanism, boisterous democracy and the mess of a thriving economy, even while losing thousands of people yearly into the churn of the American dream.

By 1867, Macdonald had succeeded in pushing through an amalgamation of Nova Scotia, New Brunswick, Upper Canada and Lower Canada into the kernel of a new country. He handily won the election in the fall of that year, with the Conservatives claiming 101 of the 181 seats, and Parliament convened in the partially completed buildings in Ottawa on November 7, cementing his role as Canada's first prime minister. He would serve in that position for nineteen of the next twenty-four years, until his death in 1891. But he had still grander ambitions: to extend the boundary of this new country many thousands of kilometres west until it reached the Pacific Ocean, to make it a continental nation just like the United States. These were remarkable ambitions for anyone, let alone the middle child of a failed Scottish shop owner.

CHAPTER FIVE

THE DREAMER
AND THE DREAM

———

B orn in Glasgow in 1815, Macdonald was five when his father emigrated to Kingston seeking a new start in life after his business failed. In Upper Canada, the family endured several other failed businesses, and Macdonald ended his formal schooling at age fifteen. He began clerking with a local Scottish lawyer and before he was twenty he had taken on several placements and begun practising law in Kingston, quickly earning a name for himself with high-profile criminal cases. A year before he entered politics, he married Isabella Clark, six years older than him and already in her thirties when they had first met in Scotland; when she travelled to Kingston to visit her sister, the two courted and, after a few months, married in 1843. They had two sons: the first, born when Isabella was thirty-nine, died after thirteen months, and the second, Hugh John, went on to a distinguished career in law and politics. Isabella and John enjoyed only two years together before she became afflicted with an unknown ailment that left her mostly bedridden with brief relapses, despite expensive medical attention in

New York. Her health, which had never been good, took a turn for the worse after her first pregnancy and never really recovered. Her heavy prescription of opium left her mentally as well as physically distant, and Macdonald threw himself into his work. She lingered on with bouts of illness until she died, at age forty-seven, in 1858. After her death, seven-year-old Hugh John, who would later become a premier of Manitoba, was mostly raised by his aunt and uncle.

In addition to his invalid wife, Macdonald was responsible for his mother, who had suffered a stroke and needed care, and his two sisters. His was not a fulfilling home life, but his loyalty and sense of responsibility kept him deeply involved with his family and their needs. It was during this time that Macdonald turned to hard drinking and politics, and he remained devoted to both for the remainder of his life.

Macdonald was and is sometimes mockingly known for his predilection for a wee dram of an evening, and of an afternoon, and at other times. Sometimes he was entirely in thrall to the insidious affliction of alcoholism, disappearing for days without notice, dysfunctional and unable to discharge his duties, carried out of meeting rooms or politely ignored as he mumbled and twitched in his chair. These days it is recognized that severe alcoholism is a debilitating disease, but in the later nineteenth century hard liquor was prevalent in society in a way most people today would find disturbing. There were many alcoholics, and drinking on the job was not uncommon, even around industrial machinery, when dealing with horse-drawn transport or farm equipment, and working on the railways. There were injuries. Liquor was the downfall of many families. American whiskey traders were plying their trade in the North American West after the ending of the Civil War discharged thousands of soldiers into a moribund eastern economy. So, while Macdonald was merely one of many succumbing to the allure of hard drink, it didn't make his life, or the life of his family and colleagues, any easier.

Macdonald remained unlucky in family matters. He married his second wife, Agnes Bernard, the sister of his private secretary, whom he first met when she was twenty, in 1856. Ten years later they had met again in London, when Macdonald was in town for the political business of finalizing the British North America Act, which would create the country of Canada. She was lively, vivacious and religious, and her attachment to her church deepened in correlation with her husband's drinking. After a courtship of several months, they married in February 1867; he struggled with his alcohol abuse, which he knew she disapproved of, seesawing between spiralling binges and months-long bursts of temperance. Their sole child, a daughter born less than two years later, after a prolonged and painful delivery, suffered from substantial physical and mental handicaps, including encephalitis, a swelling of the brain. Yet Macdonald remained ever loyal and a devoted husband and father. He thrived in politics in spite of his family obligations.

Macdonald was known for a lively wit, sense of humour and deep sense of caring toward the people of the land. Liberal MP Charles Langelier described him in the 1880s: "His eyes lively and his look pleasant. A charming smile, an enormous mass of curly hair, a slim build, his walk an elegant nonchalance, and a nose that made up his whole glory." There is a great abundance of literature about Macdonald, analyzing every aspect of his personal and professional life. In sum, he was a wily, strategic genius with a deep and intuitive understanding of the hearts, passions and needs of ordinary people. His political sense was seldom wrong even if he made mistakes, lost his temper or misjudged, particularly on happenings in the West, a land he had never visited and didn't seem to understand, grasping neither the politics nor the passions, desires and aspirations of the people living there.

Macdonald wasn't a judgmental prude, mean or vindictive, but he was a bon vivant who liked dinner parties and social affairs, even more so if they could be blended with politics. He wasn't motivated by money—his personal finances were precarious because of poor investments and debt inherited from his law partner—and at times he fought to stave off the embarrassment of personal bankruptcy. Nor was he inflamed by the arbitrary execution of power for petty reasons, or by imposing social values. His singular preoccupation for many decades was his dream of a semi-independent nation, still yoked to Britain for foreign policy, but entirely independent from the U.S. Most of his political capital during nineteen years in power as prime minister was devoted to this objective: creating the skeleton of a nation, the bones upon which the remainder of the body could be affixed sometime in the future.

Power is a mountain that one is always at risk of tumbling down—a mountain not of rock and forests but of writhing, grasping people. It's a struggle just to remain in place, let alone scramble, kicking and clawing, to the pinnacle and remain there. But Macdonald was a master at turning strangers into acquaintances, acquaintances into friends, friends into money, and money into votes. It was this very trait that was to get him into trouble a few years later. Given all his foibles, it makes one wonder whether he and others like him were the great people history paints them as or whether Macdonald was just one of yesterday's mediocrities bloated by a century and a half of unearned credit to suit a popular narrative of nation making. A balanced review of history, however, mostly disabuses this claim. Whether Macdonald was a good man or a bad man is open to debate, but he was certainly an interesting one. And if you consider the creation of Canada to have any merit—including its institutions that allow for peaceful change over time (however open to corruption and manipulation, even to this day) and the robust critique of its founders and their misdeeds without reprisal—then he was undoubtedly the right person at the right time. Even after decades in politics, it still wasn't possible to determine whether he was a genius or merely odd. In any event he was right at home in Parliament.

UPON HIS ELECTION IN THE FALL of 1867, Macdonald quickly set about fulfilling his next dream, or more accurately, phase two of his original ambition: to ensure that this new Canada did not become American. He was convinced, with good reason, that if he didn't grow Canada as a semi-independent appendage of the British Empire, all of what is now western Canada would become part of the aggressively expanding American Empire, and Canada would then drain away with it. He was convinced that the new country, if it was ever to rise to his expectations of producing a semi-democratic commercial hinterland for the Canada that existed along the St. Lawrence, would need a railway to bind it together and support a shared economy. Macdonald had, of course, never been to any of the places that he envisioned as becoming protectorates of the St. Lawrence. But that didn't seem to cause him any concern—anything was better than becoming American, wasn't it?

In addition to cajoling Newfoundland and Prince Edward Island to join Canada, Macdonald was busy with negotiations to secure for the new country the vast territory of the Hudson's Bay Company. Begun as a monopoly trading grant to politically connected cronies of King Charles II, its original territory was called Rupert's Land (after the king's cousin and the company's first governor, Prince Rupert) and consisted of all territory within the drainage basin of Hudson Bay— not that anyone at the time had any idea what that entailed or how large that drainage basin was. The company was founded on the ideas of two rascally French Canadian voyageurs whose fundamental notion—after adventuring extensively deep into the heart of North America in the lands surrounding and west of Lake Superior, visiting Indigenous trade fairs and villages and observing the variety of goods

being trafficked—was to send ships into Hudson Bay and tap into
these pre-existing Indigenous trade routes via the web of river systems
that led from the bay. The company is a much-storied enterprise whose
history includes naval battles in Hudson Bay, epic overland explorations that led as far west as the Pacific Ocean and literally cutthroat
competition with the upstart North West Company out of Montreal.

During its turbulent history it developed an enviable network of trading outposts that extended like a web over most of western Canada and
much of the Pacific Northwest of the U.S. that was serviced by rivers, the
original highways. The company nurtured good relations with most
Indigenous people, particularly the Cree, a woodland people who were
linked with the company from its earliest days and expanded west with it
over the generations, occupying varied roles within the continental economy. From liaisons among fur traders and their Indigenous wives sprung
the Métis, mixed-heritage descendants who had eventually established a
decentralized community based around the Red and Assiniboine Rivers.

In the 1840s, American migrants had trooped west along what
became known as the Oregon Trail and began farming and cattle raising in the Willamette Valley, among other regions. Although both
Britain and the U.S. claimed this territory for their empires, neither
party had established a dominant claim; the Indigenous people living
there were never consulted and by this time had seen devastating population declines, essentially emptying the land of inhabitants in advance
of the arrival of American pioneers. The only commercial outposts in
the region were maintained by the Hudson's Bay Company, its principal settlement being Fort Vancouver along the Columbia River—a
sprawling community of around five hundred people, a multicultural
blending that included Haudenosaunee, Cree and local peoples of the
Pacific Northwest, as well as French, Scottish, English and even some
Hawaiians. Eventually, in 1846, the American citizens in the region
declared themselves to be a new state in the union, and the company

had no option but to acquiesce. The border was established along the 49th parallel all the way to the Pacific. The company moved its western outpost to south Vancouver Island and named it Fort Victoria. The fact that territory could be claimed so effortlessly by the expanding American union was not lost on anyone.

Much ink has been spilled about the supposedly excessive powers of the Hudson's Bay Company, but for the first 150 years of its existence this power amounted to nothing other than a protection from domestic competitors in Britain. That began to change in the 1830s and accelerated as the century progressed, under the harsh vision of company governor George Simpson and increasing pressure from the British government that the company work toward certain imperial objectives as payback for maintaining its monopoly. By the 1860s, the fur trade was in decline. A shift in consumer tastes had for the first time in centuries left the beaver-felt hat out of demand. The fickle and whimsical seas of fashion had endured a mighty storm and tossed the wreckage of past trends upon the rocks. Fur from North America had been replaced by silk from China. This had drastic and horrible repercussions on the economy of North America, repercussions that coincided with the devastation of Indigenous society from contagious disease and the incursion of American whiskey traders on the Plains and the influx of perhaps thirty thousand American prospectors farther west. The company's revenues were declining, and the old social and commercial patterns that had shaped the land were being reordered and remodelled by these powerful forces.

In the absence of overarching authority by any Indigenous polity, the British government feared the entire territory would become subsumed by the American Empire as it crept west. Indeed, the only obstacle to this dominance by one empire over the territory dubiously claimed by another empire-in-the-making was the presence of the fur trading monopoly that had existed for countless generations back to 1670. The

Hudson's Bay Company's claim over the territory in which it operated rested on shaky foundations obscured in the mists of history. By the mid-nineteenth century, the company no longer existed merely at the request or acquiescence of Indigenous societies. It had become indispensable to life, the distribution of its basic hardware goods necessary for survival. Simpson, however, sought to impose his will upon Indigenous societies weakened by disease and susceptible to manipulation and control, and the attitude of the company became more domineering and avaricious.

Many, especially the Métis in Red River, were chafing at restrictions on their commercial ambitions, on activities that the Hudson's Bay Company didn't control. It was not tenable for a shareholder corporation engaged in fur trading to be dispensing justice to tens of thousands of people throughout its commercial purview—it was like putting the fox in charge of the henhouse. It never had been a satisfactory governance solution, but the company had only recently been pushed into this conflicting role and had no real interest in furthering its involvement—governance wasn't its core business, so to speak, being complicated, expensive and unremunerative as a private activity, especially without access to tax revenues.

For many years the British government had pondered the fate of the venerable company, which strenuously argued to maintain its monopoly even in the face of the declining fur industry. By the late 1860s, the idea of the land becoming an appendage of the new country of Canada was increasingly seen in Britain as the solution to stemming the tide of American expansion and domination of North America. The scheme that most closely matched these political aspirations was for Canada to purchase the territorial rights of the Hudson's Bay Company and use this as the legal foundation to annex the vast western hinterland into the new Dominion.

This was the thinking when, on July 15, 1870, the company relinquished its monopoly for a £300,000 payout, and other land and concessions, and transferred the overarching rights to its territories to the new country of Canada, as if the entire deal was an uncomplicated real estate transaction with clear title. Essentially, multiple cultures of Indigenous peoples and others, including the Métis, were assumed to be transferable tokens on the board of the great game of empire, easily moved about or replaced to achieve other, more political objectives. No one bothered to consult them or inform them of this material change in their citizenship, freedom and independence. In fact many, if not most, despite the strains and destructions of the era, still harboured no doubts as to their own independence.

Macdonald saw the HBC territory—which had conveniently morphed in public discourse, from a commercial monopoly that gave the company protection from domestic competitors into the owner of the vast field of its operations—as being the key to his grand dream of a northern empire that linked the St. Lawrence to the Pacific.

MACDONALD HAD AN UNLIKELY ALLY in his nation-building dream, a prominent and outspoken Victoria resident who advocated for union with the Canadas and went by the unusually evocative name of Amor De Cosmos. De Cosmos was born William Alexander Smith in Nova Scotia, but he had changed his name to reflect his new philosophy. After having first converted to Mormonism, the "Lover of the Universe" headed west to join the California gold rush and then washed up in Victoria in 1858 when gold was discovered along the Fraser River. Always interested in philosophy, debate and journalism, he was a social reformer who opposed Governor Douglas and his undemocratic ways, denouncing the family-company compact that seemed to rule the new colony. In many ways Douglas was an admirable character, but an openness to sharing power in a democratic government was not one of his noteworthy traits. Power in the small community was tightly managed and doled out to serve the interests of the few.

De Cosmos, a somewhat fanciful advocate for social change, agitated for free enterprise unleashed from the constraints of the monopoly, for public education and for responsible government and an elected assembly. When he arrived in Victoria, he found to his consternation that an American newspaper, the *Victoria Gazette*, served the community. To pursue his own interests against Americans and the Hudson's Bay Company, he founded the *British Colonist*. Eccentric and flighty, with a fiery temper, a bundle of peculiar phobias and a penchant for flying into rages and attacking opponents with his fists, De Cosmos eventually became the second premier of British Columbia, in 1872, and jointly a member of the provincial legislature and Liberal member of Parliament in Ottawa, a post he held until 1882, before being declared insane several years before his death in 1897. But in the 1860s, he was a serious thorn in the side of the ruling oligarchy, which mostly consisted of former Hudson's Bay Company managers and their cronies who had resisted the transition from company rule to representative government, locking up much of the economic activity within their internecine clique, even after Douglas's retirement in 1864.

De Cosmos did not love all of the cosmos equally. He frowned at Chinese immigrants and was opposed to land rights for Indigenous peoples. "Shall we allow a few vagrants to prevent forever industrious settlers from settling on the unoccupied lands? Not at all. . . . Locate reservations for them on which to earn their own living, and if they trespass on White settlers punish them severely. A few lessons would soon enable them to form a correct estimation of their own inferiority," he wrote in the *British Colonist* on March 8, 1861. His was a limited or exclusive cosmos; some might call it diminished in comparison to its expansive possibility. His opinions dovetailed neatly, however, with those of Joseph Trutch, the chief commissioner of lands and works.

Trutch, who later became the first lieutenant-governor of the new province, was an unabashed racist who referred to all Indigenous peoples as "savages" and proclaimed that they had inferior intelligence and were lazy, violent and incapable of "improvement." He reversed the Indigenous land policies of Douglas, whose opinions dated from the old fur trade era and his decades-long interaction and affiliation with multiple Indigenous peoples and cultures over his long career, and were reinforced by his own mixed-heritage wife and children and the other company fur traders and their mixed-heritage families who formed the establishment in the early days. But the world was changing, and there was not much anyone could do to stop the tectonic population migration. Perhaps they could have, at least, tried to smooth the transition and prevent exploitation and violence. Instead, the new establishment swept the fur trade mentality away, driven by a dream of widespread farm settlement based on the European or eastern model, and had no interest in or sympathy for any aspects of Indigenous culture.

Although a somewhat odious character, De Cosmos was instrumental in pushing through the amalgamation of the colonies of Vancouver Island and British Columbia, and then for establishing the Confederation League, a loose affiliation of prominent members of the settlements who favoured a union with Canada as the best political future for themselves and the entire region. One of the other prominent members of the Confederation League was Mifflin Wistar Gibbs, a Black business owner and journalist who had arrived from California in 1858 and met with Douglas to negotiate the immigration of between five hundred and six hundred Black pioneers from California. They were worried about political oppression and their future in a land where they couldn't own property or give evidence against a white person. Douglas welcomed

Gibbs and his pioneers, and they settled in the vicinity of Fort Victoria. "British Columbia offered and gave protection to both [rights and commercial opportunity], and equality of political privileges," Gibbs wrote. "I cannot describe with what joy we hailed the opportunity to enjoy that liberty under the 'British lion' denied us beneath the pinions of the American Eagle."

These newcomers, as Gibbs noted, soon "bought homes and other property, and by industry and character vastly improved their condition and were the recipients of respect and esteem from the community." For years after, Gibbs and many members of his community threw their vote behind Douglas, ensuring his victory over De Cosmos in the 1860 provincial election. Gibbs was elected to Victoria City Council in 1867, the first Black holder of public office in B.C. After ten years, Gibbs departed Victoria with his wife and two young daughters and settled in Little Rock, Arkansas, where he became a lawyer and diplomat. He was active in the Republican Party, and in 1873 became the first Black judge elected in the U.S. One of his Victoria-born daughters, Harriet Gibbs Marshall, later established the Washington Conservatory of Music in Washington, D.C.

MACDONALD INSTINCTIVELY KNEW that he would have to offer something grand and outrageous to distract attention from the practical and legal obstacles to his vision. The promise of a railway across the continent was the greatest inducement, or bribe, that he could think of to coerce B.C. to join with Canada. Meanwhile, on the other side of the continent, prominent citizens of the Confederation League, which included De Cosmos, Gibbs and many other influential members of the community, convened a meeting, the Yale Convention, in September 1868. They advocated against independence and against joining the United States. Instead, they favoured joining with Canada, provided the eastern country built a railway to connect them to their potential countrymen, eliminating the need to have all of their economic and communication networks run through San Francisco.

Dr. John Sebastian Helmcken, Joseph Trutch and Dr. Robert Carrall were the three delegates of the government sent east to Ottawa in 1870, via the U.S. railways, along with a journalist named Henry Seelye, dispatched by the *Colonist*. Directed to negotiate the terms of union, their collective attitude and position were summed up nicely by Dr. Helmcken. "The journey from San Francisco by railway opened our eyes not a little, for a railway had been built through a mountainous country quite as bad as that of B. Columbia—if this one could be built so could one through B. Columbia. . . . No R.R. no Confederation."

But there was no need to summon such bluster and dudgeon. In Ottawa, the delegates were offered terms more favourable than they had reason to expect—survey work would start immediately, with construction to follow within two years, and the whole thing would be completed within ten years. It sounded too good to be true. They would have been content to accept a road, but they were offered a railway, and were quietly advised to publicly demand one. It would be much more advantageous for Macdonald to be able to claim that it was an outside demand that had commanded compliance, rather than his own personal dream and ambition.

Once back in Victoria, Helmcken complied. During the Confederation debates in 1870–71 he proclaimed: "It is just as well that the Dominion Government should know that there are very many people in this Colony who think that Annexation would be far more advantageous than Confederation, and who have no love for Canada. I maintain that the people of this Colony do not desire Confederation; they desire these glittering terms; take away or reduce the terms, and the people don't want Confederation—will not have it."

As a province of the new Dominion of Canada, British Columbia would gain control over public lands. While government authority to enforce control over people within that territory was not clear or undisputed, it would be required to relinquish to the federal government a large swath of land, twenty miles wide, adjacent to the new railway's right-of-way, along a route yet to be determined. This was no big deal to politicians in Victoria, since in what sense did they really own this land anyway? It cost them nothing to agree to ceding land that was occupied by others, and they could also leave the enforcement up to others.

The promise of a soon-to-be-completed rail link to the East was enticing, as it would provide vital economic and social connection to a population centre that was neither Indigenous nor American. It was sure to bolster their own colonial economic interests. But the key was that the federal government would assume the colony's debt, finance the legislature and the governor's salary, and support all federal agencies with salaried positions. There would be representation within the federation in Ottawa; it would be a responsible government rather than an appointed one. "The remaining terms," wrote Seelye in the *Colonist* in July 20, "are unimportant. They refer to the extension of the postal service, the erection of a Hospital, a Lunatic Asylum, and a Penitentiary, Protection of the Fisheries, aid to Immigration, the election of senators, the formal admission of the colony into the Union, the defence of the colony and aid to the volunteer force."

Yet joining the Dominion of Canada, although deemed the most promising means of preserving what they perceived as their British heritage, presented insurmountable geographic and economic obstacles. Victoria remained very British in culture while very American in economy—a dichotomy that caused considerable tension in the late 1860s. Although an ardently pro-union faction in Victoria sent two petitions to President Grant in Washington, stressing their natural link with the United States and requesting support for their battle to maintain that link, the majority of British Columbia's non-Indigenous, mostly white citizens were leery about shedding British affiliation. Victoria even had a cricket team where everyone knew each other; in a photo they are shown suited and bewhiskered in their mismatched and garish-looking clothing and hats posing on the rude lawn of what would become Beacon Hill Park. Members included the most prominent men of the community, including judges, lawyers, politicians and a gold commissioner. Other photos of the era depict boatloads of besuited men and bonneted women draped in heavy-looking dresses, having rowed out for a picnic along the rocky coast, artfully posed around their baskets and ground cloths, holding china teacups and napkins and small plates of dainties—many no doubt imported from San Francisco.

An election was held in November soon after the delegates returned, and federalists were elected across the board in all six ridings. On January 5, 1871, they met and approved the terms of the union. Some must surely have shaken their heads if they were at all familiar with the geography and, in particular, the mountains that blocked the path. The great new railway was to be built from both east and west to converge somewhere in the middle. It would surely provide economic stimulus to the region, which was currently losing much of its American population back to the U.S. and the economy was in the doldrums.

The declaration to make the railway a reality was a promise that soared high on the winds of rhetoric, but the truth was more sobering. It was a goal more aspirational than realistic. The Canadian Pacific Railway, as it was being called, if it could be built, would be the longest, most technically sophisticated yet financially precarious railway yet constructed anywhere. Canada's first and greatest megaproject was a political and engineering feat of staggering dimension, with over four thousand kilometres of track, much of it driven through terrain unsuitable for railways. It made political sense, from a certain big-dream expansionist point of view, but certainly not economic or geographical sense. There was no dominant overriding political or military authority west of the colonial regions of Ontario and Quebec with any true force; Macdonald hoped that the proclamation of the land transfer would usher in the very authority he boldly proclaimed for Canada—a situation that would have profound implications, leading to misunderstandings that reverberate to this day.

In any case, all talk of railways over such distance and terrain was a recent phenomenon made possible only a few years earlier by a revolutionary invention from a sickly young Swedish chemist.

PART TWO

—

THE PLAN

CHAPTER SIX

CONQUERING GEOGRAPHY

———

I n April 1866, a standard shipping crate, one among thousands, had been sent by steamship from New York, by rail along the future route of the Panama Canal, and by ship again up the Pacific coast to San Francisco. It was labelled "general merchandise." When a man working in the Wells Fargo warehouse compound noticed the crate was leaking a strange oily substance onto the ground, he grabbed a hammer and crowbar while some others gathered around to see what was inside causing the leak. "The explosion was so powerful as to shake the earth like an earthquake for a circuit of a quarter of a mile. Every window in California Street, between Montgomery and Kearny, were demolished and panes of glass were shattered even afar as Third Street," declared the *Placer Herald* on April 21. The thunderous explosion destroyed most of a block of buildings, killing ten and injuring dozens. The article contained the following disclaimer:

WARNING!
THE FOLLOWING DESCRIPTION OF
THE RESULTS OF THE EXPLOSION
IS EXTREMELY GRAPHIC.

Fragments of human remains were found scattered in many places. In the auction room of Cobb and Stinton, on the east side of Montgomery Street, a human brain, almost intact, and other fragments of the body near it, were found. A piece of human vertebrae was blown over the buildings on the east side of Montgomery Street, where it was picked up in front of Squarza's, on Leidsdorff Street. A piece of skull was lying on California Street, east of Leidsdorff, with other fragments of human remains, and a human arm struck the third story window of the building across the street.

It was the latest in a series of mysterious civilian explosions that had killed dozens in 1866. Earlier that same month, fifty crates had erupted aboard the *European*, a ship in Panama bound for San Francisco, killing over fifty workers. Along the Central Pacific Railroad in the Sierra Nevadas a similar blast tore through a work camp. In New York City, a hotel worker dragged a forgotten suitcase from storage into the street; it was seeping acrid vapour and it soon blew a massive hole in the pavement, shattering windows along the block and injuring eighteen people. A warehouse in Sydney, Australia, erupted, killing twelve. A factory in Germany was demolished, and a month later so was a factory in Norway. In Bremerhaven, on Germany's north coast, the steamship *Mosel* exploded, killing twenty-eight and injuring nearly two hundred in an instance of insurance fraud; it involved the same substance that was implicated in all of the other explosions—a staggering chain of deadly detonations, occurring seemingly at random.

All the deaths and millions of dollars of property damage were soon linked to two words most people had never before heard: nitroglycerine and Nobel.

NEVER IN ROBUST HEALTH, Alfred Nobel was a frail, nervous man whose receding hairline exposed his protuberant forehead, and his slightly bulging eyes were framed by rather large ears. Shy in public and socially awkward, he had a curious retiring manner and preferred the solitude and regimen of his work to social functions.

Lonely and isolated, and with no formal education, he put in herculean hours in his chemistry laboratory, which was a major component of his Paris mansion, often working all night or until he became overwhelmed by toxic fumes; for some reason he worked with poor ventilation. He didn't look old and yet, when he was in his mid-forties, referred to himself as elderly. Since his youth, he had devoted nearly all of his time to his experiments and to expanding his business, leaving him a somewhat melancholy individual without family or friends and with deep regret for his life choices. He nevertheless became one of the world's wealthiest people, before donating it all to his now famous prizes in physics, chemistry, medicine, literature and peace. One of the great ironies of his life is that he developed a heart condition called angina that during his lifetime began to be treated with nitroglycerine pills.

Born into a family of inventors and entrepreneurs—his father worked on underwater gunpowder mines for the Russian government in St. Petersburg, while his two older brothers made a fortune developing the vast petroleum deposits in Baku, Azerbaijan, along the Caspian Sea—Nobel had a morbid fascination with explosives. After his family returned to Stockholm from St. Petersburg when he was in his late twenties, he and his younger brother Emil Oskar began experimenting with nitroglycerine, trying to control it or make it more predictable and safe. Nitroglycerine had been accidentally invented sixteen years earlier by the Italian chemist Ascanio Sobrero. Sobrero ceased his explorations of nitroglycerine after several dangerous experiments demolished parts of his laboratory. He nearly died himself after placing a drop on his tongue, causing a pulsating, violent headache and a general weakness in his limbs that lasted several hours. As test subjects, his dogs didn't fare so well; they flopped to the floor, foaming at the mouth, violently shuddering and vomiting, banging their heads against the ground until they died.

Nobel's first great patent was for the blasting cap, a device that used a smaller, controlled explosion to trigger a larger one, transforming nitroglycerine from a dangerous curiosity into something of great practical power. His blasting caps used controllable mercury fulminate, heralding an era of high explosives that radically changed the world in the late nineteenth century. It was the spark that unleashed the civil engineering revolution, which in turn fuelled the industrial and political revolutions.

Naturally there were setbacks, particularly the explosion that destroyed his early manufacturing facility and killed his younger brother. But business soon boomed, scaling up rapidly as he licensed his patents throughout Europe and the world, with many nitroglycerine factories popping up to meet the escalating demand. The revolutionary new product was marketed as Nobel's Blasting Oil. Unknown at the time was that nitroglycerine is sensitive to heat and the slightest impact, which led to the deadly explosions of 1866.

SINCE THE DAWN OF HISTORY, muscle, fire, wind and water were the only energy sources. It wasn't until the thirteenth century that gunpowder, a mixture of sulphur, charcoal and saltpetre, was added to the list. Not surprisingly, soldiers and civil engineers adopted it quickly, for it was certainly more powerful than shovels and pickaxes. Black powder, as it was sometimes called, was revolutionary and made possible the blasting of great troughs for canals for shipping, levelling hilly ground for roads and railbeds and even digging the first subaqueous tunnels. The Languedoc Canal, or Canal du Midi, in southwestern France, which linked the Mediterranean and the Bay of Biscay, stands out as one of the great public works enabled by black powder. Completed in 1681, it was around 220 kilometres long, with 119 locks to manage water levels. It included a 165-metre-long tunnel and reached an elevation of nearly 190 metres above sea level. It was a phenomenal feat of imagination and technical sophistication rivalling the aqueducts of ancient Rome.

These types of industrial projects were on the increase throughout the nineteenth century, slowly and painstakingly transforming Europe and eastern North America. Constructed between 1817 and 1825, the Erie Canal was a 942-kilometre-long waterway that linked Buffalo and Albany and thence the Hudson River to New York and was used for the transport of bulk commodities, especially grains, by barge, supplying growing cities with a reliable food source. The Welland Canal linked Lake Ontario to Lake Erie, bypassing Niagara Falls. Fresh fruits and vegetables could now travel quickly to key urban centres, and bulky commodities like coal could be shipped from mining regions to industrial centres.

By the early 1860s, the demands on gunpowder had exceeded its capacity. The Central Pacific Railroad alone was consuming three to five hundred kegs of gunpowder every day, with workers piling them up awkwardly at rockfaces, lighting the fuse and running for cover. But having teams of men heap barrels of gunpowder against rockfaces was inefficient and deadly. Progress was slow and dangerous and expensive; injuries and deaths were legion. The quantities needed to break hard rock were too great, and it couldn't easily or safely be placed in cracks to improve its efficiency. The world was on the verge of a golden age of engineering but was tethered to the limited explosive capacity of black powder. Black powder had become obsolete for any large-scale project except those guaranteed to be profitable. When Nobel's Blasting Oil burst onto the scene it opened a door to a new world. Once the properties of the new substance became known, international demand soared. Its uses for blasting in civil engineering were as obvious as its military applications. It was almost too good to be true, and no one had time for safety checks.

AFTER THE DEVASTATING EXPLOSION in San Francisco, the State of California banned the transportation and shipping of nitroglycerine, and other jurisdictions in the U.S. were considering following suit. It was even suggested that possession of the deadly substance should be a hanging offence. Countries throughout Europe likewise quickly leapt to ban it and shut down production. Ships wouldn't transport it because they couldn't get insurance, nor would railways carry it. The Central Pacific had to revert to the dangerous and inefficient black powder until they hired a chemist to work on site, blending the glycerine with nitric and sulphuric acids each day in a hastily erected lab in a rickety shed, powering the final blast through the granite of the Summit Tunnel. It got the job done, but it still wasn't safe or efficient.

Nobel realized nitroglycerine could never be entirely banned, for it was just too useful. But it could easily bankrupt the first company to market and manufacture it. He once again threw himself into his work. He spent months locked in a factory lab in Germany trying to stabilize the substance; meanwhile his budding commercial empire teetered. Finally, he settled on kieselguhr clay as a stabilizing agent. The inert and malleable putty absorbed the nitroglycerine and neutralized its volatility. Nobel called his new product dynamite—after the Greek *dynamis*, for powerful or potential—and marketed it as Nobel's Safety Powder, to allay fears that it was in any way associated with the deadly nitroglycerine. It could be shaped into sticks and coated with stiff paper, perfect for sliding into predrilled boreholes to trigger the explosion within the rock instead of on the surface.

Throughout the remainder of the century, Nobel and other chemists fine-tuned and perfected multiple variations of nitroglycerine-based explosives to achieve more power, better-controlled explosions and explosives that could be detonated underwater or acted as smokeless propellants for use in guns and artillery. Some of the famous names of the era include Blasting Gelatine, Atlas Powder, Hercules Powder, Judson Powder, Ballistite, guncotton and cordite. What once would have taken a thousand labourers a century to complete could now be done in months.

Dynamite and its subsequent improvements and variations made possible the modern industrial world. It was a catalyst for the grandiose dreams of a wildly optimistic age. Concrete and cement became common construction materials once gypsum and lime deposits could be affordably blasted. Fields could be easily cleared of stumps and rocks for agriculture, which allowed the use of machines to improve harvest yields. Ruined buildings could easily be demolished and cleared away. The landscape could be transformed, causing a radical shift in the way civil engineering projects were conceived and executed. In the years after 1867, shipments of dynamite doubled annually, and Nobel had factories around the world and licensed production to other companies in North America. In Canada, the two main producers of dynamite at the time were the Hamilton Powder Company and the Acadia Powder Company, which were owned by Nobel Industries.

All of the famous monumental projects that defined the era were conceived and completed within decades of the invention of dynamite and the blasting cap. For generations it had been a dream to blast a hole through the Saint-Gotthard Massif between Italy and Switzerland, but it was only after the invention of dynamite that it became feasible to consider a sixteen-kilometre-long railway tunnel. It took ten years and over a thousand tons of dynamite to complete nineteenth-century Europe's greatest engineering feat. Not to mention countless lives.

Work continued relentlessly twenty-four hours a day, month after month, as the workers drove through the solid rock in the ill-lit gloom of the mighty tunnel. Thunderous explosions shattered tons of rock from the mountain while hundreds of men scampered over the piles of pulverized boulders to clear the way for the next blast. Water gushed from the cracks and boreholes, soaking the men and occasionally requiring them to drag boulders and debris from the tunnel face while wading up to their knees. Labourers dropped from heat exhaustion. Rock dust, deadly fumes, the stale exhalations of men and pack animals and the heat brought on an array of debilitating afflictions such as silicosis, bronchitis and pneumonia. The tunnel eventually claimed more than 277 lives and seriously maimed thousands of workers. There was on average one death every two weeks, and countless other deaths in the labour camps from disease and malnutrition. Several months of work weakened a man, and a year usually left him sickened. French, German and Swiss labourers refused to work in the tunnel and so the work was generally left to more desperate Italian peasants.

The U.S. consul general to Switzerland and Italy, Samuel Byers, made a trip to see the famed engineering feat in 1878, when it was still years from completion. He was appalled by the conditions. "My guide and I got on the front platform of one of these air engines, and were shot into the tunnel for miles through a black cloud of smoke and gas that I thought would kill me, or cause me to fall off the engine. It was Cimmerian darkness. The engineer said: 'You shall now see a glimpse of the bowels of hell.' I saw nothing for miles, and then suddenly we came to the weird lights, the big air machines boring into the granite walls, and the half-naked workmen. It was a gruesome picture in there, with the yellow lights, the racket of the machines, and the occasional explosion of dynamite. The water in places burst from the rocks in streams as big as my arm, and with force enough to knock the workmen from their feet. . . . Far in, where the compressed air left the pipes, the ventilation seemed better, but it would kill most men to stay in there at all for any length of time. It is well known that the health of these unfortunate workmen is being ruined. An early death stares every one of them in the face."

Even Louis Favre, the Genoese mining contractor who rashly put up his personal finances to back the project, succumbed to the inhumane conditions. After years of scurrying in the gloom with his men, sleeping and eating there while inhaling the noxious air, he clutched his chest, sank to his knees in the mud and was dead before he could be brought out of the fume-infested tunnel, leaving behind a now destitute daughter who was provided a meagre pension by the company.

After its completion, however, the railway through the mountains cut travel time between Milan and Lucerne to five hours from over twenty-seven before, an enormous economic boon.

THE ENGINEERING TRANSFORMATION of Western society as it rapidly industrialized included other famous projects that increased trade and travel and created the modern economy. On September 24, 1876, the rocks at New York's Hell's Gate, a giant submerged outcropping that blocked the channel between the East River and Long Island Sound, the source of treacherous currents that damaged about 2 per cent of the vessels that travelled the waterway and made the channel unnavigable to larger ships, was detonated in a grand display. In the preceding years, 48,000 pounds of dynamite and blasting gelatine had been strategically situated in boreholes and caves surrounding the outcropping. After the mighty explosion, "the odors of combusted nitroglycerine swept over unfortunate Yorkville—as though a hundred tallow factories were on fire," according to the *New York Times*. They did it again nine years later, on October 10, 1885, with an incredible 283,000 pounds of dynamite and blasting gelatine, creating the modern New York river infrastructure that vastly expanded the channel for shipping, opening "a new highway for the commerce of the world."

Other famous industrial engineering projects of the era included the Severn Tunnel in western England, completed after thirteen years of work in 1886; the 1.5-kilometre-long Musconetcong Tunnel in Pennsylvania in 1875; the 7.6-kilometre Hoosac Tunnel in Massachusetts in 1875, with two hundred recorded deaths in blasting accidents; and the 19.8-kilometre Simplon Tunnel through the Alps in 1906, with only thirty-two deaths and eighty-four permanent maimings. There were also the 6.3-kilometre-long rock trough of the Corinth Canal, separating the Peloponnese from mainland Greece and linking the Ionian and Aegean Seas; the 193-kilometre Suez Canal, a commercial link between the Mediterranean and Red Seas that obviated the lengthy sail around Africa, which was rapidly finished with dynamite in 1869; and the Panama Canal, begun in 1882 but not completed until 1914—82 kilometres across the Isthmus of Panama, connecting the Atlantic and Pacific Oceans, which ended the circuitous and dangerous voyage around Cape Horn, shaving weeks off sailing times between eastern and western North America. Dynamite also made possible the London Underground and the New York subway.

The Canadian Pacific Railway belongs to this pantheon of transformative industrial megaprojects.

DYNAMITE AND STEAM TECHNOLOGY augmented each other, like relay racers handing off the baton before each new spurt of speed, taking over from the flagging energy and rushing onward with renewed vigour into the future. Each improved the efficiency and practicality of the other, making possible further advancements. The idea of steam power led to the need for more blasting, while more blasting improved the benefits of steam transport, which in turn led to even more blasting with better and more powerful explosives, which created more demand for coal and metals, which in turn required more explosives, etc.

The Industrial Revolution began in Great Britain in the late eighteenth century, initially with textile mills and later iron production. The productivity gains from mechanization were incredible, and it is generally considered one of the most intense periods of human technological improvement since the domestication of crops and animals at the dawn of the agricultural revolution thousands of years earlier. What previously had to be done by hand could now be done with the aid of machines operating independently of individual workers. The machines needed many knowledgeable engineers to design them and skilled workers to operate them, which in turn led to greater technical proficiency and specialization that created further improvements.

The spike in population growth and increase in economic output resulted in an overall wealthier society, but at horrendous social cost: devilish working conditions and injured and killed workers, displaced from rural villages into congested urban slums. The increased productivity came with an increase in tedious and repetitive jobs in unpleasant environments. The filth, poverty and squalor of rural peasant life were replaced with the filth, poverty and squalor of congested tenements in urban slums, where the miasmic clouds of coal smoke produced a stagnant fug that clogged streets with damp, acrid fumes, a mélange of industry and humans, bodies congested with phlegm, coughing and spitting. It's hardly surprising that respiratory ailments such as tuberculosis were rampant. In pre-industrial Europe, and indeed much of the world, malnutrition and hunger were common and life expectancy was barely forty, though it approached fifty in the United States.

Steam power was a mighty new source of energy in an era when everything had been accomplished, tediously, dangerously and slowly, with horses, oxen, wind and water. Iron became the new structural material for bridges, displacing wood and stone. Now, instead of the

odour of horse excrement and woodsmoke and the clang and thud
of pickaxes, there were shadowy workers shuffling through the gloom of
foundries and the eerie red glow of molten metal being poured. Coal
was piled in great heaps in factory yards. Belching smoke issued from
chimneys, and the daily sounds were piercing screeches, deep grinding
growls, rumbles and metallic bangs. To some it was the sweet sound of
money being made. To others it was hell on earth. But as the processes
became more refined and efficient, these technologies began to change
the landscape.

The Industrial Revolution brought us a great many new mass-
produced materials, such as chemicals for bleaching cloth, bulk glass,
soap, paper, cement and gas lighting and a host of other items previously
made by artisans at significant expense. The benefits to agriculture
came from mechanized plowing, seeding, harvesting and shipment.
In mining, efficiencies came from coal-powered steam engines pump-
ing water and hauling heavy carts from the bowels of the mine. But it
was transportation that saw the greatest changes. Previously a few
inland waterways could be barged and ships plied the coasts; otherwise
there were rutted roads for horse-drawn wagons, mired in mud and
notoriously unreliable for bulk transport. With iron production came
the ability to roll out iron rails, which a heavy, powerful, mobile steam-
powered, piston-driven engine with metal-flanged wheels could roll
on, quickly hauling incredible quantities of goods, bulk commodities
and people. Beginning with the Liverpool and Manchester Railway in
1830, soon Britain and later Europe and the eastern U.S. were gripped
by railway mania. More than ten thousand kilometres of rails were laid
in the 1840s in Britain, and the same by 1860 in the U.S., and increasing
every year.

Railways in the U.S. were spearheaded by the United States Army
Corps of Engineers, who surveyed routes and imposed the rights-of-
way through laws of eminent domain, which allowed railways to

proceed even in the face of property owners' objections. They organized the manufacture of uniform track and other civil infrastructure, so that by 1860 nearly every major city along the Eastern seaboard and as far west as Ohio was connected by a network of rail lines. President Abraham Lincoln oversaw the Pacific Railway Act of 1862 as a means of creating cohesion in the nation during and after the Civil War, by opening new markets and connecting regions. The first American cross-continental railway was completed in 1869—a combination of the Union Pacific Railroad and the Central Pacific Railroad. It linked the country through a rapid mechanized transportation corridor that radically transformed the economy and population of the West, replacing the old wagon trains popular in the mythology of the Oregon Trail.

Railway development was slower in the territories of British North America. Most of the capital in the sparsely populated region was tied up in canals. But the benefits of rail transportation were quickly grasped, since roads were poorly engineered quagmires impassable for much of the year and waterways were frozen for five months of the year, severely limiting the options for travel and shipping and hampering economic development. As early as 1836 a collective of Montreal merchants financed the Champlain and St. Lawrence Railroad, which was little more than a twenty-six-kilometre "portage" to get from Montreal to Lake Champlain in Vermont. The Montreal and Lachine Railroad in 1847 provided a similar service twelve kilometres long to get around rapids and aid water transport. The Albion Mines Railway in Nova Scotia was a similarly short ten-kilometre stretch to haul coal.

After the colonial government passed the Guarantee Act, which provided for a government grant guaranteeing interest on railway bonds, railway construction surged. In 1854 there were the Great Western Railway, connecting Niagara Falls to Windsor, Ontario; the Ontario, Simcoe and Huron Railway in 1855; and the St. Lawrence and Atlantic Railroad, between Montreal and Portland, Maine, which was completed in 1856, as well as a smattering of others. But the most ambitious project was the Grand Trunk Railway from Montreal to the Atlantic, using British capital and imported engineers and surveyors. Unfortunately, it was a poorly conceived mess and ran into serious financial difficulties before being bailed out by the government. Nevertheless, by 1867 it managed over two thousand kilometres of track linking Nova Scotia, New Brunswick and the northern New England states to Sarnia and Montreal.

Railways were huge, coddled sponges for public support—land grants, interest guarantees, rights-of-way legislation and outright cash giveaways. But the promise was that they would open travel and commerce to new regions and improve efficiency, and provide access to timber and mining regions; as well, new farmland could be developed once there was access to a market. It also spurred industry to mine and smelt all the raw materials and manufacture them into the components required by railways. Toronto grew rapidly as a hub for most of the big railways. Canada's first locomotive was built there. Techniques and innovation in manufacturing for railways were then applied to other products and civil engineering projects. The building of bridges and tunnels created the technical know-how to tackle other engineering problems related to urban development. Railways also created demand for coal or wood at the stops along the route, and those stops provided employment in service centres, hotels, track yards and stations.

Railways had cultural and social benefits too, creating a network for commerce and travel that could strengthen cultural and national ties and foster a sense of community. Macdonald sought to emulate the rationale of the American cross-continental railway and apply it to his new country. The idea of creating greater connections between people in disparate regions resonated with the larger idea of connecting all of British North America to create a network distinct from the one being created in the U.S., enabled by the twin powers of dynamite and steam power. Macdonald dreamed of a cultural, technological and transportation bubble, a hinterland from which "all roads led to Rome," primarily to the benefit of the new latter-day Romans with their capital in Ottawa.

But politics, at times, is like engineering. As a law of systems, engineering builds in safeguards for failures. Yet when there are an inestimable number of variables, something in the safeguards themselves can cause even the best laid plans to fail.

CHAPTER SEVEN

THE INCORRIGIBLE "LABRADOR" SMITH

———

I t is one of the most iconic photographs in Canadian history. A cluster of men, clad variously in dungarees and brimmed caps or suits and top hats above the prodigious beards fashionable in the era, some artfully posing with construction tools, huddle around an elderly man bent over and wielding a hammer, or, more accurately, holding its handle as it rests upon the symbolic last spike. Two steel tracks run through the centre of the congregation on the overcast morning of November 7, 1885, at Craigellachie, in Eagle Pass, British Columbia. It was a staged grouping, rather small for its historical import, but reflecting the precarious finances of the Canadian Pacific Railway. These weren't the labourers who had built the railway—a lesser-known photo taken on the same day at nearby Donald shows a decidedly more raggedly clothed and motley crew of actual workers. Rather, the iconic photo shows eastern financiers and management, including many of the luminaries responsible for overseeing the completion of the first transcontinental railway north of the border: the rotund CPR manager,

William Cornelius Van Horne; the route finder, railway engineer and inventor of time zones, Sandford Fleming; the famed ascetic and surveyor, Major Albert Bowman Rogers; and the legendary Sam Steele of the North-West Mounted Police.

But the central character is the old, bewhiskered yet otherwise unremarkable man who is the focus of the photograph. Timorous and uncomfortable-looking, he at first had swung and struck a glancing blow, bending the first spike without driving it into the wooden tie. Only on the second, more forceful, strike did the cameras flash. The unobtrusive man with the feeble swing was Donald Alexander Smith, the shadowy force that had driven the enterprise since the early 1870s. Appearances to the contrary, Smith, later 1st Baron Strathcona and Mount Royal, was one of the most influential individuals in late nineteenth-century Canada.

His many prestigious, honorary or ceremonial roles included governor and principal shareholder of the Hudson's Bay Company, with whom he would work in some capacity for seventy-five years; president of the Bank of Montreal; founder of the Royal Trust Company; Canadian high commissioner to the United Kingdom; chancellor of McGill University (1889–1914) and the University of Aberdeen (1902–14); and co-founder of the Canadian Pacific Railway. In addition to a long career in Canadian provincial and federal politics, he established the Donalda program for the purpose of providing higher education for Canadian women, founded Royal Victoria College and was a prominent philanthropist who disbursed generous endowments to universities and hospitals on both sides of the Atlantic. He had also ingratiated himself, on account of his extreme wealth, with British royalty. Smith never ceased working to increase his own fortune and position, far beyond the point of any meaning, since he was one of the wealthiest people in the British Empire. He cultivated an air of aloof respectability, giving the appearance of a man impervious to vice and temptation, guiltless and morally superior. Yet he was so

overcome with remorse and the need to appear respectable that he publicly married his wife four times, always attempting to quell the rumours
that she had been married to a remote northern Labrador fur trader at
the time of their first marriage, which she had been.

For decades Smith, with his curious gnomelike posture, elfin stature, ragged white beard and tufted eyebrows, dominated Canadian
commerce and politics. He seldom spoke, preferring to bob his head
and raise his palms to convey that others should continue talking.
Enigmatic, self-serving and greedy, he could sometimes veer into
unethical waters; at least he was not overly introspective when it came
to his own business dealings, preferring to let his contrived edifice of
respectability conceal his underhanded manipulations of others unfortunate enough to attract his attention. He saw little distinction
between his occasionally disingenuous business dealings and his grand
yet self-serving political ambitions, so long as he benefited in some
way. He disliked putting anything down in writing, and for good reason, since his schemes were often flying close to the sun, as they say;
he once took a steamship across the Atlantic to meet in person rather
than send a telegram. Over the years he had betrayed many of his
political and business associates, beginning with his fellow fur traders
in 1870, and he never stopped acquiring power and wealth until he
died, at the age of ninety-four, in 1914.

In the late nineteenth century, the British Empire was in its ascendancy. It held sway over nearly a quarter of the world, and its prosperity
was rising rapidly with industrialization: crop yields were increasingly
making food cheaper and more reliable, lifespans were lengthening,
and people were flocking from the countryside into cities and towns
to take up jobs in manufacturing and services. The moral justification
for imperial rule—or exploitation, depending on how you look at it—
was to elevate "inferior" races and cultures from their gloomy bogs of
superstition and ignorance and deposit them onto the sunny uplands

of enlightenment and civilization. The Earl of Carnarvon, secretary of state for the colonies, while delivering an address to the Philosophical Institution of Edinburgh in 1878, mused that the world was a big place and in need of the civilizing hand of the Empire, for there were "races struggling to emerge into civilization . . . vast populations like those of India sitting like children in the shadow of doubt and poverty and sorrow, yet looking up to us for guidance and for help. To them it is our part to give wise laws, good government, and a well-ordered finance. . . . This is the real fulfilment of our duties; this, again, I say, is the true strength and meaning of imperialism." It was a sanctimonious era, not unlike today's, where people believed in the righteousness of their cause and consequently committed or overlooked great injustices in pursuit of ideological purity. They willingly trampled on some rights in order to champion others, solved some problems while creating new ones that would in turn have to be dealt with by future generations. And Smith was a man steeped in the pious certainties of his age, an unethical man preoccupied with propriety and virtuous appearances, living in an unethical era that seldom questioned itself.

Few would have predicted that Smith was destined for the upper echelons of the British Empire or Montreal high society. He was born in the small Scottish town of Forres in 1820. A middle child in a family of six, he emulated his industrious mother rather than his alcoholic father, who struggled to manage a general shop. Initially apprenticed to a clerk to copy documents, he took greater inspiration from his maternal uncle, who told stories of his many adventures and his life with the North West Company in western North America, managing fur trade posts and exploring with Simon Fraser as far as the Pacific Ocean. Wanting to escape the myopic life destiny seemed to have in mind for him, Smith secured a letter of introduction to George Simpson and in 1838 set off in a small sailing ship on the seven-week voyage to Montreal.

The city would expand dramatically over the course of Smith's life, soaring to become British North America's largest and most dynamic urban centre. At the time of Canadian confederation, thirty years later, it was a city of over a hundred thousand, trailed by Toronto and Quebec at merely sixty thousand each. The population of both the Canadas would triple during that time, from around 1.2 million to over 3.5 million by Confederation. But when Smith disembarked from his ship and strode down the docks, Montreal was a rough-at-the-edges boom town of about thirty thousand filled with ramshackle buildings, the people serenaded by the incessant ping of sledgehammers and buzz of saws, enshrouded by a lingering cloud of construction dust.

Smith found his way by foot to the Hudson's Bay Company's unofficial North American headquarters, which was George Simpson's mansion in Lachine. The "Little Emperor," as Simpson was called, was away on his annual tour of the company's domain, being propelled by a crack team of Haudenosaunee voyageurs along the network of rivers that linked the 170 or so fur posts that extended throughout the northwest as far as the Pacific Ocean, where the former Quebec surgeon Dr. John McLoughlin ruled Old Oregon like a feudal baron. Despite Simpson's absence, Smith was hired based on his uncle's recommendation and his Scottish heritage, which counted for much within the company's ranks, and set to learning the basics of fur warehousing and quality sorting in the Montreal warehouse. Here he had the unfortunate luck to befriend Simpson's much younger wife, Frances, who "took a friendly interest in the 'indentured young gentlemen,' as they were called, [and] was attracted by the simplicity and gentle address of the new-comer's manners." She invited him for tea and "commanded his escort" on boating excursions on the river throughout the summer, until the return of the imperious and jealous Simpson put an end to Smith's pleasing sojourn in Montreal society and precipitated his banishment for the better part of the next three decades. Simpson commanded young Smith to an audience, where the governor was overheard yelling "in a highly pitched treble" that he would not tolerate "any upstart, quill-driving apprentices dangling about a parlour reserved to the nobility and gentry."

Smith was perfunctorily ordered to Tadoussac, a post along the Gulf of St. Lawrence known as career purgatory, which was usually followed by a transfer to Labrador, an even more remote career-stifling jurisdiction. He had hoped to be transferred west to the mysterious and romantic Columbia District where his uncle had served. Nevertheless, a stoic man, he persevered and set off for his official posting, where he would remain until he was forty-nine, in 1869. Promotion was indeed slow, his career a series of unfortunate setbacks precipitated by critiques from Simpson right up until the governor's death in 1860. It was not until 1862 that Smith was promoted to the position of chief factor in charge of the Labrador District. And not until after a voyage to London in 1865, where he made a favourable impression on the company's senior management, was he finally transferred to the Montreal office, in 1868. During his time in Labrador, Smith earned a reputation for competence but also for a willingness to betray his fellow traders, and even his senior manager, to further his own advancement.

He introduced new farming techniques with hardy northern grain species from the Orkney Islands. He took an avid interest in animal husbandry and bred several hardy species of cattle and chickens that thrived in the harsh climate of Labrador, and expanded the company's interests to include a salmon fishery and seal oil factory. He reported consistent profits in his district, yet he caused hardship and perhaps even starvation among the Naskapi people by denying them credit for ammunition to hunt caribou. He also married the daughter of his manager when the man retired and departed south, even though she was already married to another company officer. Isabella Hardisty was the daughter of a Scottish trader, Richard, and a mixed-heritage mother,

Marguerite Sutherland. Smith took pains to stem the rumours that she had been formally married to her former husband (even though they had a son together) and insisted that his own marriage to her was legitimate and not just a "country marriage" of convenience. This was the era when Simpson was discouraging the long-standing practice of company traders having Indigenous or mixed-heritage wives and families, and denying or delaying promotion to officers who didn't cast off their country wives, while refusing to promote to senior positions the many employees of mixed heritage who swelled the company's ranks. Smith and Isabella weathered the moral storm and remained together until her death, in 1913. They had one daughter, named Maggie. Isabella had two older brothers in the fur trade out west who occupied respectable senior positions in the company and in the commercial and political elite of Calgary and Edmonton. Whatever else happened to the many in that family line, Isabella became one of the richest women in the world's most powerful empire, and her daughter married into the upper echelons of the Anglo-Scottish commercial elite of Montreal, then Canada's most prominent commercial and urban centre.

By the late 1860s, Smith foresaw the decline of the fur trade, coinciding with the expansion of railways and the flood of settlement occurring around Montreal and elsewhere, which he beheld during a trip to Boston, New York and Montreal. He and Isabella were growing weary of living in remote Labrador and were seeking broader fields. With his spare pay Smith had been quietly buying up stock in both the HBC and the Bank of Montreal and found himself, perhaps not unexpectedly, one of the principal shareholders of both institutions. He was an odd fellow, though. On a trip to Montreal, he went to visit his well-positioned and successful cousin, George Stephen, who through tireless and crafty manoeuvring had risen through the Montreal business community, starting in the drapery business, which led him to banking, which introduced him to many others in Montreal.

Isabella of course worried that her husband's peccadilloes might derail his prospects. After all, he hardly cut the figure of a worldly man of finance and power—that would come later. They had gone shopping earlier in the day before the meeting with Stephen, and Smith had become obsessed with a bright red carpet bag—an odd frivolity that somehow induced him to open the tight fist that gripped his money. A companion recorded that "as Mrs. Smith had some shopping to do, we all went into the city together."

> I gave him Mr. Stephen's address, and we parted company. A couple of hours later I met all the Smiths in St. James's Street, loaded down with parcels, and Mr. Smith carrying a rather gaudy carpet bag. He stopped to show me the bag, and asked my opinion of it. "It's just the thing for the Labrador," he said. "It'll make a great hit with the Indians there."
>
> I inquired if he had met his cousin, Mr. Stephen. "Oh, yes," he said. "I went in and had a few moments' conversation with him."
>
> "I suppose he was glad to see you, eh?"
>
> Mr. Smith seemed a little embarrassed at the question, but his wife burst forth. "He wasn't glad at all. Why should Mr. Stephen be glad to see country cousins like us—all the way from Labrador? I wish," she added shyly, "I wish he had waited until he had met Mr. Stephen before buying that red carpet bag. But he wouldn't let me carry it, and the rest of us waited outside."

The odd couple returned to the remote Labrador outpost while they dreamed of new horizons. They didn't have to wait long. The company had moved its headquarters west from Montreal to Red River a decade earlier, to be closer to its primary operations, and so the Montreal District was much reduced in importance, though still a step up compared with operations in Labrador. When the chief factor of the

Montreal District retired in June 1869, the natural man to replace him was "Labrador" Smith.

Smith had only been in his position in Montreal for a few months when, on November 29, he was called to a meeting with Prime Minister Macdonald in Ottawa. Macdonald was under the mistaken apprehension that the secretive company must be ruled from Montreal, just as it had been during Simpson's epochal era, and Smith was the highest-ranking official within travel distance of the new capital. Though technically only a junior or district manager, and Montreal being the smallest and least important of the company's districts, and himself having never travelled west of Lachine and not being particularly knowledgeable of the company's operations, Smith was near at hand. There was a serious problem, Macdonald told him, arising with the transfer of the company's lands to the new Dominion of Canada, which was slated to occur on December 1. The problem went by the name of Louis Riel, a hitherto unknown leader of the Métis who had somehow pulled off a remarkable diplomatic and legal coup that placed the transfer of the company's western territory to Canada in jeopardy. Smith listened and nodded, somehow made a favourable impression, and was hastily appointed Dominion Commissioner to Inquire into the North West Rebellion. His instructions were to immediately depart for the West by train (through the United States) and then take barge and horse cart, or whatever means of transportation presented itself, north to Red River to try to meet with Riel, resolve the difficulties and ensure that the land transfer to Canada went ahead as planned.

CHAPTER EIGHT

NO PAWN TO EMPIRE

———

Colonel John Stoughton Dennis arrived at the Red River Settlement with a survey crew in August 1869. No one had been expecting him or his surveyors and he was quickly looked upon with suspicion by the Métis after he took up residence at the home of John Christian Schultz. Schultz was a prominent but unscrupulous business leader whom the Métis held in low esteem for his demeanour and annoying proclamations, including his vociferous support of annexation by Canada. The Red River community consisted of around ten thousand Métis and one thousand English Canadians led by Schultz. Most of the people of Red River did not think of themselves as Canadians—not the Métis bison hunters, their predominantly English-speaking mixed-heritage compatriots who had recently turned to farming, or the descendants of the Selkirk settlers.

Dennis, a United Empire Loyalist and former cavalry commander with a patchy record, had been appointed by William McDougall, the minister of public works in Macdonald's government. Dennis's official instructions were to bring some order to the parcels of land in the community in preparation for their transfer from the Hudson's Bay Company in four months' time. The legal ownership of these old properties was often sketchy, dating to the time of the Selkirk settlers early in the nineteenth century, and occasionally augmented by incremental grants from the company or merely acknowledged by virtue of prior use—unfavourably known by government officials as squatting. The government's plan was to make the land appealing to eastern settlers, who it was hoped would come from Ontario, settle the territory and remain loyal to Ottawa, thereby staving off American annexation.

Unfortunately, Dennis was somewhat tone deaf and rigid in his interpretation of his duty, and he proceeded to survey the region in the style of large blocks suitable for grain farming, which ran counter to the prevailing seigneury survey style, common in Quebec, which involved long, narrow plots of land that fronted the Red and Assiniboine Rivers so that each had access to water and at least some richer, moister soil. Dennis was later reprimanded, since he wasn't supposed to do anything that might agitate the local people before the land transfer.

The two most prominent leaders of the fractious community at Red River were the governor of Assiniboia, William Mactavish, and the head of the influential Catholic church, Bishop Alexandre-Antonin Taché. Unfortunately, Mactavish was seriously ill with tuberculosis, listlessly pondering his waning life, while Taché was away in Rome on some form of church business. At the time of greatest need, there was no respected person to offer a semblance of central authority around which the people, already divided by race, religion and economic interest, could rally. There was no one who could unify the people or help them weather the storm of uncertainty caused by the impending land transfer. Dennis's arrival and his belligerent and ham-fisted efforts to survey land that didn't belong to him or his government, in a manner that ran counter to local customs—otherwise known as trespassing—gave the impression that land rights which had existed for generations would count for nothing if Canada gained control. No one wanted their interests to be sacrificed to the power of the new Dominion, a political force far to the east where most had never been.

Everyone in the settlement was living in a state of anxiety and apprehension. For the Métis, it was another assault on their way of life, already being threatened by the declining bison herds in recent years and the political agitations of a cluster of inflexible Orangemen who were trying to dominate the affairs of the community. On October 11, when Dennis's survey crews expanded beyond the boundaries of the generally English-speaking regions and encroached upon the Métis lands, specifically at the farm of André Nault, it became a flashpoint for conflict. Nault, a French speaker who was unable to communicate with the men surveying his lands and whom he thought may have intended to seize it, hurriedly sent a messenger to his cousin Louis Riel, who spoke English. Riel, twenty-five years old and recently returned from the East, where he had spent several years at a seminary school in Montreal, came galloping across the prairie with fifteen Métis. He dismounted, boldly marched up to the surveyors, placed his booted foot on the survey chain and pronounced: "You go no further." Dennis and his men fumed, observed the stony countenances of the Métis riders who surrounded them, packed up and departed. But the event sparked an opposition that quickly coalesced around Riel and his council, which was based on the communal buffalo hunts so famously part of Métis heritage.

The events of the first Red River uprising are possibly the most well-studied story in Canadian history, routinely debated and pondered. The choice for the Métis was between resistance and grudging acceptance of the inevitable change that was being forced upon the land, in part by global forces no one could fully appreciate and in part by the bungling dictates of an amateur eastern political establishment intent on

territorial expansion against people they clearly wished to brush aside
to fulfill their ambition.

The leader who rose to prominence in this struggle was Riel, and he
had the support of the Métis at Red River, as well as many Indigenous
peoples who had not been consulted over the plan to place them under
the control of a distant aspiring empire. They all refuted, and dismissed
as ridiculous, the notion that they were now going to be under the
authority and control of some place called Canada, far to the east, just
because a company they traded with had signed a paper and received a
payment. The Canadian government, the HBC and the British government had colluded to pass off the transfer as an agreement between the
parties with official standing; Riel proved otherwise.

The eldest of eleven in a deeply religious Catholic family, he attended
a seminary but never completed his studies. Departing after the death
of his father, he had worked his way back to Red River by 1868. Tall
and muscular, with a mane of wavy black hair, Riel had charisma and
magnetism—an aura of authority that was immediately apparent to
those who met him. Although one-eighth Chipewyan, he was thoroughly culturally Métis despite never having been a hunter or ever
travelling nomadically. Most Métis, a blend of French and Anishinaabe,
Saulteaux or other Indigenous people, or of Scottish and Cree, were
illiterate. Riel was educated and thus was being called upon to protect
the interests of his people, which the Canadian government had sig-
nalled were to be sidelined in the new order. Riel, at least at this point
in his life, was a reasonable person, which means he was viewed with
suspicion by government agents, reasonable people often being seen as
threatening to the ambitious, the partisan or the ideological.

One of Riel's first directives, with his hastily assembled council, was
to send Nault and a band of between 250 and 300 armed and mounted
Métis south to the border to erect a barrier around the road to prevent

the new eastern official, Lieutenant-Governor William McDougall, and his entourage from crossing the border into the territory from Pembina in the U.S. McDougall was a pompous and inflexible man chosen for his perceived ability to knock some sense into the "wild" Métis and bring them to an acceptance of the new order. As the first lieutenant-governor-to-be of the lands Canada desired, he set a precedent that lingered far beyond his minor turn on the stage of history. He was directly responsible for galvanizing Métis hostility toward an eastern takeover of their territory. He was well educated but rabidly anti-Catholic and condescending toward the Métis, viewing them as semi-savages who needed a good wallop to bring them into line. Despite his impressive political résumé with both the Liberals and Conservatives in Canada, it is a challenge to imagine a poorer choice to usher in a peaceful transfer of political authority in Red River. His inclination was toward stubborn autocracy; he expected to be obeyed. A snob with an elevated opinion of his position, and his position over others, he believed that his superiority demanded respect and deference without his ever having earned it—particularly from the people at whom he disdainfully sneered.

He arrived in the West with a sizable entourage, including a government-in-waiting that contained no local representatives. He appeared more like a conqueror than a conciliator. But McDougall never got beyond Pembina, although he did briefly set foot on soil north of the 49th parallel.

Riel's blockade of McDougall's official entourage was possible because of a quirk of geography dating from the fur trade era. Because the Hudson's Bay Company had resisted any form of outside settlement for generations, there were only three access routes into the territory it was "selling" to Canada. Two of these routes—by ship across the Atlantic to York Factory on Hudson Bay, and the arduous canoe and portage route west from Lake Superior—were controlled by the company. The third access was by way of the U.S., coming north from Minnesota. It was easy for Riel to surmise where the officials would be arriving from, and he sent men to await them along the road.

McDougall, the viceregal contingent and various hangers-on trundled unsuspectingly toward the border on November 2. Carts were loaded with necessaries, including exotic foodstuffs, liquor, copious chests of fine garments and groomed hunting dogs, as well as the new throne of authority. They were shocked to see men clustered around the border. One of these men rode forward and handed McDougall a letter from Riel's committee, refusing him entry into the territory. Meanwhile, Riel himself moved against the company's administrative centre at Upper Fort Garry with a contingent of around 120 Métis cavalry. Accounts vary, but Governor Mactavish may have welcomed them in— he was head of a company, after all, not a police force or government. The Métis rode in and assumed authority without conflict, confining Mactavish to his quarters, where he mostly dwelt anyway on account of his advanced tuberculosis. Riel anticipated armed resistance, however, from Schultz and other Protestant Canada supporters.

Meanwhile, in Ottawa, Macdonald had written to McDougall several times throughout November, cautioning him to have patience above all and to take no rash actions. Macdonald provided McDougall with careful instructions: he was to find the two most important Métis leaders and "take them into your Council. This man Riel, who appears to be the moving spirit, is a clever fellow, and you should endeavour to retain him as an officer in your future police. If you do this promptly, it will be a most convincing proof that you are not going to leave the half-breeds out of the law." Macdonald's advice was to try to bring the people together into a new governing council so that they felt their voices would form part of the new order, rather than being controlled from afar. Placate those whose feathers were being ruffled, he suggested, and create a more diverse council that could represent the varying views on the future that were clashing in the community.

Macdonald informed McDougall that in his capacity as lieutenant-governor he could call on the people of Red River to unite and support the law and to get the insurgents to disperse. But he was to be careful to judge the situation to ensure they heeded his suggestions. It would be very well if he was obeyed, Macdonald cautioned; "If, however, it [the proclamation] were disobeyed, your weakness and inability to enforce the authority of the Dominion would be painfully exhibited, not only to the people of Red River, but to the people and Government of the United States. An assumption of the government by you, of course, puts an end to that of the Hudson's Bay Company's authorities. . . . There would then be, if you were not admitted into the country, no legal government existing, and anarchy must follow. In such a case, no matter how the anarchy is produced, it is quite open by the law of nations for the inhabitants to form a government *ex necessitate* for the protection of life and property . . . which might be very convenient for the United States, but exceedingly inconvenient to you." And inconvenient for Canada, he could have added. All the U.S. would have had to do then was acknowledge the new government, and the project of Canada would be, in railway parlance, dead on the tracks. Most importantly, Macdonald advised McDougall against impatience.

But McDougall couldn't wait. On December 1, in the midst of a freezing blizzard, he crossed the border from his rustic lodgings on the U.S. side to an abandoned company fort and began a furtive ceremony. First, he wrote up a false royal proclamation that listed himself as the new authority; then, with his seven deputies present, he withdrew the forged document from his waistcoat and read it aloud into the blustery night, after which he retreated unceremoniously to his American encampment. McDougall had assumed that the transfer of the HBC lands had taken place as planned. It had not.

Macdonald had reasoned that if Canada simply refused the land transfer from the company it would be the responsibility of the imperial government in London, not himself in Ottawa, to remedy the situation, to subjugate or placate the rebels to keep the Americans out. The company, naturally, just wanted its money on December 1 and was perturbed when Macdonald sent a telegram to London informing the governing board of the unrest, as far as he understood it, based on his patchy and out-of-date dispatches from the remote region. He also informed them that since the Canadian representative couldn't enter the territory because of the actions of the Métis, Canada wouldn't be dispatching the payment until they, as the previous authority, had regained some semblance of peace in the territory. Macdonald could be a wily character; he informed the board that the Canadian government had naturally assumed it would be given "peaceable possession" in exchange for its substantial payment. While Macdonald negotiated, McDougall had done exactly what he had been instructed not to do: proclaim his governorship, which effectively deposed Mactavish and the company; and then he retreated, leaving the territory without a legally recognized head of government.

Macdonald was apoplectic. McDougall, he fumed, "has ingeniously contrived to humiliate himself and Canada, to arouse the hopes and pretensions of the insurgents, and to leave them in undisputed possession until next spring." This final act in a series of stupid, unnecessary blunders was another wasted opportunity to begin the new government on a positive footing. Macdonald ordered McDougall to return to Ottawa; he would never, in fact, ever take up his appointment. But before he departed, McDougall sent off a letter to Mactavish letting him know that the company no longer had any power, and then another note to surveyor Dennis, appointing him, on dubious authority, in charge of maintaining the peace and deputized him to march on Fort Garry and remove the rebels by force. It was a crazy and foolish series of dictates guaranteed to result in increasing conflict and produce the opposite result of his instructed mission.

The Métis under Riel's leadership were not to be treated like pawns in Canada's imperial gambit, which many felt would open up immigration from the east and swamp their culture and way of life. There already existed among the Métis a feeling that perhaps they were being swept away by the tide of history, and they vowed not to go down without a fight. Theirs was an oxbow lake of culture, seemingly cut off from the main flow of history, and they would do nearly anything to preserve themselves. And if the Métis were feeling this way, imagine what the Cree, Nakoda (Assiniboine), Anishinaabe and Niisitapi were feeling.

MACTAVISH WAS A DYING MAN who had little vigour and enthusiasm. He hadn't left the company's headquarters since Riel had taken possession of them months earlier. (Mactavish did eventually leave Red River, to return to Scotland, where he died on July 21, 1870, two days after he arrived following a long, arduous journey.) But when Riel called a meeting in early December to discuss the political future of Red River, Mactavish dragged himself into the room and informed the gathering—mostly Métis delegates, both French and English, and some company workers—that McDougall's proclamation rendered his own authority obsolete, and that as the head of a private company, he no longer considered himself to have any authority over anything political. With no one present in the territory claiming to have any right to represent the community, Riel was voted president of the provisional government of Rupert's Land and the North-West, and hoisted a new flag over Fort Garry—the Métis flag, a green shamrock and a golden fleur-de-lis on a white background. Mactavish had no great affinity for Canada or the HBC anymore, a sentiment not uncommon among the company managers since they had been cut out of receiving any of the payment from Canada for the transfer of the company lands. He was of the opinion that the best interests of Red River lay in eventually joining the U.S., a view, if not widely embraced, at least not strongly opposed either.

Macdonald was accurate in his assessment that the Americans were intent on annexing the territory that is now western Canada. And pressure was applied to Riel from that direction as well. Annexation was not just an idle fear. In 1869, Congressman Ignatius Donnelly, one of many adherents of the philosophy of manifest destiny, advocated for the annexation of Red River. "If the revolutionists of Red River are encouraged and sustained by the avowed sympathy of the American people, we may within a few years, perhaps months, see the Stars and Stripes wave from Fort Garry." Newspapers likewise cried out for this iteration of manifest destiny. "The Red River revolution," proclaimed Joseph Wheelock in an editorial in the *St. Paul Press* on February 8, 1870, "is a trump card in the hands of American diplomacy, if there is statesmanship equal to the opportunity, by which, if rightly played, every vestige of British power may be swept from the Western half of the continent." The Métis recognized no international border, and indeed many of them lived on either side of it. The commerce and culture of the region were dominated by links to the south. Trade with St. Paul in buffalo hides was strong, and many Métis had voted in favour of statehood for Minnesota a decade earlier.

Macdonald himself was nearly overcome with anxiety. "I would be quite willing, personally, to leave the whole country a wilderness for the next half-century, but I fear that if Englishmen do not go there, Yankees will." He also admitted the solution to his fears: "The United States Government are resolved to do all they can, short of war, to get possession of the western territory, and we must take immediate and vigorous steps to counteract them. One of the first things to be done is to show unmistakably our resolve to build the Pacific Railway." Just as the delegates from Victoria were planning their trip to Ottawa, other newspapers expressed this same sentiment. The Toronto *Globe* pronounced on March 23, 1870, that "with the construction of the railway the country will be populated by Englishmen; without it by Americans." Out on Vancouver Island, the *British Colonist* declared on February 20: "If the railway scheme be Utopian, so also is Confederation. The two must stand or fall together." Riel's uprising was fuelling the discussion of the transcontinental railway.

Riel and his new council issued a "Declaration of the People of Rupert's Land and the North-West," which dismissed the authority of distant Canada to control or govern them or any of the territory of the northwest on the pretense that since there was at present no legally recognized government in the territory, the people living within it had the inalienable right to choose their own. The new provisional government would negotiate with Canada and see if any terms could be agreed upon. It was around then that Macdonald's delegation, which included Smith, arrived to try to settle things down. Macdonald opted for a two-pronged approach to pacify the Red River country, and hence Rupert's Land: negotiate with Riel via the unassuming Smith, while also organizing a military troop to arrive the following summer. Smith's job was to talk up the benefits of Canada and persuade Riel to send a delegation to Ottawa, and to delay any hasty decisions made in the heat of opposition.

Smith arrived on December 27, the final stretch of his otherwise pleasant journey through the U.S., by horse-drawn sleigh north into the disputed territory across the windswept, freezing prairie. When Smith refused to promise not to undermine the authority of the provisional government, Riel ordered him confined to a small room in the fort. Smith spent nearly two months in the cramped space but hosted numerous visitors, and with his affiliation with the HBC, his background living in remote Labrador and his wife Isabella's family connections to several Red River families, he was able to establish a network of people sympathetic to the moderate cause of at least hearing the proposals of the Canadian government. He also tactfully deployed several thousand dollars in bribe money with which Macdonald had supplied him, including job offers and notes of credit at company stores.

Riel was persuaded to convene a congregation of the Métis settlement outside the fort on January 19 to hear the official position of the eastern government. Over a thousand people clumped together on the freezing wintry day while snow blew about and the sun hung low and weak on the horizon. Bundled in buffalo robes, stamping their fur boots around sputtering fires, with dogs placed out of the wind and horses tended to, Riel and Smith stepped up onto the crude wooden platform. Smith spent the next five hours reading documents aloud in a monotonous, soothing voice informing them of the foreign government's intention to respect all religions, property and customs, with Riel dutifully translating his speech into French. The meeting adjourned on account of the extreme cold but resumed the next morning. "Gentlemen," Smith proclaimed, "Canada is prepared to respect the people of this country and grant them everything that is just."

In the end it was Smith who won over the assembly with his slow, ponderous pronouncements and steady, weathered appearance and demeanour. Fifty and bearded, with a lifetime spent in remote Labrador as a company manager, he just seemed trustworthy and experienced. And his family ties, however distant, went a long way to soothing anxious hearts and paving the way for an acceptance of Canada's overtures—or at least the idea that Canada might be preferable to the United States, the other empire eying their lands. Riel seemed to accept the inevitable and publicly moved for twenty French and twenty English Métis delegates to draft a list of grievances and demands, which would be forwarded to Ottawa. English and French, hunters and farmers, Protestant and Catholic voted to enumerate these concerns, and on February 10 they selected three delegates to make the long journey east. At this point there was no consultation with the Indigenous Plains people.

Sadly, Riel soon made the worst political misstep of his life. There was still opposition to the Métis plans, chiefly from John Schultz and the Canada Firsters, rabid Orangemen from Ontario who disparaged Catholics, French and Métis. Schultz tried to rally supporters for armed opposition to Riel, but the Métis firebrands eventually put down all opposition and had Schultz's men loosely imprisoned at Fort Garry. There had been no bloodshed until mere days before Smith was to depart for Ottawa with his news. Then an odd string of events that involved an accidental shooting and a violent beating resulted in the death of the bigoted Irish Protestant racist Thomas Scott, a well-known twenty-eight-year-old agitator and hater of the Métis. Scott spat on his guards, who sighed with stoic forbearance. He continuously insulted them for their language, heritage and religion and he once lunged at Riel, trying to assault him. Faced with conflict among his more ardent followers, who were already frustrated by his release of most of the other prisoners, and who informed Riel that they might just kill Scott if he didn't do something about the infuriating man, Riel instructed that Scott to be taken from his cell and put on trial for insubordination. Hardly surprisingly, Scott was found guilty and condemned to death.

Smith tried to persuade Riel to relent, but he wouldn't budge; he was losing authority over the most militant of his followers and feared a backlash if he allowed a man as hated as Scott to escape punishment. No doubt Scott was a bigoted, hard-drinking, violent racist, but did he deserve to die by firing squad? It's hard to say. The times were different, and many people wanted him dead as a message to Canada that the Métis were to be taken seriously. In any event, he was blindfolded, led out of the fort with his hands bound and placed in a ditch in front of six Métis riflemen. He was struck six times by bullets but somehow didn't die, so another Métis militant strode up, placed a gun at his temple and fired a shot at close range that erupted from his mouth. He was dragged over to and loaded into a primitive coffin and carried to a nearby outbuilding, where he lay moaning and delirious for several hours before expiring.

Scott's death changed the narrative instantly. Riel was no longer a romantic defender of his people but a despised murderer—and the peaceful land transfer that Macdonald had sought became impossible. Schultz quickly fled Red River to the U.S. and made his way back to Ontario, where he toured Orange country delivering fiery speeches denouncing Riel and the Métis and the French and Catholics, carrying with him a rope that he falsely claimed was the one used to unjustly tie the innocent Scott's hands behind his back. People in Quebec, naturally, quickly rallied to the French and Catholic cause, elevating Riel and his cohorts nearly to the status of folk heroes in opposition to Ontario, which they perceived, mostly accurately, as bigoted toward both the French language and the Catholic religion.

Macdonald faced a dilemma. It was impossible to placate both sides in an escalating conflict that had no palatable solution. So much damage had been caused for no real benefit. All Macdonald wanted was his empire, and to fend off the advances of the Americans, but the obstacles to its creation kept piling up.

IN APRIL 1870, THE MÉTIS DELEGATES who had been sent to Ottawa were arrested several times on trumped-up charges meant to harass them, and each time were promptly released by a judge. Finally, in mid-May, holed up in a private home in Ottawa, they negotiated the Manitoba Act, which created a rather small "postage stamp" province on July 15. The act guaranteed rights for the Métis, protected the French language and Catholic church schools, and gave a significant land grant to the Métis—not a collective grant as Riel had sought that would "preserve the existence of our people" but rather individual grants that quickly changed hands as people moved farther west and dispersed. Nevertheless, in the short term, the Métis, with 1.4 million acres of land, could pursue their traditional way of life even as white eastern Canadian settlers began to move in around them. Riel never could secure an amnesty for himself and fled to the U.S., dashing out of the gates of Fort Garry mere hours before Macdonald's expeditionary force arrived on August 24.

Macdonald had been considering sending troops to put down the uprising, as many urged him to do, with the typical sentiment of "how dare they oppose British power," but he had been reluctant to follow through, knowing full well that violence would not forward the interests of a peaceful westward expansion for his new nation. Even if a military solution could achieve his goals by force, it would be expensive to maintain, and in any event, the eastern establishment underestimated the military capability of thousands of skilled marksmen and hunters, essentially an irregular cavalry with intimate knowledge of the land, who dominated many thousands of kilometres distant from Canada's logistical supply lines. How would Canadian troops even get there anyway? The only established route was through the U.S., south of Lake Superior, but for obvious reasons the U.S. wouldn't want foreign troops transiting through their territory. And there was sobering suspicion in Ottawa—not without merit—that these Canadian troops would see the greater opportunity for advancement in the U.S. and desert before arriving in Red River. But a show of force might perhaps send a message to the U.S. that Canada and Britain weren't about to abandon the continent easily.

Macdonald's expeditionary force was inexplicably led by Colonel Garnet Wolseley. Although a competent and experienced officer with an eye to logistics, Wolseley was another bigoted anti-French and anti-Catholic Ontario Protestant, and many of his force were of similar creed. Their instructions were to take over the fort that Riel was already prepared to hand over peacefully. Wolseley led a large contingent of soldiers and voyageurs on a gruelling ninety-six-day trek west. The troop included seven hundred Canadian militia and four hundred British regulars, as well as civilian voyageurs to assist in getting the troops and their equipment through the swampy lowlands and over forty-seven portages. It was rife with angry Ontario Orangemen who were openly proclaiming their intention to round up and lynch the Métis leaders, overjoyed at the exciting prospect of crushing a "rebellion."

Once he heard the growing rumours of the calls for his murder at the hands of the "benevolent constabulary," Riel knew he had to flee, barely a year after the arrival of Dennis's aggressive survey party that had precipitated the entire affair. The Canadian troops, frustrated that Riel had slipped away before they could exact vengeance, began a series of assaults on local Métis leaders and their families, plundering and destroying homes and raping young women—the typical actions of an army after a brutal siege. Some of the troops openly declared their vow, proclaimed even before leaving home, to seek revenge by shooting any French person who was in any way connected with the event. One young officer, William Francis Butler, later wrote in his memoirs of the "wild scene of drunkenness and debauchery" that followed the arrival of the troops in Winnipeg in late August 1870: "The miserable-looking village produced, as if by magic, more saloons than any city of twice its size in the States could boast of. The vilest compounds of intoxicating liquors were sold indiscriminately to every one, and for a time it seemed as though the place had become a very Pandemonium. No civil authority had been given to the commander of the Expedition, and no civil power of any kind existed in the settlement. The troops alone were under control, but the populace were free to work what mischief they pleased."

Some Métis were shot, some stoned to death, others beaten during the five-day rampage before the expeditionary force turned back east in September—the land now pacified. After some negotiation, Riel was denied the right to live in his homeland, and on February 23, 1872, he was escorted out of the country with a payoff—he couldn't just be killed because of the political ramifications in Quebec. The Orangemen of Ontario still maintained a mighty $5,000 price on his head. In 1875, he was formally exiled for five years. Under pressure from Quebec, Macdonald refrained from additional action. While in exile, Riel was elected to the Canadian Parliament three times in the Red River riding of Provencher, but could never take his place in the House of Commons because of the bounty placed on his head. In 1874, he did sneak into Parliament and sign the ledger before again fleeing. But neither history, nor the railway, was done with Riel.

THE PIECES OF MACDONALD'S PUZZLE were still coming together despite all the setbacks—all he needed now was to somehow push a railway through to the Pacific. A wily schemer, he worked tirelessly toward this seemingly impossible goal; the ends justifying the means seems to have been his guiding philosophy. He wanted the land connected to the eastern political and financial centre to bind a nation, not just service a hinterland. Canada officially obtained the western lands from the HBC roughly around the time B.C. agreed to join Confederation, and the fledgling country was immediately faced with the staggering challenge of how to go about financing and constructing the promised railway to the Pacific.

The Wolseley Expedition's ninety-six days of struggle through the wilderness of northern Ontario emphasized how laughably difficult it was to access these new lands if one didn't travel through the U.S. It certainly wasn't a contiguous piece of geography, and in some ways it may as well have been a different continent. The lands north of the Great Lakes were a formidable geographical barrier that blocked passage between the two regions. The Métis problems also highlighted just how important it was to have a railway to control the territory, and as many feared, the eagle was always hunting for new prey. Riel unintentionally lit the fire of ambition for the railway by highlighting the need for speed, just as he would save the project fifteen years later. In some unintentional way, Riel was one of the great progenitors who galvanized an action plan for the railway dream, by demonstrating the practical benefits of the business plan.

When Wolseley and his troops arrived back in the East they spread rumours of the quality of the new lands Canada had just claimed, including their estimation of the potential productivity of the dark, rich soil of the river valley. Wolseley then penned a memoir of sorts of his adventure for *Blackwood's Edinburgh Magazine*. While criticizing the Canadian government for its incompetence, he lauded the prospects of the land itself. "As far as the eye can see," he rhapsodized, "there is stretched out before you an ocean of grass, whose vast immensity grows upon you more and more the longer you gaze upon it . . . [producing] a feeling of indescribably buoyant freedom [that] seems to tingle through every nerve, making the old feel young again. Old age and decrepitude belong to civilization and the abodes of men. . . . Upon the boundless prairies, with no traces of man in sight, nature looks so fresh and smiling that youth alone is in consonance with it."

Purple prose, to be sure, but who wouldn't want to feel young again, to see sprawling vistas of undulating golden grass stretching to infinity, into the future, making people feel, fountain-of-youth-like, as if they had regained their early vigour and vitality? All they had to do was save up for a ticket and board a comfortable train heading west— through the U.S., unfortunately. Then they could settle in for a lengthy and bone-jarring horse-drawn cart ride or a freezing dogsled trip back north into the new regions of Canada. So simple! A century after the invention of the steam engine, the northwest was still reliant upon horses, ox carts, birchbark canoes and wooden York boats—or walking—for all transportation.

Nonetheless, soon after the Red River incident, the tiny trickle of migrants heading west turned into a moderate stream of thousands yearly.

CHAPTER NINE

OCEAN TO OCEAN

———

"**L**abrador" Smith arrived back east from Red River an unexpected hero, his career in the ascendancy after decades of purgatory. Suddenly he was a known entity in high circles with a reputation for dependable competence. Though barely removed from the remote wilds of Labrador, he was now a respected member of the upper management of the Hudson's Bay Company and a member of the Canadian political elite, with the ear of the sitting prime minister. He had defused a volatile uprising, and those skills would be necessary in dealing with the western territories in the years ahead. He was also now respected by all the parties in the northwest: the Métis, the company's field officers, the settlers and the Canadian government. Everyone except the nomadic bison-hunting Plains people, who had mostly moved farther west, following the dwindling herds of once plentiful bison.

At age fifty, Smith calmly set off on a new career trajectory. After treading water for decades, he had suddenly awakened and began swimming vigorously. Most interestingly, his eye fell on the railway he rode in the U.S. on his first journey west, and it set his mind on a tangent that had little to do with furs and more to do with the newly fashionable industrial reworking of the continent. Railways became his new great interest, transforming him into one of the richest people in the world and giving him an outsized role in the development of the country of Canada in the coming years. When he rode the rails north of St. Paul, before disembarking when the tracks ended and continuing north to Red River by ox cart, he beheld the fertile land and noted how farms and communities surrounded the tracks. It was rich, dark soil, ideal for farming, and he assumed domestic cattle surely could replace the bison, which were basically gone from these regions by then. The huge tracts of land the Hudson's Bay Company was poised to gain from selling their monopoly had the potential to be staggeringly valuable—if they could be linked to a railway system that would bring in settlers and remove the products of their labour, at first primarily grain and beef.

Smith was soon back in Red River fulfilling his new role as head of the company, and at the annual meeting of the field partners at Norway House in the summer of 1870, he heard from many their grievance of not being offered a share of the £300,000 paid by the Canadian government for the company's lands. As partners rather than employees, they felt they deserved it—after all, they had finally been awarded a share of the proceeds the company received for relinquishing its territories in Old Oregon to the U.S. government decades earlier. "From our isolated position and want of unison and unanimity," wrote Chief Factor Roderick MacKenzie to his colleague Roderick MacFarlane in the Peace River country, "the directors and share-holders are doing all they can to deprive us of our heritage. . . . The sharks are numerous and powerful, and it will need our united action to escape their ravenous gullets."

Smith promised to present their case to the company's directors in London, which he did in 1871. The field partners' position was that their pay came essentially from a share of profits, and with the fur trade in decline and without pensions, how could they ever retire? But the company was no longer a monopoly controlled by an aristocratic elite board. Instead, it was now a public enterprise traded on the London Stock Exchange, and respect for long-standing fur trade traditions was subsumed beneath the mighty dollar: company policy now was just a numbers game. Smith, however, persuaded the directors to enter into a new deal with the field partners—give the partners their 40 per cent share of the government windfall, with one key provision: that they would forever relinquish any future claim on company profits derived from the sales of land. The negotiations were tense and acrimonious, and neither side gained what it wished or felt was deserved, but in the end that is what was agreed.

For a country bumpkin barely two years from a life in the remotest outposts in Labrador, Smith was curiously astute at detecting which way the winds were about to blow. Animal fur, already in decline as a valuable commodity, was certainly not the future source of the company's income. But the vast segments of land to which it was entitled were a different story altogether. By shutting out the field partners from this future source of wealth, he gained the respect and support of the London financial elite, who better understood such things, and he retained the respect of the field partners, who perhaps wouldn't realize what they had signed away until many years hence, but were meanwhile pleased to be gaining a payout sufficient to ameliorate the hardship of an impoverished retirement after their lifetime of service in a declining industry. Smith was cheered by many of the unsophisticated and unsuspecting field partners, while the company promoted him and awarded him a handsome pay raise.

Not everyone was quite so sanguine about signing away their rights to obtain a payout to which they were already legally entitled. A handful of senior traders resigned over the matter. Chief Trader James Lockhart wrote in March 1872: "It is all very well for Donald A. Smith, with his £2,000 secure annually, to puff the new arrangements. But 'fine promises butter no parsnips,' and you will all find yourselves fooled. . . . I hope things may turn out all right, but I do not expect it, and would advise you to do as others have done, i.e. send back their commissions with the note 'Declined with thanks.'"

Right after the Manitoba elections had given some stability to the land, Smith bought himself a mansion he named Silver Heights, outside of Winnipeg, which was incorporated in 1873. He and Amelia and their daughter moved into their new temporary home (most of their time would be spent in their stately stone mansion on Dorchester Street in Montreal). In 1874, Smith resigned his management position with the Hudson's Bay Company and devoted his energy to land speculation, becoming the company's first land commissioner, surely a conflict of interest, as he took the company's salary and used the knowledge he gained through this position to advance his personal schemes. With his connections to the Montreal banking and financial networks and a reputation for sound investment decisions, Smith had been personally managing the savings of many of the field partners, as George Simpson had done previously. He had acquired a significant book of business by the 1870s. He placed these funds with the Bank of Montreal, of which he was a director.

Smith was also the president and principal shareholder of the nascent Royal Trust Company, which he had established as the financial vehicle to legally manage these funds held in trust for the partners. He agreed to guarantee their capital and pay out a 3 per cent interest on it for their retirement. He in turn used this capital pool to purchase additional HBC shares on his own account when those shares plummeted after the loss of the monopoly. He knew that the company owned extremely valuable land, even if the other directors didn't truly appreciate its potential value; Smith instinctively realized the stock had more value than commonly acknowledged. Using insider knowledge, complex legal structures and personal connections, Smith paid out 3 per cent on investments that eventually earned him in excess of 1,300 per cent capital appreciation, let alone the huge dividends paid out to shareholders, of which he was a major one, eventually taking a controlling interest. Being privy to information that others lacked and abusing the privilege was not illegal in those days. Despite these eye-popping returns, however, this venture wasn't even Smith's most lucrative scheme.

Although not an introspective man, Smith no doubt was an adherent of the philosophy that principles are like clothes—you have to change them to suit the audience, and he was now playing to a new group of select wealthy power brokers in distant cities. His conscience was impervious to his memory. In any case, this betrayal of the field partners, as well as other shareholders and directors, would not become apparent for many years. Meanwhile, Smith had his eyes on grander things: politics and railways, which in this era were much the same thing.

He became interested in politics not as a means of directing or improving society but rather to become an insider privy to decisions from which he could personally benefit. First elected to the Manitoba legislature in 1870, he decided to shift to federal politics for better access to the key decision makers; he wanted political connections that could lead to lucrative private investments or access to public subsidies. He was elected to the House of Commons in 1871 and retained the seat until 1880. His was the inverse of the usual pattern: he sought not to spin wealth into political influence but to transform political influence into wealth.

Smith did little to benefit the Hudson's Bay Company during the 1870s, though he cashed the paycheques for his services. Despite his knowledge, he provided no good advice or direction to his employer. He didn't even bother to explain to the London directors, even when his position was land commissioner, that they had considerable value in land holdings, and he mostly ignored the company and his responsibilities to it as no longer being the primary vessel for his ambitions. Better opportunities presented themselves.

MEANWHILE, SOON AFTER BRITISH COLUMBIA had voted itself into Canada in July 1871, parties of survey engineers were dispatched from Victoria across the Salish Sea and east toward the mountains, and other teams were dispatched west from the upper Ottawa River "into trackless, inhospitable regions, obliged to carry their provisions on their backs over swamps, rocks, and barriers . . . to do their best to find out all they could, in as short a time as possible."

The land that had seen rebellion by the Métis was not transitioning smoothly into its new iteration as a subsidiary of the new eastern empire; it was too isolated. What seemed obvious and simple on paper, when scrutinizing charts and dreaming big dreams, was considerably messier and more challenging on the ground—not surprising, really, given that Macdonald himself had never been west of the settled parts of Ontario and had no idea what the rest of his Dominion encompassed. Not the least problem was where, in the vastness of the new Canadian appendage, a railway should be situated for the greatest political gain, or where it had to be situated to accommodate geography. Where it would be permitted by local people whose lands it would traverse wasn't even a question being considered yet; this was a mere secondary concern, barely an inconvenience compared to the grandness of the dream.

Many of the early travellers to the northwest were either unreliable or concerned more with their personal situation than the concerns of eastern politicians: Viscount Milton and Dr. Walter Butler Cheadle first worked their way across the prairies and into B.C., arriving in time for the Cariboo gold rush in 1862; William Francis Butler, an English army officer without a commission, wrote *The Great Lone Land*, a romantic idolization of many Indigenous peoples oddly combined with a mild

casual racism; and James Carnegie, the Earl of Southesk, was a gour-
mand who toured the land shooting, cooking and eating everything he
could find: "As a matter of curiosity I had a hind-leg of the skunk for
breakfast," he recalled. "It tasted like sucking-pig; very white, soft, and
fat, but there was a suspicion of *skunkiness* about it that prevented me
from finishing the plateful." Carnegie did, however, attempt to explain
his unusual preoccupation with the uncommon foodstuffs of the frontier: "Let me here, once for all, deprecate censure from fastidious readers,
in regard to the minuteness of my gastronomic details. No question is
more frequently asked of the traveller, than—What is such and such a
beast, bird, or fish fit for as an article of food? Being able, through my
careful note-keeping, to meet, in some degree, the general wish for this
sort of information, ought I—O considerate critic!—to deprive the
many of a boon, out of deference to the probable or possible objections
of the few?"

Between 1857 and 1860, Captain John Palliser was sent by the British
government to explore the country west of Lake Superior to the Rocky
Mountains, with the intention "'to ascertain whether any practicable
pass or passes, available for horses, existed across the Rocky Mountains
within British Territory, and south of that known to exist between
Mount Brown and Mount Hooker,' known as the 'Boat Encampment
Pass.'" Boat Encampment Pass is Athabasca Pass. Although in use as
a major fur trade "portage" between the Athabasca and Saskatchewan
river systems, which eventually connected to York Factory on Hudson
Bay and to the Columbia River, which led to the Pacific, the pass is a
steep and unremitting slog along craggy, windblown track bounded by
glaciers strapped to the rockfaces of gloomy and forbidding mountain sentinels; it would have been entirely unsuitable for any mode of
transportation other than mule train or dogsled. Palliser was pessimistic
about the practicality of a gradual graded route suitable for a road
through the "Canadian" Rockies: "The knowledge of the country, on the

whole, would never lead me to advise a line of communication from Canada, across the Continent to the Pacific, exclusively through British Territory."

Nevertheless, despite Palliser's gloomy advice, Macdonald persevered. One of the first moves was to send out a survey party to scout and make suggestions in an effort to take the railway proposal out of the realm of pure speculation and political promise and advance it into the realm of possibility—to give something concrete for engineers and financiers to grasp on to, a skeleton upon which to hang the body.

The person chosen for the job, Sandford Fleming, was an unpretentious bearded man of slight stature with kind eyes and a thoughtful countenance. This unprepossessing individual's career trajectory was now unexpectedly set to arc across history's stage. Born in Scotland and trained as a surveyor, he emigrated to Canada in 1845, at age eighteen, together with his older brother, bouncing between Quebec City, Montreal and Kingston before temporarily halting his peripatetic ways in Peterborough, where others of his family had settled. A curious and inventive personality led him to found the Royal Canadian Institute, a broad general society for promoting science, in Toronto, and he also designed the first postage stamp for the Province of Canada as it existed in 1851, sixteen years before Confederation. One of his most noteworthy achievements was to use the prime meridian as the base for the twenty-four-hour clock, and the correlated concept of time zones, to facilitate accurate communication and scheduling between distant locations. He also later became chancellor of Queen's University in Kingston.

Fleming was employed for many years as a general surveyor, principally for the Grand Trunk Railway, working up from assistant engineer to the position of chief engineer at the Northern Railway; in 1862, he became a government surveyor for Nova Scotia, the same year he proposed the concept of a cross-continental railway. Several years later he became the chief engineer of the Intercolonial Railway, which had the objective of linking Nova Scotia and New Brunswick to Montreal. His unconventional ideas included building all the bridges using stone and iron rather than wooden timbers, which was expensive but proved more durable and fire resistant.

By 1871, when the government founded the Canadian Pacific Railway, Fleming had become so well known and respected that he was offered the post of chief engineer. He initially balked at the overwhelming responsibility. A devoted husband and father who had married the daughter of family friends in Peterborough, Ann Jane Hall, with whom he would have nine children (seven survived to adulthood), Fleming was in the midst of middle age with family responsibilities. But he couldn't resist the temptation of a once-in-a-lifetime opportunity with the greatest railway project yet conceived.

By mid-1871, Fleming had dispatched twenty-one survey parties of nearly eight hundred men across the country to begin the arduous and painstaking task of narrowing down the route from a general idea to a more specific corridor. The job was enormous—to chart a viable track through the rock and bog of the Canadian Shield, find a convenient path across the immensity of the prairies that took into account all the people living there, and wind a circuitous passage through the forbidding and foreboding passes, canyons and mountain ranges of British Columbia. Fleming's early survey crews laid their preliminary reports before the House of Commons in the spring of 1872, and Fleming then embarked on his own scouting tour of the vast territory to assess their progress, with his teenage son Frank Andrew in tow. Of course, there was to be an election in the fall, so to whom he would be reporting in the House was an open question. But in any case, Fleming wasn't political; he was a practical engineer and dedicated to his job.

As his travelling companion and secretary, he enlisted the garrulous and energetic Presbyterian minister George Monro Grant, a member of the strong Gaelic-speaking Highlander population of Pictou County,

Nova Scotia. Then in his late thirties, Grant was married to Jessie Lawson, daughter of one of the prominent merchants in Halifax; they had two children, but only one survived to adulthood. As principal of Queen's College in Kingston, in 1879 he strove toward the admission of women to regular courses. He also worked to establish the Women's Medical College in 1883, as well as expanding science education in general. A prolific writer and polemicist, he vociferously championed Indigenous rights in British Columbia and denounced restrictions on Chinese immigration. Grant was an ardent proponent of Confederation, a believer that the independent colonies had a better future grouped together than alone. Despite having only one hand (he had lost the other in a farming accident in his youth), he proved to be the ideal companion for a rugged and uncertain trek across the continent, through variable weather and via a multitude of modes of transportation that included railway and steamer at the luxury end, down to canoe, horseback, ox cart and foot when the speedier and more restful options were unavailable, which was most of the time once they were west of Fort William, at the end of Lake Superior.

With a prodigious beard, penetrating eyes and an orator's voice polished by many years in the pulpit, Grant was also a talented writer and storyteller who diligently kept a lively diary of their trials and foibles, which he later turned into a bestseller titled *Ocean to Ocean*. The book was a thinly disguised booster for the concept of the new Canada as a dominion with a hinterland stretching to the Pacific. "By uniting together," he claimed, "the British Provinces had declared that their destiny was—not to ripen and drop, one by one, into the arms of the Republic" but to become "the grandest Empire in the world."

"TRAVEL A THOUSAND MILES up a great river; more than another thousand along great lakes and a succession of smaller lakes; a thousand miles across rolling prairies; and another thousand through woods and

over three great ranges of mountains, and you have travelled from Ocean
to Ocean through Canada." So begins Grant's account of his and
Fleming's grand cross-continental trek. "All this Country is a single
Colony of the British Empire," he continued—as indeed it was in the
minds of eastern politicians who had proclaimed it so—"and this
Colony is dreaming magnificent dreams of a future when it shall be
the 'Greater Britain,' and the highway across which the fabrics and
products of Asia shall be carried, to the Eastern as well as to the Western
sides of the Atlantic. Mountains were once thought to be effectual barriers against railways, but that day has gone by; and, now that trains run
between San Francisco and New York, over summits of eight thousand
two hundred feet, it is not strange that they should be expected soon to
run between Victoria and Halifax, over a height of three thousand
seven hundred feet."

Lest readers be tempted to believe their task was a simple one, Grant
disabused them right away: "No white man is known to have crossed
from the Upper Ottawa to Lake Superior or Lake Winnipeg. There
were maps of the country, dotted with lakes and lacustrine rivers here
and there; but these had been made up largely from sketches, on bits of
birch-bark or paper, and the verbal descriptions of Indians." He continued: "In a word, the country between Old Canada and Red River was
utterly unknown, except along the canoe routes travelled by the Hudson
Bay men north-west of Lake Superior. Only five or six years since, a
lecturer had to inform a Toronto audience that he had discovered a great
lake, called Nepigon, a few miles to the north of Lake Superior."

"It will be sufficient for our purpose . . . to begin at Toronto," Grant
wrote, reflecting what would become a recurring theme of frustration
for the Atlantic provinces, although the Nova Scotian did then admit
that they had passed over "all that may at any time be seen on the line
from Halifax to Truro, and northerly across the Cobequid Mountains
to Moncton," and that to the west of Moncton "there is much along the

line worthy of description, but thousands of Railway tourists will see it all with their own eyes in a year or two;—the deep forests of New Brunswick, the noble Miramichi River with its Railway bridging on a somewhat gigantic scale, the magnificent highland scenery of the Baie des Chaleurs, the Restigouche, and the wild mountain gorges of the Matapedia." But, he sighed, they rushed ever onward "without delaying even to catch a forty or fifty-pound salmon in the Restigouche" along the shores of the great St. Lawrence. At Rivière-du-Loup they boarded a Pullman car and trundled past the cliffs of historic Quebec, then crossed the St. Lawrence on "that magnificent monument of early Canadian enterprise, that triumph of engineering skill, 'The Victoria Bridge,' opposite Montreal." They "necessarily" spent two days in the sweltering, uncivilized humidity of Ottawa before pressing on south to Toronto by July 15. From there they boarded a series of boats and railways and a steamer through Georgian Bay and along Lake Superior to Fort William, where the real adventure began.

On the steamer near the end of July they noticed a curious slight Irishman scurrying off the boat in the evenings: John Macoun, "a gentleman, out for his holidays on a botanical excursion to Thunder Bay," who befriended Grant, Fleming and young Frank. They were to become fast friends and continue westward together. They soon set out along the Dawson Route, the horrifically chaotic and ill-manicured track that traversed the rock and muskeg north of Lake Superior. Trending upward over undulating terrain by horse cart, they were pleased to note that "the mosquitoes are not more vicious than in the woods and by the streams of the Lower Provinces," and yet they were astonished that they encountered barely six settlers over days of travel. "How many cottars, small farmers, and plough boys in Britain, would rejoice to know that they could get a hundred acres of such land for one dollar an acre, money down; or at twenty cents per acre after five years settlement on it?" But the land soon turned rocky and the timber poor, and the road even poorer.

"The road was heavy," Grant related, "varying between corduroy, deep sand, and rutty and rooty stretches, over which the waggon jolted frightfully." The travellers switched to canoes and endured frequent portages along the series of lakes, with Haudenosaunee and Anishinaabe (Ojibwa) canoe masters guiding their progress and helping to carry their mounds of equipment. The lead guide was an older man with steel-grey hair named Ignace Mentour. He had a quiet demeanour and a "broad, handsome" face and he commanded quiet respect from the others. Mentour, it turned out, had been Sir George Simpson's guide for fifteen years and was a gifted storyteller who enlivened the evenings around the fire with tales of his exploits. "These Iroquois, and most of the Ojibbeways we have met, are men above the medium size, broad shouldered, with straight features, intelligent faces, and graceful, because natural, bearing." The Haudenosaunee (Iroquois) were distinguished by their short hair and neat clothing, the Anishinaabe by long, straight hair in two braids, feather adornments and colourful sashes.

At one clearing along the rugged route, they met a gathering of around eighty who spoke neither English nor French, who were awaiting more of their fellows to congregate for a powwow and a signing with a Dominion Indian commissioner. (This would have been for Treaty 3, formalized in 1873.) But as Grant observed, the negotiations were taking longer than anticipated, as "the terms on which they would allow free passage through, and settlement in, the country . . . were considered extravagant." He expressed insight as well as the common sentiment of imperialists who dreamed of empire: "Poor creatures! not much use have they ever made of the land; but yet, in admitting the settler, they sign their own death warrants. Who, but they, have a right to the country; and if 'a man may do what he likes with his own,' would they not be justified in refusing to admit one of us to their lakes and woods, and fighting us to the death on that issue? But it is too late to argue the question; the red man, with his virtues and his vices,—lauded by some as so dignified, abused by others as so dirty—is being civilised off the ground. In the United States they have, as a rule, dealt with him more summarily than in British America, but it comes to pretty much the same in the end, whether he is 'improved off,' or shot down at once as a nuisance. His wild, wandering life is inconsistent with modern requirements: these vast regions were surely meant to maintain more than a few thousand Ojibbeways."

Grant, the great nation booster, who truly and passionately believed that there would be better prosperity in unity under Canada's umbrella, possessed a curious insightful empathy for the plight of the land's original inhabitants and the uncertain future they faced. "Whatever the benefits that have been conferred on them, or whatever their natural defects, they surely have rights to this country," he wrote,

> though they have never divided it up into separate personal holdings. They did not do so, simply because their idea was that the land was free to all. Each tribe had its own ground, which extended over hundreds of miles, and every man had a full right to all of that as far as he could occupy it. Wherever he could walk, ride, or canoe, there the land and the water were his. If he went to the land of another tribe, the same rule held good; he might be scalped as an enemy, but he ran no risk of being punished as a trespasser.
>
> And now a foreign race is swarming over the country, to mark out lines, to erect fences, and to say "this is mine and not yours," till not an inch shall be left the original owner. All this may be inevitable. But in the name of justice, of doing as we would be done by, of the "sacred rights" of property, is not the Indian entitled to liberal, and, if possible, permanent compensation?

They also met one of Chief Blackstone's three wives "sitting on a log, with two or three papooses hanging round her neck" and were sympathetic to the plight of the exhausted-looking woman. "She was dirty, joyless-looking and prematurely old. All the hard work falls to the lot of the women: the husband hunts, fishes, paddles, or does any other work that a 'gentleman' feels he can do without degradation; his wife is something better than his dog, and faithfully will he share with her his last morsel; but it's only a dog's life that she has." Both Grant and Fleming had, however, gone on their jaunty adventure leaving their many children behind to be tended by their wives, apart from Frank, and there is no record of whether the teenager was finding the trip edifying or adventurous, or was merely irritated to be stuck with the oldsters away from his friends.

They continued onward through a sparsely but consistently populated land of lakes and channels in three canoes powered by their hearty and genial guides, under the direction of Ignace, with several friendly races each day and Haudenosaunee voyageur songs to liven the monotony as they pushed west and north toward the open land of the prairie. Each night, before the fire was lit for the evening repast, the guides turned the three bark canoes over, inspected them for damage and reapplied resin on the seams. "The Indians grow on us day by day," wrote Grant, who, like Fleming, had previously never met any. "It is easy to understand how an Englishman, travelling for weeks together with an Indian guide, so often contracts a strong friendship for him; for the Indian qualities of patience, endurance, dignity and self-control, are the very ones to evoke friendship."

Only occasionally did they meet other travellers or some "road" construction crews. At Fort Frances they observed the construction of two small steamers soon to be plying the waters along the Rainy River and Lake of the Woods. It was a herculean task, but the route was slowly being transformed. The botanist Macoun continued to amuse with his enthusiastic antics whenever he spied a new species of plant to document for his collection. One morning he was ecstatic to note twenty-four new wildflowers, eight of which he had never seen before. On another morning, on the verge of the prairie, he awoke early, rushed around frantically, and exclaimed, "Thirty-two new species already; it's a perfect floral garden."

At the far end of the Lake of the Woods, on July 29, they bid adieu to Ignace and their Haudenosaunee voyageurs and disembarked "in the dirtiest, most desolate-looking, mosquito-haunted of all our camping grounds," where a small gathering of voyageurs, Anishinaabe and road construction workers were congregated. The next morning, they loaded their goods aboard a horse-drawn cart and set off through the rain to the northwest on a rugged newly built road. It was "a flat country, much of it marshy, with a dense forest of scrub pine, spruce, tamarack, and, here and there, aspens and white birch. On both sides of the road and in the more open parts of the country, all kinds of wild fruit grow luxuriantly; strawberries, raspberries, black and red currants, etc., etc., and, as a consequence, flocks of wild pigeons and prairie hens are numerous."

The soil began to change into a dark loam they noted would be sure to be productive for agriculture. And the naturalist Macoun was ecstatic over yet more new findings in the world of plants and flowers. "Great was the astonishment of our teamsters, when they saw him make a bound from his seat on the waggon to the ground, and rush to the plain, wood, or marsh. At first, they all hauled up to see what was the matter. It must be gold or silver he had found; . . . he came back triumphantly waving a flower or bunch of grass, and exclaiming: 'Did you ever see the like of that?'" to the "disgusted" Scottish teamsters, who jocularly called him "the Professor" after one particularly exuberant day of hauling armfuls of vegetation back to the trundling cart.

Their first sight of the prairie was met with amazement. They emerged from the forest during the night and made camp, and when they awoke it was with astonishment that they beheld a "sea of green sprinkled with yellow, red, lilac, and white. None of us had ever seen a prairie before, and, behold, the half had not been told us! As you cannot know what the Ocean is without seeing it, neither can you in imagination picture the prairie." The route to Fort Garry passed uneventfully apart from the change in food; now they dined on tomato soup and fresh bread with wild blueberry jam and other such rarities at the various staging stations, or roadhouses, along the new road. All seemed to be run by newly arrived Scottish immigrants or Métis, some dreaming of saving their wages to acquire farmland in Red River. The general talk was about the prospects of the new railway and the need to settle land treaties to avoid conflict.

The road was much improved on the prairie. They struck directly for Winnipeg and quickly arrived at the settlement. It had taken them merely three weeks, a great improvement on the three months it took Wolseley and his troops the previous year, although Fleming and Grant travelled with far less baggage and equipment. The bustling settlement of Red River, and its sprawling hinterland of farms, now had a population of fifteen thousand, mostly of mixed heritage. Grant noted that the French-speaking Métis were generally selling their land and moving farther west, while the Scottish and English Métis seemed to be settling down to farm. He interviewed people, seeking their opinions on the frost, rainfall and farming potential to report back to prospective emigrants. "The wealth of vegetation and the size of the root crops astonished us, especially when informed that no manure had been used and very little care taken. The soil all along the Assiniboine is either a dark or light-coloured loam, the vegetable or sandy loam that our gardeners are anxious to fill their pots with; a soil capable of raising anything."

But they didn't linger too long, as Fleming wanted to get to the Rocky Mountains for his principal task of finding a pass suitable for the railway. "If Canada is to open up her North-west to all the world for colonisation, there must be a road for troops." After visiting Smith at his mansion Silver Heights, the quartet joined a congregation of travellers in six Red River carts and two flatbed carts that were setting off northwest across the grasslands, along the Carlton Trail to Portage la Prairie, Fort Ellice, Fort Carlton and Fort Edmonton. It would have been impossible for them to cross the land without the Hudson's Bay Company forts, the only stations on that long route where horses could be exchanged, provisions bought and information or guides obtained. Their Métis guide was named Emilien, and he worked with six other Métis who tended the nearly two dozen horses, several used to haul the carts and the tents, equipment and provisions and others as spare mounts. Emilien set a gruelling pace throughout August, from dawn to dusk, the carts screeching and generating clouds of dust through fields of golden grass enlivened by vast clusters of wildflowers and the occasional giant sunflower beneath a clear blue open sky.

Near the Qu'Appelle River they met a Scots Métis named Mackay and his family, hauling six carts of buffalo meat and hides, who told them a vast herd of the shaggy animals was roaming several days' travel to the north. Sadly, the men couldn't spare the time to see what was becoming an uncommon sight. They met several other Métis over the journey, hauling their bounty in their squealing carts from their summer hunt back to the vicinity of Fort Garry, as well as encampments of Sioux searching for buffalo. But the herds were much diminished from former days. Once, they came upon a band of Saulteaux with a team of loaded horses and carts and were able to barter for some dried buffalo steaks in exchange for some tea. "The men had straight delicate features, with little appearance of manly strength in their limbs; hair nicely trimmed and plaited. Two or three young girls were decidedly pretty, and so were the little pappooses. The whole party would have been taken for good looking gypsies in England." At Tortoise River they stopped near Horse Hill, the site of a famous battle between the Niisitapi (Blackfoot) and Cree forty years earlier, when a Niisitapi party that had ventured far east of their traditional territory was returning after a

successful raid and had been lured into a valley where they were surrounded by Cree warriors and forced to drop all their plunder and flee.

Around the campfire at night many other tales were told of the battles
and deeds of former days. "The characteristic of the Blackfeet braves,
however, is daring. Many a stirring tale of headlong valour they tell round
their camp fires, as, long ago in moated castles, bards sang the deeds of
knights-errant, and fired the blood of the rising generation. Such a story
we heard of a Chief called 'the Swan,' once the bravest of the brave, but
now tho' in the prime of life, dying of consumption. Dressing himself one
day in all his bravery, he mounted his fleet horse and rode straight for the
Cree camp. A hundred warriors were scattered about the tents, and in the
centre of the encampment two noted braves sat gambling. Right up to
them 'the Swan' rode, scarcely challenged, as he was alone, clapped his
musket to the head of one and blew his brains out. In an instant the camp
was up; dozens of strong arms caught at the reckless foe, dozens of shots
were fired, while others rushed for their horses. But he knew his horse,
and, dashing through the encampment like a bolt, made good his escape,
though chased by every man that could mount."

They continued across the sea of grass toward Fort Edmonton, now
into the more northern region, with islands of aspen verdant along the
creeks and rivers, feasting finally on tender buffalo steak and new potatoes
in delicious gravy. Around campfires more stories were told beneath the
stars while the wolves howled in the distance. Several times they traded
tea and flour for fresh ducks, trout or berries with bands of Cree. Grant
noted that "they were handsome fellows, with well cut, refined Italian
features—handsomer than any of us," and friendly and helpful. But "the
farming is on a very limited scale, as the men prefer hunting buffalo,
fishing, or freighting for the Company to steady agricultural labour."

At Fort Edmonton everything was loaded onto pack horses. It was
a sad leave-taking from many of the guides who had seen them across
the prairie, especially for young Frank, who had been learning Cree

from Souzie, one of their Cree guides. On the day they were to depart, "Souzie mounted his horse and waited patiently at the gate of the Fort for two hours, without our knowledge. When Frank came out he rode on with him for a mile to the height of a long slope; then he drew up and putting one hand on his heart, with a sorrowful look, held out the other; and, without a word, turned his horse and rode slowly away."

It was also at Fort Edmonton that the botanist went north to scout the Peace River country and to proceed west along a different route, while Grant, Fleming and Frank continued along the Saskatchewan River west into the forested hills before the mountains. They hired new guides, familiar with the region. Unlike when Catherine Schubert and her Overlanders passed through a decade earlier, now there were also seven hundred or so people at a nearby settlement called St. Albert, a missionary and farming outpost of mostly French Métis that had recently lost three hundred to smallpox. From there it was around six hundred miles to Kamloops, through rugged woods, marshes and mountains, with no guaranteed opportunity to resupply or obtain fresh horses. Gone were "the luxuries of white-fish, fresh eggs, cream, butter and young pig bountifully served up," Grant lamented.

They headed west into the wooded foothills, so far following, as they generally had been, the same route taken by the Overlanders on their trek to the goldfields of Barkerville. Key to a railroader's ambition, Fleming spied abundant outcroppings of coal, which the party occasionally burned to cook their dinner—and to test it out for future railway use. Valad, their Cree guide, informed Grant that many people used coal as a fuel when wood was wet or they were near to a promising exposed seam. "The simple fact is that the coal deposits of the North-west are so enormous in quantity that people were unwilling to believe that the quality could be good. Here then is fuel for the future inhabitants of the plains, near water communication for forwarding it in different directions."

The small pack train ambled along the "road" through heavily wooded hills with autumn tints to the underbrush, the red and yellow evidence of early frosts, although there would be nearly three months yet before winter. Now into September, the days were beautifully warm but nights were getting colder as they trended ever upward and ever west. In the mornings they could often see a good fire blazing when they woke and by it sat Valad, smoking and looking pensive.

> He might have been sitting there for centuries, so perfect was the repose of form and feature.
> Brown enquired if he had seen the horses and the answer was a wave of the hand, first in one direction and then in another, not only enough to say that he had, but also where they were, without disturbing any of us who might be asleep.
> He looked more like a dignified Italian gentleman than an obscure Indian guide.

They ate wild cranberry jam with each meal, freshly gathered as a complement to the pemmican, pork and pancakes. It was slow and tedious travel along a surprisingly well-trodden trail that was unfortunately littered with deadfall. After two weeks of hard travel they reached the now mostly abandoned HBC outpost of Jasper House, formerly a bustling place and the staging ground for the infamous and brooding Athabasca Pass, and the party continued west by the broad but forested track along the Miette River. The scenery was stunning, an open valley with serrated rocky ridges and snow-dusted peaks. "There is a wonderful combination of beauty about these mountains. Great masses of boldly defined bare rock are united to all the beauty that variety of form, colour, and vegetation give. A noble river with many tributaries each defining a distinct range, and a beautiful lake ten miles long, embosomed three thousand three hundred feet above the sea, among mountains twice as high, offer innumerable scenes, seldom to be found within the same compass, for the artist to depict and for every traveller to delight in." No wonder it is now a famous international tourist destination.

The travel was hard, through tangled scrub brush and masses of fallen timber scratching and tearing at clothes, and miring in bogs with horses' hooves sinking, the trail indistinguishable from the rock slides and shores of murky ponds. At the terrifying fording of one swollen river, where the water rose to their horses' shoulders and nearly swept them away, they spied signs of shod horses, perhaps the first evidence of the survey parties that Fleming had been hoping to see, which had been tasked with scouting the route east toward Jasper. After a bit more travel along some ponds and past a cluster of pine trees, a Secwépemc man quietly rode into their camp along the river and, after shaking hands all round, handed a slip of paper to Fleming. The letter was from Walter Moberly, Fleming's survey engineer, informing them that he was ahead and hoped to see them soon. Valad tried to talk to the man in Cree, to no avail. But he was able to speak the old company fur trade jargon called Chinook and learned that there was a big camp with many horses and plenty of food a few days to the west.

When they met up with Moberly and shared food, it was a cornucopia of delights: "delicious Java coffee, sweetened with sugar from the Sandwich Islands, that now supply a great part of the Pacific coast with sugar; and crisp bacon, almost as great a luxury to us as pemmican to Moberly's men." Valad and two other guides returned east with the horses of their pack train, while Grant and the others were provided with a new set of horses for the final stretch of their journey. They followed a well-marked trail west to Tête Jaune Cache and then along the North Thompson River to Kamloops. It was still a struggle in places but the way was slowly being cleared along the route first scouted and blazed by Moberly's Pacific party. They continued onward toward the coast, reaching Yale in early October. There they met the famous Judge Begbie, who was then returning from the Interior to New Westminster, stopping along his way in all the towns along the Fraser River. They continued on to Victoria, crossing the Salish Sea and arriving after nearly one hundred days of hard travel.

Victoria, the farthest-flung outpost of empire, one year after Confederation with Canada, intrigued them, as it was unlike any towns and cities along the St. Lawrence. "A walk through the streets . . . showed the little capital to be a small polyglot copy of the world. Its population is less than 5,000; but almost every nationality is represented. Greek fishermen, Kanaka [Hawaiian] sailors, Jewish and Scotch merchants, Chinese washerwomen or rather washermen, French, German and Yankee restaurant-keepers, English and Canadian officeholders and butchers, negro waiters and sweeps, Australian farmers and other varieties of the race, rub against each other, and apparently in the most friendly way. The sign-boards tell their own tale: 'Own Shing, washing and ironing'; 'Sam Hang,' ditto; 'Kwong Tai & Co., cigar store'; 'Magasin Français'; 'Teutonic Hall, lager beer'; 'Scotch House'; 'Adelphic' and 'San Francisco' saloons; 'Oriental' and 'New England' restaurants."

After feasting their eyes upon this smorgasbord of amicable ethnicity, in mid-October they boarded a steamer to San Francisco and cruised four days south. They then purchased tickets on the Union and Central Pacific Railroad and within days were breakfasting in Ottawa.

CHAPTER TEN

THE PACIFIC SCANDAL

———

While Fleming was scouting and wandering the vast land over which a railway would have to traverse, Macdonald was grappling with unforeseen problems arising from the financing and corporate structure of his ambitious project. For obvious reasons, the railway had to be constructed within Canada and not rely on American branch connection lines, which would surely result in the territory becoming Americanized in culture and economy, and eventually politically. The American railway from Boston to Puget Sound near Seattle, called the Northern Pacific, would roll west with the segment crossing the prairies running suspiciously close to the international border. Obviously, the intention was to run branch lines north to siphon commerce and travel to the U.S.

The main problem with a Canadian-only route was the thousands of miles of track that would have to be laid to the north of Lake Superior, land of rock and bog. It was unproductive land from a farming point of view (the vast mineral potential was unknown at the time and in any case was of little value without a means to get it to market). Back then, railways were financed by governments giving the railway companies substantial grants of public land surrounding the track before it was built, which was then sold at the most opportune time to secure enough money to pay for the track—a creative solution to the old chicken-and-egg conundrum. It was ingenious if the land could be easily sold; a brow-furrowing problem if not. (Even more of a quandary if the government granting the "Crown" land had no underlying title to it.) Investors in Macdonald's scheme were not pleased with his demands that the line traverse the northland before reaching the deep, loamy soils of Red River. These were economic objections, rather than political or nationalistic ones. In this region, the project just couldn't pay out. The Canadian Shield was an insurmountable geographical, and hence financial, barrier to the expansion of the Canadian Empire. Given the different topographies, applying the ingenious American financing model to the Canadian railway could not fully work. In 1871, Macdonald had turned down an offer to construct the line from a predominantly American conglomerate of investors because they were also involved in the Northern Pacific in the U.S. He feared their intention was to dawdle on the Canadian Shield section while building the much-feared spurs south to connect to their own railway, all the while making good with government subsidies—which is precisely what they did intend.

George W. McMullen, the Ontario-Chicago business promoter associated with the Northern Pacific, and Jay Cooke, a Philadelphia financier, were two of this group of prominent American investors. Although he turned down their proposal, Macdonald pointed to their interest as leverage to get more local investors, who did in fact emerge, although the shadowy presence of McMullen and Cooke was never distant.

THE HUGE, DARK PORTRAIT shows a fearsome balding aristocratic-looking gentleman glaring at the viewer. His pose is aggressive, as if he is striding forward to strike, his hair long and beard prodigious, his eyes fierce, as if glowering at the little people. In 1870s Montreal, everyone was a little person when compared with Hugh Allan.

The son of a Scottish shipmaster who regularly sailed the waters between Clyde and Montreal, he dropped out of formal education when he was thirteen and went to work in shipping, moving to Montreal when he was sixteen, in 1826. Through unstinting labour and unusual perspicacity, determination and instinct, he rose rapidly within a firm of shipbuilders to become a senior partner. In the early 1850s, along with his younger brother, he shifted to steamship construction and expanded the enterprise into one of the world's great commercial shipping and passenger fleets, the Allan Line, making Allan the richest man in the Dominion. He naturally expanded his industrial investments into coal, railways, cotton, tobacco and steel, while keeping leading politicians in his pocket with "bonifications"—more crassly known as bribes—that smoothed the passage of lucrative government contracts in his direction, for mail delivery and for shipping immigrants west across the Atlantic and then natural resources east, to the chagrin of his competitors. His was one of the largest dwellings in the nation: a thirty-four-room Montreal mansion that he titled Ravenscrag, whose property sprawled across ten acres on Mount Royal. The house boasted interior plumbing, gas lighting and heating, and eleven live-in servants. His ascent to the pinnacle of society and business was aided by his wife, Matilda Caroline Smith, of Montreal's merchant elite, and they had nine daughters and four sons; incredibly all but one survived to adulthood to carry on the family legacy, including their son Montagu, who significantly expanded the family mansion in the 1890s.

Ravenscrag had its own seventy-five-foot tower from which Allan could leisurely get behind his brass spyglass and observe the comings and goings of his ships along the St. Lawrence, small in the distance; or, if he looked downward toward Old Montreal, he could perhaps scrutinize the dark industrial bulk of his cotton mill, which hulked ogre-like in the east, where children as young as ten toiled barefoot amidst the gloom, inhaling fibrous dust and cringing at the screech of machinery. With virtue and social standing, appearance is everything. Allan was the type of man who would squeeze his partners and senior employees in private so they could do the more visible squeezing in public. He understood that child labour for poverty wages was bad in principle. But this sweatshop and others like it were far away from where he lived. Things often seem smaller when viewed from afar, even the suffering of children.

Arrogant, condescending and single-mindedly preoccupied with his fortune and social standing, Allan was naturally drawn to the national railway project when he got wind of it in 1871. Not only would it funnel a profitable feedstock of goods from British Columbia and Asia toward his shipping empire in the St. Lawrence, but the cachet of being the man who made it happen—a glorious nation-building link in the expanding chain of the British Empire—was sure to land him a further title. He was a respected man, envied for his riches, admired for his business acumen and connections and lauded for his prominent role in his church. Yet so far, at age sixty-one, to his chagrin he had achieved only a single knighthood. He was the obvious man to lead a Canadian consortium to build a railway to the Pacific.

In Montreal in the fall of 1871, Allan met with McMullen and Charles Mather Smith, a Chicago banker, and the men agreed to form an apparently Canadian corporation that would actually be beholden for finances and direction to the same American investors Macdonald had rebuffed earlier, including the American financier Jay Cooke. They would enlist additional prominent backers for a syndicate. Of course, the membership would be politically unpalatable, so their arrangement had to be kept secret. "The act will provide for building a north shore road to Fort Garry merely to calm public opinion," wrote Cooke to his business partner. Their actual plan was that "the American agreement has to be kept dark for the present on account of the political jealousies in the Dominion, and there is no hint of the Northern Pacific connection, but the plan is to cross the Sault Ste. Marie up through northern Michigan and Wisconsin to Duluth, then build from Pembina up to Fort Garry and by and by through the Saskatchewan into British Columbia." They would maintain the pretense of the northern route around Lake Superior for as long as possible before announcing it was untenable. What they envisioned was a sort of hidden union between the Canadian Pacific and the Northern Pacific.

By mid-1872 two railway syndicates were competing for the lucrative government contract, Allan's and one in Toronto led by David Lewis Macpherson, who was vehemently against any American meddling in the Canadian railway. Macpherson's party was incorporated as the Inter-oceanic Railway Company of Canada and Allan's as the Canada (later "Canadian") Pacific Railway Company. A general election called for August 1872 seemed a perfect time to settle the matter. In the railway-crazed era, there was fierce competition for the contract to survey and construct the great railway amongst those who imagined piles of government money, with perhaps deliberately minimal oversight, attached to its distribution. Both syndicates schemed under the misapprehension that such a contract would be lucrative, with plenty of government support, because of a deep-seated underappreciation for the technical challenges ahead. Allan wasn't one to let fate intervene; he took direct action, in the manner to which he was accustomed when pushing business ventures: bribery. He secured a slush fund from the Americans to distribute to key ridings, to promote pliable politicians and gain the contract for his consortium.

It was a hard-fought election, bitter and divisive. The Liberal leader, Alexander Mackenzie, a former stonemason from Sarnia, denounced the railway scheme as impracticable and a swindle. The Riel uprising and the overgenerous promises to induce British Columbia to join Canada were damaging Macdonald's popularity in Ontario. Money was running low for both parties to finance their campaigns. But there was no secret ballot in 1872, and consequently bribes were lavish and common, since it was easy to ascertain their effectiveness. Allan, directly and indirectly through businesses he owned or controlled, dispensed funds liberally to Macdonald's campaign, including having the Merchants Bank, which he had founded, write off all of Macdonald's considerable personal liabilities. In all, Allan flooded the campaign with perhaps $360,000—in those days a huge amount. When the dust settled, Macdonald had scraped out a victory with a mere two-seat advantage.

The world moved on. Macdonald spent the next several months trying to cajole, persuade, flatter and threaten Macpherson into merging his Inter-oceanic Company with the Canadian Pacific. But Macpherson was like a huge ill-situated rock; he wouldn't budge. No Americans should be involved in the railway, he believed, and there was nothing Macdonald could do to change his mind; Macpherson told Macdonald that he knew there must be American money involved in the CPR proposal and he wouldn't stand for it. Macdonald then went to Allan and informed him that he must provide confirmation that McMullen and Mather Smith and the other Americans were not involved. Macdonald was shocked to learn that Allan had misrepresented the extent of American backing and control over his Canadian Pacific Railway syndicate; that he had, in fact, lied. This presented Macdonald with a problem, since Allan and his foreign financiers had been massive backers of his and his party's campaign and expected the agreed-upon payoff.

Nevertheless, Macdonald told Allan he wouldn't get the contract if the Americans were involved. Allan, evidently believing that he would be insulated from the fallout by his signed documents disclosing his distribution of funds for the election—documents that, if made public, would construe that he was "purchasing" the contract illegally—sent a telegram to Chicago informing McMullen that their deal was off; they were not to be allowed in on the consortium, and neither would their money be refunded. McMullen was stunned and then furious. He rode the train from Chicago to Montreal to confront Allan, to no avail. He threatened to go to the prime minister with all of his incriminating evidence, to no avail. He did ride the train to Ottawa and met Macdonald on New Year's Eve 1872. He did present his documents, but Macdonald wouldn't budge—though he sweated. Now he had seen the evidence of the bribes Allan had paid, mostly in Quebec, to Macdonald's Quebec lieutenant, George-Étienne Cartier; he had seen the signed agreement between Allan and Cartier detailing the distribution of funds and alluding to their "agreement." To Macdonald, this was all scarcely creditable, enough to drive a man to drink, which it certainly did. He was astonished, almost incredulous, at what had been going on and what he was now caught up in.

Certainly, the Pacific Scandal was one of the most detailed and incredible instances of bribery in Canadian politics. It was all unfolding the same summer that Grant and Fleming were scouting the route for the railway, ascending the Yellowhead Pass, camping under the stars and noting the best location for the route without ever dreaming of the corruption, swindles and backstabbing that were occurring among their political masters back east.

But McMullen and Cooke were people unaccustomed to being unceremoniously ditched after years of planning and significant financial investment. They weren't shy about letting Macdonald know that they would reveal their financial involvement in both the railway scheme and the election. Before Allan departed for London in early 1873 to try to drum up alternative investors, he somehow calmed the pair down. But he received only a lukewarm reception when he presented to London capitalists the opportunity of investing in the great Canadian railway.

And then, by the spring, the scandal was again burbling in the press, threatening political and perhaps financial disaster for those involved. On April 2, a Liberal member rose in the House of Commons and announced that he had evidence of corrupt dealings between the government and Allan, and worse, that these dealings involved the American railwaymen and the election; indeed, he suggested that Allan had purchased the contract for the western railway by contributing huge sums to the Conservatives to pay for their election win. The railway consortium was set to gain a great deal for their investment, including $30 million in taxpayers' cash up front and fifty million acres of land on the prairies, in addition to the promise that the government would clear the title to the land with Indigenous peoples.

The most damning, and the most famous, piece of correspondence between Macdonald and Allan's lawyer was a call for money: "I MUST HAVE ANOTHER TEN THOUSAND—WILL BE THE LAST TIME OF CALLING. DO NOT FAIL ME. ANSWER TO-DAY—J.A. MACDONALD." To which Allan's lawyer, John Abbott (later Canada's third prime minister), responded: "DRAW ON ME FOR TEN THOUSAND DOLLARS." Unfortunately, the telegram was mysteriously stolen from Abbott's office and sold for $5,000 to the Opposition Liberals, who naturally passed it on to their partisan news organs, the *Montreal Herald* and the Toronto *Globe*, which began to publish this and other evidence of bribery and corruption involving Allan and the American money and the disbursements to Macdonald and his party officials during the election. There could be no denying the collusion, although they tried, and Allan published a carefully worded rebuttal and justification for his no doubt out-of-context correspondence: it was merely a misunderstanding, there was no undue pressure. McMullen himself got his revenge by spilling the beans on his version of the entire affair, including details of the payoffs and secret agreements. Of course, he was one of the dastardly Americans at the heart of the affair, so his credibility was suspect.

But more damning, an inquiry established by Parliament found evidence of bribery. Macdonald, after disappearing on a lengthy drinking binge, in mid-August tried to deflect from the scandal in the time-honoured tradition still in practice today: by proroguing Parliament for two months. But to little avail.

In the end it was the vote of Donald "Labrador" Smith, mockingly referenced as the "Member for the Hudson's Bay Company," who was then representing Selkirk in Manitoba, that turned the tide. He rushed back to Ottawa from Silver Heights—by Red River cart south into the U.S. and then by railway—and arrived in late October. Macdonald had never repaid Smith for the money he used to bribe Riel and his senior followers. When Smith mentioned the oversight to Macdonald, who had been drinking, Macdonald, instead of apologizing for the delay and seeking forgiveness, puffed up and strutted about, swearing and daring Smith to make the bribes public. The abstemious Smith was not impressed. And although a few days later Macdonald did agree to pay him, the damage was done. During the fateful parliamentary sitting of November 3, Macdonald rose in the House and gave a long, windy, booze-soaked speech, limply defending himself and his government's actions. "If we had had the same means possessed by hon. gentlemen opposite; if we had spies; if we had thieves; if we had men who went to your desk, picked your lock and stole your note books, we would have much stronger evidence than hon. gentlemen think they have now. We were fighting an uneven battle. We were simply subscribing as gentlemen, while they were stealing as burglars."

"By their line of action," Macdonald intoned,

the gentlemen opposite have postponed for some years the building of that railway, and they have besmirched unjustly, dishonourably, the character of the Canadian Government and of the Canadian people. If there be any delay, any postponement in the completion of that great system of railways, I charge it to the hon. gentlemen opposite. Long after this quarrel is over, it will be recorded in the history of this Dominion of Canada that there was one body of men in this country willing to forget self, to forget Party, to forget section to build up a great interest and make a great country, and they will say that there was another Party who fought section against section, province against province, who were unable to rise to the true position of affairs, and I say the history of the future will be our justification and their condemnation. . . .

I have fought the battle of Confederation, the battle of Union, the battle of the Dominion of Canada. I throw myself upon this House; I throw myself upon this country; I throw myself upon posterity, and I believe that I know that, notwithstanding the many failings in my life, I shall have the voice of this country and this House rallying round me. And, Sir, if I am mistaken in that, I can confidently appeal to a higher Court, to the Court of my own conscience, and to the Court of Posterity.

Unmoved by Macdonald's grand words, Smith slowly rose and cast his vote with the Liberals, officially bringing down the government. Smith couched his stance in the rhetoric of high morals, which was particularly amusing given who it was coming from: he claimed that he would be most willing to vote confidence in the Government, if he "could do so conscientiously," but "for the honour of the country, no Government should exist that has a shadow of a suspicion of this kind resting on them," and for that reason, he could not give it his support. Pandemonium best describes the scene that followed. Amidst the yelling and shoving, Macdonald strode calmly toward Smith, the crowd opening before him, and began spewing invective while reputedly drawing back his arm and planting two blows upon Smith before being restrained.

Macdonald then took to his sickbed and the government fell, and in the general election that followed in early 1874—the first with secret ballots—Macdonald and the Conservatives were relegated to the Opposition benches. Smith won in his old riding, but this time as a Liberal supporting Alexander Mackenzie. Afterward he became one of Mackenzie's principal advisors, but not before being pelted with raw eggs during the election campaign in Winnipeg. But he didn't mind. He wasn't in politics to make the world a better place or to pursue a grand national vision like Macdonald. For some, politics was a means to fuel political or religious objectives, to force their will upon others, a more intimate and subtle form of mastery—always for the benefit of the people, naturally, and sometimes it even worked out that way. But Smith seems to have pursued politics as a means to meet people who could help him increase his personal fortune.

In any event, it's worth noting that Smith, his cousin George Stephen—the well-known financier, director and, within three years, president of the Bank of Montreal—and a consortium had only recently applied for the charter to run a railway the one hundred kilometres or so between Pembina on the U.S. border and Winnipeg. If Allan and his American promoters and the Canadian Pacific Railway Company had won the railway contract from the federal government, they would have run a branch line north from their Northern Pacific line instead, putting a damper on Smith's own railway ambitions and risking his investment.

Macdonald resigned the day after the momentous debate, and the first Canadian Pacific Railway Company died in sympathy. The events bring to mind the old saying "to regret the methods, you first have to win." Macdonald was now, at least for a while, a politician free from power, and hence dilemmas and disappointment, especially since the country soon descended into a major economic recession that correlated with Mackenzie's taking office. But Macdonald, the consummate politician, was already planning his return.

PART THREE

THE REALITY

CHAPTER ELEVEN

MASSACRE IN THE CYPRESS HILLS

———

I n the summer of 1873, while parliamentarians in Ottawa yammered and jousted and frothed their indignation or innocence, a group of ill-kempt American wolfers based out of Fort Benton, Montana, went on a liquor-fuelled rampage and murdered dozens of people, shooting them down with Winchester repeating rifles. Such killings were not uncommon in the American western territories in the 1870s, the destination of choice for many thousands of battle-hardened former soldiers discharged after the Civil War, inured, as they were to violence and bloodshed, maiming and sickness. Seeing comrades stabbed in the guts with a bayonet or their legs blasted off by a cannonball, or swooning from the sickly sweet rot of gangrene from an amputated limb, or enduring the knifing pain and screaming while black frozen toes slowly thawed takes a toll on a person's mental state. And it showed in their behaviour, shadowing the history of the era with a taint of inhumanity.

But this massacre didn't happen in the American territories. It occurred in the Cypress Hills of what would later become Alberta and

Saskatchewan. And the massacred people were Nakoda (Assiniboine), ostensibly Canadian citizens, though they probably didn't think of themselves as such. Afterward, the killing accomplished, their bloodlust satiated and the liquor supply running low, the gang mounted their horses and fled back south to American territory. The massacre was the culmination of events that had begun earlier that spring.

WOLFING WAS A DISREPUTABLE PROFESSION, and the wolfers were disreputable folk, universally scorned and reviled by all Indigenous people, Métis and most white traders as well. Their ranks were filled by footloose men who, at that point in their lives, had nowhere else to go. They had reached the bottom. Not fit for any other occupation by dint of personality, temperament or personal history, and with no war and therefore no army in need of their specialized skills, they turned to wolfing in the wild lands along the upper Missouri River, now being plied by small steamboats—boats that were hauling out wolf pelts and buffalo skins gathered by this new breed of frontiersmen who were invading the territory of the Sioux, Numakiki (Mandan), Crow (Absoraka), Cheyenne, Atsina (Gros Ventre) and Niisitapi. Since gold had been discovered in the 1860s in Montana, dozens of steamboats plied the river, bringing in vagabonds from New Orleans, Memphis and St. Louis. But as usual the boom was short-lived and had petered out by 1870. The ragged men who had hauled wood to the shores of the Missouri, who had endured a constant low-level warfare with surrounding Indigenous Plains peoples, now sought new opportunities, as did the erstwhile miners. Once the illegal rotgut whiskey trade was saturated and had taken in the best of this lot, the remainder turned to wolfing.

These men banded together into heavily armed gangs and pushed into territories where they were not welcome, with plenty of ammunition and casks of strychnine. They would shoot a buffalo, cut it open and douse the corpse with poison, wait until the rotting scent of death drew wolves from the valleys and hills, and then either shoot the weakened animals, if the wolfers were present, or wait for them to be caught in leghold traps and die. Wolf fur was fashionable attire for status-conscious grandees of the eastern cities, and perhaps thirty thousand pelts were shipped east yearly in the 1870s from Fort Benton, the old fur trade and now U.S. Army outpost, at the height of navigation on the Missouri River.

Poisoning wolves was cowardly, despicable work, disdained by all, and the wolfers were loathed for their methods and their demeanour. Many semi-domestic dogs kept by the Niisitapi were poisoned, dying in agony, as was every other animal and bird in the vicinity. This "profession" basically amounted to dumping poison all over the country and then coming back to take the few animal pelts that could be sold back east.

In general, the wolfers tended to shoot from a distance anyone resembling an Indigenous person whenever they could. Hardly surprisingly, a general state of warfare existed. Wolfers murdered hundreds of mostly Niisitapi people. Sometimes the wolfers banded together in groups as large as sixty and engaged in gun battles with any encampments they encountered across the Plains, firing even at women and children. As the warfare intensified, the wolfers began threatening the traders, demanding that they refuse to sell guns to the Niisitapi and demanding protection money, even killing some who refused to acknowledge their authority. More like a criminal gang, they were swept away by their cruelty and self-importance. The international border then being an imaginary thing, with the traditional territory of the Niisitapi peoples on both sides and the bison migrating indiscriminately along with the wolves, the killing and other depredations of the wolfers frequently extended north into Canada.

In May of 1873, a band of Northern Cree were exploring the Plains much farther south than their habitual territory when they came upon a congregation of wolfers, carts laden with carcasses and dozens of horses corralled for the evening. The gang included Thomas Hardwick, a Civil War veteran and psychopathic murderer, particularly of Indigenous people, and their leader John H. Evans, an erstwhile army captain; the remainder of the gang could in general fit the description of desperadoes, outlaws or horse thieves so common in the American West at that time. Naturally the Cree were tempted by the horses and quietly snuck away in the night with about forty of them, inflicting a serious blow to the wolfers, who now had to drag their own carts into Fort Benton, much to their humiliation. When their calls for justice were met with indifference by the authorities, they went on a drinking binge and decided to take the law into their own hands. It was quite easy to follow the Cree and the stolen horses; concealing so many tracks would have been nearly impossible, and in any case the Cree were running north as fast as they could, concealing nothing, until at some point across the border they must have dispersed, since all trace of their passage disappeared. The disgruntled wolfers in pursuit then decided to head east toward the Cypress Hills, which were a congregating place for many different peoples, believing that perhaps some of the Cree had gone there.

Rising unexpectedly from the prairie and visible from many miles across the otherwise flat land, these pine-covered hills were a source of timber and water from the wetlands, as well as protection from the winds that often blew unobstructed across the prairie. The terrain surrounding them was prime bison country even with the diminished herds of the 1870s. The hills were not in any claimed Indigenous territory but mostly open to all comers, from Niisitapi, Cree, and Atsina (Gros Ventre) to Nakoda, Saulteaux (Plains Ojibwa), and Sioux. Several hundred Métis had also congregated there after the Riel uprising two years earlier and dwelt in a large village of bison-hide lodges, from which they sallied forth to hunt and to trade with their compatriots to the east in Red River or north in the Qu'Appelle Valley. It is from them that the hills got their current name. Although each of the peoples had their own name for the iconic hills, the Métis called the lodgepole pine trees *cyprès*, and the English later adopted the name Cypress, although no cypress trees grew there.

There were two trading posts in the Cypress Hills in the summer of 1873, on opposite sides of the aptly named Battle Creek: Fort Farwell, Abe Farwell in attendance, on the west bank and Fort Solomon, Moses Solomon in attendance, on the east. They could yell back and forth to one another and even observe each other attending to nature in the nearby bushes. Often there were several additional traders living in canvas tents and doing business from the back of their buckboard wagons. In all there were perhaps fifteen or twenty American traders and a handful of their Indigenous wives, all financed by and supplied from Fort Benton. These traders, who dealt primarily in whiskey, were not an extension of the fur trade as conducted by the Hudson's Bay Company, where, even in the 1860s and 1870s, strong social and familial ties existed between the traders and their customers (although much dismantled by the racist policies of George Simpson during his long reign as head of the venerable monopoly); most of the people who worked for the company were of mixed heritage and knowledgeable in perhaps multiple Indigenous languages and customs. The whiskey traders, on the other hand, were more akin to invaders, operating defensive military-style forts, and were heavily armed. They traded not in a smorgasbord of practical and decorative implements and wares but in rotgut whiskey, cheap trinkets and pots, tobacco and a few poor-quality blankets, usually through a small opening in the gates.

The "whiskey" itself was not brandy from Montreal, watered down or adulterated. It was a toxic concoction of pure alcohol, ink, tobacco juice, pepper, laudanum and any other thing tossed into the pot to make it bitter and strong, boiled down to concentrate it. The people who drank it were poisoned as well as intoxicated. The so-called whiskey traders were more like drug pushers than anything else, and they contributed to great destruction on the Plains.

"The Indians are evidently decreasing," observed George Grant during his cross-continental trek with Sandford Fleming, "'dying out' before the white man. Now that the Hudson's Bay monopoly is gone, 'free traders,' chiefly from the south, are coming in, plentifully supplied with a poisonous stuff, rum in name, but in reality a compound of tobacco, vitriol, bluestone and water. This is completing the work that scrofula and epidemics and the causes that bring about scrofula and epidemics were already doing too surely: for an Indian will part with horse and gun, blanket and wife for rum. There is law in abundance forbidding the sale of intoxicating liquor to Indians, but law, without force to execute law, is laughed at by rowdies from Belly River and elsewhere." The Montana whiskey traders were ubiquitous by the mid-1860s, an ever-present culturally corrosive influence that was fuelling deadly fights, drunken deaths by freezing and outright murder by the traders. Many Indigenous people were known to have reduced themselves to penury after trading away their horses, buffalo robes and sometimes even their lodges while intoxicated.

Trading whiskey to Indigenous peoples was illegal in Montana in recognition of the devastation it caused to civil society, and it was also technically illegal in the new Canadian territory, but of course there was no one to enforce the edict north of the border. And so American traders had established dozens of small posts throughout the Canadian prairies, including the infamous Fort Whoop-Up, to the west of the Cypress Hills, along the Oldman River near the present-day city of Lethbridge. Dozens of people died each year after trading for whiskey at Whoop-Up, hundreds throughout the territory. Whoop-Up was a more substantial establishment than most, made from squared timbers, with sentry towers hosting cannons and several stout buildings inside. Great teams of ox carts trundled north on the two-week journey from Fort Benton, hauling whiskey and guns.

AS HARDWICK AND EVANS and their gang, which contained some Métis and Canadians as well as American wolfers, rode down into the valley where the two forts were situated, they spied Nakoda nearby. About a month earlier, the weary, bedraggled band of around 150 people under the leadership of an older chief named Little Soldier had arrived in the vicinity after a deadly winter march without enough provisions. The bison they relied upon had disappeared from their hunting grounds several hundred kilometres to the east. Dozens had perished on the journey, and the others were staggering and weak; most of their horses were dead as well. About 100 other destitute Nakoda soon joined them, looking for shelter and food, and the 250 or so were camped in about forty lodges nearby. Their horses were still sickly and skeletal, their guns were old muskets. What they sought was some shelter and some good hunting, and perhaps some whiskey, before they moved off on their summer migrations.

The wolfers took note of their camp near the whiskey forts and became suspicious, even though there was no evidence of their own horses anywhere. Most of the wolfers didn't bother to make any distinction between "Indians"—they hated them all and killed them indiscriminately. The outlaws rode toward Fort Farwell, and Abe Farwell warily told the heavily armed band that he hadn't seen any Cree or anyone with forty horses. Moses Solomon told them the same. The traders, perhaps foolishly but also perhaps having little choice, furnished the gang with jugs of whiskey, which they quickly began to drink. The wolfers were not readily welcomed; there was an edge to their behaviour, unpredictable and dangerous, and now they were drinking heavily, with an attitude. The Nakoda were also somewhat restless after perhaps being swindled with mouldy flour, damp gunpowder and diluted firewater. They had already traded away nearly all they had of value and were angry. One intoxicated young man shot a bullet toward Fort Solomon; sensing trouble, the trader locked himself and his people inside and refused to conduct any further trade.

June 1 dawned with an edge to the weather, with wind and clouds. The wolfer gang began swilling whiskey right after breakfast and continued throughout the day. Little Soldier tried to persuade his people to break camp and move, but some of the young men mocked him and called him a coward. So, for whatever reason, he abandoned common sense, retrieved a jug of whiskey and also began drinking, joined by many others. One young man had stolen a horse from George Hammond, a Métis trader, and then returned it, demanding a bottle of whiskey as his reward. Hammond, a loud braggart, later stumbled toward the wolfers and proclaimed that his horse had been stolen again. He stamped off with some of them to confront Little Soldier, who denied it and actually pointed out the horse grazing peacefully nearby. He offered one of his own horses as compensation but was rudely rebuffed by the drunken Hammond. Accounts vary. An alternative version of the story has Hammond drunkenly grabbing his gun and swearing that he will exact restitution while marching directly to the Nakoda camp, followed by the wolfers, who seemed to sniff trouble and wanted in on the action. Of course, the wolfer gang didn't speak or understand any Indigenous languages, so communication was limited.

Farwell rushed after Hammond and tried to urge calm, pleading with Little Soldier and Hammond to put their weapons away. Women and children began scurrying toward the fringes of the camp and young men began to undress, the traditional preparation for battle. The wolfers took up semi-concealed positions along a coulee. Then either Hammond shot his rifle or one of the Nakoda warriors shot his—many contradictory witness accounts emerged over the subsequent years—but soon there was shooting all round. The wolfers were heavily armed with repeating rifles and plenty of ammunition, while the Nakoda village consisted mostly of unarmed family units, the young men using out-dated single-shot rifles with damp gunpowder, or bows and arrows. The wolfers began firing into the crowd as they retreated to higher ground, working their way back to the whiskey fort. Then they regrouped, rushed the Nakoda camp and began destroying everything: lodges, cooking pots, clothing, sleeping robes. They discovered Little Soldier, or another elderly man, despondent in his lodge and dragged him out, cut off his head, placed it on the end of a pole and left it to mark the spot. Dozens of others were hit by bullets as they fled under the rain of shot from multiple directions, leaving most of the Nakoda wounded, some grievously. Some of the wounded were then beaten to death. For years the bones of several dozen murder victims lay strewn about.

One of the wolfers was shot dead, a French Canadian named Ed Legrace, but they had killed dozens of Nakoda before nightfall—some claim it was hundreds, though this seems unlikely. The surviving Nakoda fled in the darkness. Farwell's wife, a Crow (Absoraka) named Mary Horseguard, grabbed a loaded pistol and rushed to save a teen-aged girl from some of the drunken wolfers, but several other women were raped throughout the night, including Little Soldier's wife. In the morning, the wolfers rode toward the abandoned village and burned all the possessions and lodges. Then they fled south.

Abe Farwell reported the incident to authorities in Fort Benton, who sent the information east to Washington, while other Métis witnesses took the information back to Red River. News of the event belatedly reached Ottawa more than two months later, in late August.

Macdonald had anticipated the need for a territorial police force ever since he cast his covetous eyes across a map of North America and envisioned his empire creeping west to absorb the varying people of those lands. Originally the force was to be a small elite cavalry of perhaps fifty men, "Pure whites & British & French Half Breeds." Alas, he had become distracted by the Riel uprising and then by the railway and his own self-inflicted political wounds from the Pacific Scandal. At any rate, with the Treaty of Washington in 1871, the Americans had already acknowledged the existence of the new Dominion of Canada's western territory, and so his anxiety over an imminent invasion had been shoved to the background, and along with it the plans for the western police. He continued to dither even while reports of the devastation caused by American whiskey traders percolated east through the channels of the Hudson's Bay Company outposts, and apparently stalled over which politically affiliated personage should be awarded the plum position to head up such an institution.

"Old Tomorrow," as he was nicknamed, was still dithering about creating this police force—and financing it—when news of the Cypress Hills massacre reached him in Ottawa. Details were scarce, but the fact was that people had been killed by an incursion of armed Americans. Would there be an Indigenous uprising in protest? Would more Americans come flooding in? No one seemed to know. But things now moved quickly. By September, officers had been named, newspapers announced the new force, and enlistment of recruits began. They would need about three hundred, and the credentials would have to be somewhat malleable, given the sudden need for haste.

It looked so grand on paper, but reality is a hard mistress sometimes. Colonel George French, the Irish former army officer dubiously honoured with leading this new frontier police force, scoffed in disgust when he beheld the sorry state of his recruits. The requirements stipulated that the men had to be able to read and write in either English or French—which on its own disqualified many potential recruits, since most people at the time were functionally illiterate—and to be of good character, a criterion difficult to vet in an era of slow communication, particularly given the barely two-week time window to get the force mobilized. And, since they were to be a mounted police, charged with patrolling tens of thousands of square kilometres, they had to possess familiarity with horses and an ability to ride. The mounted aspect was where many of the selected men had perhaps inflated the scope of their expertise; one of French's, and his junior officers', hair-pulling and somewhat amusing tasks was improving the recruits' riding proficiency and knowledge of proper animal care. The three hundred men would be supported by a series of forts that would be sprinkled from Manitoba to the Rocky Mountains, concentrated primarily in the south near the border. Pay was low, at seventy-five cents a day for entry-level sub-constables, but the adventure surely would compensate for the poverty. Their uniforms would not camouflage them, blending in with the land, but would be scarlet, to stand out and make a statement.

Perhaps most important, the force was intended as police, not military. The U.S. Cavalry was then wreaking havoc among the Indigenous peoples in the south and had earned a bad reputation, launching assaults on the Plains tribes and herding them onto reservations. To keep the peace and try to prevent uprisings and bloodshed, it would not do to replicate any aspect of that despised cavalry. In the aftermath of the Civil War, the dregs were what had washed up in the West, shell-shocked, dissolute and generally anti-social. Soldiers, or ex-soldiers, were not generally respected. "There is nothing so little thought of in that part of the country as a soldier. There are only two creatures who look upon a soldier here without scorn and contempt, and they are little children and dogs," wrote a Montana resident to the editor of the *New York Herald* on May 10, 1878. The Canadian mounted police were intended to bring some form of order into an increasingly chaotic and shattered world.

The creation of the North-West Mounted Police would be a political statement. The Cypress Hills massacre provided the impetus for the funding and a political cover for the financial expenditure: in the East the NWMP would allay fears of a larger American invasion of "our" new territory, while in the West, to the Indigenous peoples who were beginning to negotiate a series of land treaties, it would demonstrate how the new central government could be trusted to make their world less violent, a better, safer place under the Dominion than without. The NWMP was a public relations gesture that would make the treaty efforts easier and timelier—and the dream of a railway one step closer to fruition.

Once a central authority was established, in the U.S. and Canada, it expanded outward, providing an overarching set of laws and customs, subsuming disparate, less populous peoples and cultures as it went, reordering smaller groups into a commonality that, once begun, kept gaining momentum like a snowball getting larger as it rolled downhill, consuming smaller entities and bringing them into the fold. This somewhat organic process was a time-tested way by which larger cultural and linguistic groups took over the world, from ancient China, India, Persia, Rome and Aztec Teotihuacan to the more recent British Empire and the now expanding American Empire. It accelerated after the end of the Civil War and the economic recession that followed, as hordes of footloose men migrated west searching for a place in the world, and there was no central authority to stop them. It wasn't an organized or planned migration; there was just no authority capable of controlling them, just as, many centuries earlier, the Germanic tribes, harassed by the rampaging Huns in Central Asia, moved into the territory of the Roman Empire, precipitating its collapse. No one directed this post–Civil War migration, yet it can only be described as an invasion by unconventional military units, trained in war, armed with guns and the knowledge of how to use them. They suddenly appeared on the scene and began shooting, fuelled by hatred, dysfunction and addiction.

With nothing else to do and no clear path to a different line of work, these American Civil War veterans, the most dysfunctional ones who had no chance to integrate back into society, especially during an economic recession, just kept doing the only thing they had been trained to do, only now they were called outlaws, wolfers, whiskey traders; some proclaimed themselves militia, with the mission to clear the land of "redskins." They were drifting north into Canadian territory, and the fear in Ottawa was that if the generalized warfare that was tearing the U.S. West apart crept into Canada—if Indigenous defenders attacked these American interlopers—it would provide the pretext for an American military intervention to protect their citizens from unlawful attack. Since there was no overarching set of laws or stability enforced by the Canadian government that now claimed jurisdiction over the territory, the Americans would be at liberty to provide that stability themselves to protect their citizens. A police force would at least be a proclamation of order and sovereignty to blunt these sorts of arguments.

The international boundary was being marked by Royal Engineers between 1872 and 1874, from Lake of the Woods to the Rocky Mountains, in response to this fear of American encroachment.

WITHIN TWO WEEKS OF THE RECRUITMENT DRIVE in August 1873, about 150 young men had already been assembled and sent west to Fort Garry. They were a ragtag, motley assemblage of ill-suited individuals, some because of sickness and physical impediments, others lazy, slovenly or prone to heavy drink and gambling. It was not an auspicious beginning. But they were trained that winter in the use of rifles and pistols, small field artillery and equine management, some of the skills of a light cavalry unit. Meanwhile, the election whipped Macdonald from office and ushered in the Mackenzie Liberals, who decided to augment the initial troops right away and send them west. An additional 150 aspiring young police constables were sent out from Canada in the spring by rail, through the U.S. instead of by the arduous Canadian route.

Called the Great March West, on July 8, 1874, 275 Mounties, headed by
Colonel French and 22 officers, rode out from Fort Dufferin in Manitoba
toward the infamous Fort Whoop-Up. The sluggish cavalcade kicked up
clouds of dust as it plodded away on a two-month, 1,300-kilometre trek
across the grasslands. The dusty snake of men and equipment was around
three kilometres long, consisting of the recruits, 21 Métis support staff to
tend the animals and drive the carts, approximately 310 horses, 150
oxen, a small herd of cattle, 114 Red River carts, 93 buckboard wagons and
two small wheeled cannons. Non-military supplies consisted of farm
tools such as mowers and rakes to gather hay for winter horse feed. The
Winnipeg Free Press reported that the Mounties were organized into
four main troops, reorganized after the members intended for a fifth
troop had deserted before departing because of the miserable conditions they endured over the winter at Fort Dufferin.

The commander, French, didn't want the expense and humiliation of
sending out all the heavy equipment by rail to Fort Benton, in Montana
Territory, which could have easily been done by steamer, and then riding
down to retrieve it and bring it north, so instead the cavalcade carried it
all. They were ill prepared for what awaited them. The Ontario horses
they brought with them weren't suited to the prairie heat and poor forage and began to weaken and die. The pale skin of the men burned red
under the relentless big-sky sun, blistering lips. Canvas tents blew away
in the wind, mosquitoes swarmed, and the lack of firewood made cooking a challenge. Their cotton clothing was soon bleached and ragged,
and some marched without boots.

The Great March of the Mounties was an epic disaster in many
ways—starvation, disease, inadequate provisions and faulty equipment,
coupled with the poor training, morale and skills of the recruits, left
them ill equipped to contend with mighty prairie wind and hail storms
and the other rigours of a life far from the farms and towns of the

St. Lawrence. Interestingly, they had no problems with any of the people they encountered; in fact, not many of them would have thrived without aid. Luckily they were generally welcomed for the promise of stability they represented. Far from being a romantic or heroic tale, it is the ignorance, incompetence and stupidity that astonishes, however noble the stated intentions.

French, oddly, didn't provision properly, perhaps anticipating that the troops could forage en route. They carried no water bottles and nowhere near enough food, so men and animals bent down and drank from the stagnant sloughs and soon came down with digestive ailments. Marching on half rations was unpopular, and men began to desert. Horses and oxen drifted off because of poor animal husbandry. "If the people of Canada were to see us now," wrote Sub-Constable James Finlayson, "with bare feet, not one half clothed, half starved, picking up fragments left by the American troops and hunting buffalo for meat . . . I wonder, what they would say." Eventually, one troop headed northwest to Fort Edmonton to recuperate, while French and Assistant Commissioner James F. Macleod led the bulk of the force farther west. When they reached Fort Whoop-Up on October 9 it was deserted. The ragged force built a palisaded post next to the Old Man River, set up camp and dispatched a contingent south to Fort Benton to pick up additional supplies that had been sent west on the American railway. At Fort Benton, an I.G. Baker Company store clerk took one look at them and suggested they hire Jerry Potts as a guide. It was the start of a decades-long association with the enigmatic Piikuni (Peigan)-Métis war chief and pathfinder.

Potts had a profound influence on the history of the western prairies in the 1870s and 1880s. According to Mountie Sam Steele, "He won the confidence of all ranks the first day out, and when morning came he rode boldly in front of the advance guard. It was noon when the party reached Milk River, and found him there sitting near a fat buffalo cow which he had killed and dressed for the use of the force. To those new to such life he appeared to know everything." Without Potts, the effectiveness of the police would have been blunted and perhaps ineffectual, since they were more or less incompetent and unprepared for the task before them.

French then led some of the men back east and built the headquarters of the NWMP at Swan River, Manitoba, leaving Macleod in command of the frontier force, where he would become a semi-legend during the next decade, particularly for his work with Chief Crowfoot (Isapo-Muxika) of the Blackfoot Confederacy. Within a decade the NWMP numbered five hundred and had established a series of posts strung out across the land. They founded Fort Calgary and did mounted patrols, particularly in the south, to keep the peace and deter the illegal whiskey peddlers and curb the rise of American frontier mentality.

To many Indigenous Plains people, the presence of a troop of armed interlopers in their territory was probably unsettling, but the fact that this troop was engaged in eliminating their implacable foe was at least some compensation—"the enemy of my enemy" rationale. There is no doubt that the American frontier was far more dramatically violent and immediate, seemingly without any order at times, and that a constant semi-war existed between wolfers, outlaws, the U.S. Cavalry and the Indigenous peoples. The NWMP, on the other hand, and particularly in these early years, was a small force, highly mobile and visibly courting friendship, relentlessly pursuing violent criminal gangs and helping at treaty negotiations. They did initially uphold the ideals of "peace, order and good government." While the American Empire seized the western territories by right of conquest, with brutal killing and lack of legal or moral principle, in Canada there was an attempt to take over the land in a somewhat peaceful way, with a veneer of legality and principle. It didn't last long, but it began with reasonable intentions.

ONE OF THE FIRST MAJOR INITIATIVES of the North-West Mounted Police was to investigate the Cypress Hills Massacre. French selected James Macleod to lead the investigation. Macleod mounted up a small detachment and rode south across the border to Helena, in Montana Territory, to find and interview some of the men rumoured to have participated in the killing, with the intent to extradite them to Canada to face trial. Born in Scotland and educated in classical history and philosophy at Queen's College, Kingston, and law at Osgoode Hall, Toronto, Macleod practised law in Ontario for a decade, while secretly harbouring military inclinations. Restless for adventure rather than dusty tomes of precedent, he joined the Wolseley Expedition during the Red River affair as a senior officer, having previous experience in volunteer militias in Upper Canada and active service during the Fenian raids of the 1860s. In his mid-thirties when he joined the NWMP, he was a stalwart balding man with a direct gaze and a prodigious sculpted beard. It was his legal background that recommended Macleod for the investigation. Given permission by the U.S. government to enter Montana Territory, he spent months trying to arrange for the arrest of seven men, but two escaped and disappeared into the vastness of the land before they could be questioned.

In the courtroom in Helena, questions were asked, opinions bantered about, proclamations declared about what exactly had happened on June 1 the year before. The defence lawyer framed the case as an attack on American liberty by "hirelings of a Queen," portraying obviously innocent men as heroes for defending against violent Indians. Trader Farwell gave the most damning testimony against Hardwick and the wolfers in general, but his account was challenged and denigrated by conflicting testimony, and no clear account of who shot first to cause the conflict was agreed upon.

Oddly, the Montana press seemed obsessed with the differences between American and British law rather than the inhumanity of the massacre, presenting a narrative of an autocratic monarchy trampling the rights of free citizens of a republic. The *Fort Benton Record* railed against the very idea that Americans should be subject to British justice. "It will at once be seen that the liberty of our fellow citizens is for a purpose being sworn away by the perjured and paid informer, the Englishman Farwell, assisted by the half-breed sot, La Bompard. There are at least a dozen men in this town and vicinity who can swear that there is not one word of truth in the evidence for the prosecution." Another editorial stated: "There it is. Sacrificing the liberty of American citizens for the purpose of aiding the monopoly of the Indian trade by the Hudson Bay Fur Company." In such a charged atmosphere there was no chance of either justice or truth to emerge from the obscuring cloud of ignorance. But the editorialists knew the attitude of this type of man, and knew that it was not uncommon around town. They reported of one of the prisoners that he "is quite a young man and looks as if he might or might not be a murderer. He certainly looks like a frontiersman, and has probably been educated at Benton and thereabout, to believe that the killing of a few Indians is only his mite of assistance towards the march of civilization." In any case, the defence was successful in muddying the waters of testimony, the press agreed, and the judge ruled against the wolfers' being extradited to Canada to stand trial for murder.

A few months later, three of the participants in the massacre were captured on the Canadian side of the boundary, and a murder trial was held in Winnipeg in June of 1876. Just as happened in Montana, however, because of conflicting testimonies and the lack of evidence of premeditation, no convictions were ever secured.

The editor of the *Fort Benton Record* also opined that "the arrests were made to perfect a stroke of policy, to act upon the feelings of the Indians in the British territory in the grand peace measure then about to be forced upon them." Cynical to be sure, but the claim also emitted an essence of truth. As a public relations gesture, the visible and publicized arrest of what was believed in the Canadian territory to be a gang of murderers targeting Nakoda and other Indigenous peoples—and certainly many others had been killed directly and indirectly by these same people and others like them in the preceding years—would go a long way to justifying, and even making welcome, the protection afforded by the new Canadian government and its police force in a world gone mad, violent and hard.

Whatever else the NWMP brought to the West in the coming years—and it certainly wasn't all hunky-dory from the perspective of uniform justice and respect for local peoples and customs during an era when treaties were being signed and railway workers were striking— they did essentially shut down the illegal whiskey trade in the region.

MACLEOD WOULD SPEND THE REST OF HIS LIFE in the Canadian West, with the NWMP and then as a circuit judge. He was one of the most prominent citizens of Fort Calgary, which was named after a country house near where his sister lived in Scotland. Macleod tried always to keep his promises, earning a reputation for being fair-minded, and sought to keep order and maintain the peace. He was respected for maintaining good relations with the Niisitapi peoples, particularly with the most prominent chiefs, Crowfoot and Red Crow. He also participated in the touchy political situation when Sitting Bull and his warriors came north of the Medicine Line—the 49th parallel—after the Battle of Little Big Horn.

Macleod had married Mary Isabella Drever, the daughter of Red River settlers whom he had met in 1870 when she was seventeen and he was stationed there as part of Wolseley's expedition against the Red River uprising. She revealed her character and nerve during the uprising, when several of her friends and her brother were held at Lower Fort Garry by Riel. She insisted on smuggling out a dispatch to people working against Riel's forces. She hitched a horse to a small cart, tucking the note into her bosom as she rode through the gates toward the Upper Fort, where she calmly waited while her buggy was searched, evading detection before she flicked the reins, trotting away. She was tall, well educated and fluent in English, French and Cree, and many of the officers had their eye on her, but it was James who attracted her. She shared his restless urge for a peripatetic life rather than settled and predictable domesticity. They stayed engaged after Macleod was sent back to Ontario, where he unhappily picked up his law practice before he jumped at the opportunity to move west again in 1873. In July 1876, Mary and James married at Fort Garry, and she went with him to Fort Macleod in 1877. It was a rudimentary outpost with few, if any, benefits of civilization. The log walls were chinked with mud to stop the wind, the roof was prairie sod that was only partially waterproof, and the floor was hardened prairie dirt impressed with hoofprints, but Mary nevertheless enlivened the fort with music and dancing, along with the handful of other officers' wives.

Although non-Indigenous settlement was slow at this time, there was a trickle of migrants coming north from Montana. These pioneers were an eclectic bunch, such as "Auntie" Annie Saunders, a forty-one-year-old Black steamboat stewardess working the Missouri River from Fort Benton, whom Mary convinced to come north and become a nanny and housekeeper to her growing family (Mary and James would have four daughters and a son, all of whom survived). After three years with the Macleod family, Saunders went on to become one of Fort Macleod's early entrepreneurs, starting several businesses in the region, including a restaurant, a catering service, a laundry service and a boarding house for the children of ranch families attending school. Saunders died in Pincher Creek at the age of sixty-two in 1898.

Mary often accompanied her husband on his horseback ramblings across the prairies, inspecting forts, attending treaty negotiations and upholding the peace as they saw it in their time. She earned respect within the close-knit community of the police and was one of the few women to sign as witness to Treaty 7 at Blackfoot Crossing in September 1877. Macleod was appointed circuit judge of the Western Territories in 1887. He died on September 5, 1894, in Calgary, leaving Mary without sufficient money to finish raising their children, and she worked as a seamstress for several years. She died in 1933 at the age of eighty.

CHAPTER TWELVE

CLEARING THE LAND

———

The famous photograph shows a short, bowlegged, slope-shouldered man with an aquiline nose and piercing black eyes. His fashionable drooping moustache, wide-brimmed western hat perched at a jaunty angle, neatly trimmed hair, collared shirt and tailored trousers are counterbalanced by knee-high moccasins, distinctive beadwork belt pouches and a fringed leather jacket. He holds a double-barrelled long gun, butt down, pointed skyward—and he always packed a concealed handgun and several knives strapped around his body. But in the staged photo he looks casually bored or uninspired, either from a cultivated disdain or genuine sentiment. No man is all he appears to be. Life is a dash—the line between when we are born and when we die. The interesting part is what happens in between.

Jerry Potts, or Ky-yo-kosi, Bear Child, was certainly one of the most interesting characters of his generation, a complex man of many contradictions who lived his life against the backdrop of extreme change and dislocation for his people. He did what he felt was necessary to navigate the debris of the times. The son of a Scottish fur trader named Andrew Potts and a Kainai-Cree mother from the Black Elks Band named Namo-pisi (Crooked Back), Potts was equally at home in either culture, later becoming a member of many secret Niisitapi warrior societies and a respected chief, while also being the foremost scout and guide for the North-West Mounted Police in the 1870s. He was fluent in seven languages and dialects, yet he was nevertheless famously laconic. When one NWMP officer he was guiding asked what was beyond the big hill in front of them, Potts looked over and replied, "Nudder hill," either a dismissive assertion of the obvious or a passive-aggressive cue to be left alone. No one who knew him or his reputation dared to challenge him—in fact many steered a wide berth, especially if they were wolfers or purveyors of rotgut whiskey, whom he was known to track down and shoot. Yet, oddly, he was fond of whiskey himself, and his moustache was sometimes stained red at the tips from the dye in the lower-end product he occasionally imbibed.

Jeremiah "Jerry" Potts was born in 1840 near an American Fur Company post named Fort McKenzie on the upper Missouri River in Montana. His father died when he was young, shot in a case of mistaken identity by a disgruntled Piegan who had been insulted by one of the fort's other traders. There was a knock at the wicket in the stockade wall through which goods were passed, and when the senior Potts opened it to converse, the man stuck his gun through and fired, killing Potts instantly. A hard, vengeful and violent man named Alexander Harvey then claimed Crooked Back and the baby. She fled when he became abusive, leaving the child behind, and for five years Jerry was mostly neglected until Harvey was recalled to St. Louis and fired at the request of his own fellow traders, who were frightened of him. He had once shot in the leg a young Niisitapi man who was trying to steal one of the fort's cows, and while the man lay in agony clutching his wound, Harvey casually walked up, lit a pipe and smoked a little before passing the pipe to the terrified man, who took a final puff as Harvey cocked his pistol and shot him in the head.

When Harvey was fired, young Potts was taken in by Andrew Dawson, an old friend of his father's who gave him a stable upbringing, taught him to read and write a little in English and encouraged him to mingle with the visiting Niisitapi at Fort McKenzie to learn their customs as well. Potts eventually left the fort to live with his mother's people for several years, so he became adept and culturally fluid in both worlds, moving back and forth between them as he pleased. He earned his name, Bear Child, during the Sun Dance ritual, a warrior initiation ceremony. Elders worked his skin free from his rib cage and inserted rawhide thongs underneath, then tethered him to a pole at the centre of the congregation. He remained stubbornly silent, enduring days of pain and deprivation in the burning sun before ripping out the tethers and stumbling free. After earning great honour for his fortitude, he joined many secret warrior societies where he learned tactics and strategy, and took on the role of policing the camps and bringing order to the bison hunts.

In his youth, Potts earned a reputation as either a crazy rabble-rouser or beloved of the spirits. There are countless outlandish stories that don't necessarily cleave too close to the truth. In one perhaps apocryphal tale, the young Potts set off north on a quest to find and kill his father's murderer. The journey took him to a Tsuut'ina (Sarcee) encampment near present-day Calgary, where he spied the man, One White Eye, and challenged him to a duel. After a few minutes circling each other with knives and axes, both bleeding from wounds, Potts lunged for the kill and scalped the man, avenging his father. Another story tells of how, when off duty at Fort Benton, he and George Star, one of his young mixed-heritage companions, would bolster their courage with whiskey and then stand across the compound from one another and take turns "trimming" the other's mustache with their bullets.

Potts was sought out as a cultural mediator between the Niisitapi and the increasing number of white gold seekers and traders flooding into the Montana Territory in the 1860s. Though he preferred to live as a warrior and hunter, he occasionally drifted into the traders' orbit; he understood their ambitions, desires and beliefs. Rancher W.S. Stocking said of Potts, "Jerry was about the most decent specimen I ever met with. . . . certainly a remarkable man, one with the sinews of a panther and the heart of a lion. . . . he had a camp of six or eight lodges . . . peopled by his Piegan relatives by marriage." For many years, Potts lived there with his wives and children whenever he wasn't nomading around for the NWMP, hunting whiskey traders and running horses.

He had several wives over the years, a Crow (Absoraka) woman who bore him a son named Mitchel and later two Piikuni (Peigan) sisters, Spotted Killer and Panther Woman, who kept his lodges in Montana, where they raised many children and grew wealthy from horse trading. Potts maintained one of the largest herds on the western prairies, and he could always produce bills of sale that attested to the legality of his horses, though the brands were varied. He knew where to sell horses of questionable pedigree.

By the 1860s, Potts was dividing his time between working as a hunter for the American Fur Company and his foster father Dawson, and travelling with the Niisitapi pursuing the buffalo. He believed in spirits or destiny the way some people believe in luck or money. One night at Fort Benton he had a dream about a cat that informed him it would defend him against bad spirits. When he woke, he searched the fort until he spied a cat sleeping in a patch of sun. He killed and skinned it, and always wore its fur under his clothing. Fortified by this "medicine" and other special talismans and charms, he earned a reputation as a fearless warrior, bold in action and free of self-doubt. He possessed an unerring instinct for survival and a crafty sense of the treachery that lurks in men's souls. He was proficient with bow, knife and rifle and famous for near-reckless bravery in a chaotic, violent era when two worlds collided spectacularly.

The Kainai, or Blood Nation, are one of the three nations of the Blackfoot Confederacy, along with the northern Piikuni (Peigan) and the Siksiká. In that turbulent era when whiskey and guns were stressing the long-standing allegiances, culture and politics of the western Plains, a near-constant state of warfare existed not just with the invading settlers from the eastern U.S. but between the Indigenous nations as well, with the Blackfoot Confederacy set against enemies on all sides of their territory. The Niisitapi peoples shared the same language and culture, whereas the the Tsuut'ina (Sarcee) were linguistically separate but had a similar culture and economy. To the north and east, it was the Cree and the Nakoda; in the west it was the Ktunaxa (Kootenay), Interior Salish and Kalispel (Pend d'Oreilles); to the south it was the Atsina (Gros Ventre), Crows (Absoraka) and Snakes. By the mid-1860s, the southern Piikuni were in a mighty struggle with invading miners, wolfers and the U.S. Cavalry.

The Niisitapi peoples had always remained somewhat aloof from the economy of the fur trade. Their life had revolved around a Plains economy. Most of the other Plains people of the nineteenth century, such as the Cree, Nakoda, Sioux and others of similar linguistic and cultural backgrounds, were recent arrivals on the Plains, coming from woodlands farther east toward the Great Lakes, the valleys of the Red River, the aspen parkland to the north or along the Mississippi to the south. They had either migrated west because of their association with the Hudson's Bay Company and the fur trade economy or were pushed west by increasing numbers of settlers. The Plains Cree territory was generally more to the north and east of the Niisitapi and extended as far east as the shores of Hudson Bay—they had migrated west along with the HBC in the eighteenth century and dominated north of the North Saskatchewan River; they were often aligned with the Nakoda and in conflict with the Niisitapi for control of the Central Plains. The Cree were wealthy from their various roles in the fur trade economy and were generally the best armed, but they had been severely reduced in population from exposure to diseases such as smallpox, measles, influenza and "great colds."

Tales of Potts's exploits against the Crow (Absoraka), Sioux and Plains Cree are legion and border on the incredible. Like the time he was hunting with his young cousin and they were waylaid by three Crow warriors, who shot the younger man. While Potts hid nearby, they discussed their plans to offer him the chance to escape if he left his rifle behind, but would then shoot him in the back as he rode off. Potts understood the Crow language perfectly, however, and played along with the plan while making himself ready. He came out of the gulch, slowly mounted his horse and began to ride away with his back turned. When he heard the sound of a rifle being cocked, he turned, drew his concealed handgun and shot the three warriors before they knew what was happening. When he looted the bodies, he found that one of them had a rifle with a blue sheen, and in honour of the day he named one of his sons Blue Gun.

Potts was present at nearly all the major battles of the era, including the epic Battle of Belly River. During the winter of 1869–70, another wave of smallpox ravaged the peoples of the grasslands, just one in a series of epidemics that regularly swept through the land. The nations of the Niisitapi confederacy were particularly hard hit: a staggering 1,400 or so people died in this single wave alone. The traditional enemies of the Niisitapi, the Plains Cree and the Nakoda, for whatever unfathomable reason, had been largely spared from this particular epidemic. To their prominent chiefs, Piapot, Little Pine, Big Bear and others, this was an opportune time to press their own territorial ambitions against their usually more aggressive neighbours by seizing control of the refuge of the Cypress Hills.

Born in Saskatchewan around 1825, Big Bear (Mistahimaskwa), was a respected Cree warrior and hunter who ascended to the leadership of his clan when he was forty. He had a face disfigured by smallpox, contracted when he was a child. Stern, serious, proud and introspective, he was unyielding and implacable in his antipathy toward the Niisitapi peoples, and one of his early pastimes was going on raids against them. The call to war mustered an impressive army of between six hundred and eight hundred young men, who congregated along the South Saskatchewan River before riding west into the lands of the Niisitapi and setting up a war camp along the banks of the Little Bow River. From there they sent scouts to search the land westward for what they hoped would be weakened encampments in the Belly River region. On October 24, 1870, riders returned with news that a large band of Kainai (Blood) were indeed congregated in the valley bottom, unsuspecting.

But in their eagerness to strike quickly, the Cree scouts had galloped back without searching farther afield. Had they done so they would have discovered another band of Niisitapi, a camp of Piikuni who were armed with modern repeating rifles, which far outstripped the primitive and outmoded Hudson's Bay Company single-shot muzzle-loaded muskets with which the majority of the Cree force were equipped. Moreover, the Piikuni were in a nasty mood, having recently retreated north from Montana after a bloody battle with the U.S. Cavalry.

The battle started with a surprise assault as a select band of warriors slunk in under cover of darkness; they rushed between lodges, slitting the bison hide open and stabbing sleeping Niisitapi. Then Cree war bands charged in, and the shooting lasted throughout the night as each side took cover and fired at their foes. As the sun rose, the dismay on the Cree side was palpable. Mounted riders thundered over the ridge as the Piikuni warriors galloped in to assist the Kainai, firing their guns. It quickly became a rout, and over three hundred Cree and Nakoda warriors were killed, while the Niisitapi losses were barely forty. Potts was in the thick of it, leading his warriors to high ground and then firing repeatedly at Cree warriors as they tried to flee by swimming across the Belly River. Potts alone took sixteen scalps: "you could fire with your eyes shut and be sure to kill a Cree," he recalled.

The Battle of Belly River was the final battle on the Plains between the Niisitapi and the Cree, an end to the multi-generational conflict. The next year, their respective dignitaries met beside the Red Deer River to solemnly smoke the peace pipe and conclude a century of bitter raids and warfare. There were now so many other problems arising that neither side could afford more losses of young men.

IT WAS WHILE HE WAS TRADING horses and supplies at Fort Benton in the fall of 1874 that James Macleod was first introduced to Potts's skills and hired him as a special guide for the NWMP, where he would remain employed for the next twenty-two years, until his death. He was drawn to the force because of their mission to rid the land of illegal whiskey traders. Potts had seen first-hand what the whiskey trade had done to his mother's people and how many people had been lost to the ravages of addiction and the poison. His own mother had been murdered by a man drunk on rotgut whiskey, and afterward Potts, although he was notoriously fond of hard liquor himself, declared a personal war against the traders. He killed over forty whiskey runners, including his mother's killers. When the NWMP came west in 1874, he was more than happy to help them bring an end to the calamitous traffic that was destroying the Niisitapi nations.

"The fiery water flowed as freely, if I may use the metaphor, as the streams running from the Rocky Mountains, and hundreds of the poor Indians fell victims to the white man's craving for money, some poisoned, some frozen to death whilst in a state of intoxication, and many shot down by American bullets," wrote Father Constantine Scollen, an Oblate priest who, although apparently having no interest in money, did want something else from the people: their souls. There were so many quarrels among the people of the Plains that they became afraid to meet each other, fearing revenge and retribution, so they lived in smaller, more isolated bands, growing more impoverished as they traded away everything of value, including their horses, for more liquor. Disease had created the initial social breakdown that enabled hard liquor to proliferate, which in turn created more social breakdown in a vicious negative feedback cycle, each fuelling the other. "Ten years ago," the Methodist missionary George McDougall wrote, "the Blackfeet were rich in horses, and no observer could visit their camp without being struck with their fine physical appearance as a body of natives; now they are an impoverished, miserable-looking race."

Potts was always highly paid for his services, triple the rate of a constable. There were few significant expeditions or patrols during the era that he didn't lead. Present at treaty negotiations, he could turn a long-winded metaphorical narrative speech, replete with boasting, flattery and eloquent entreaty, into a few words—a feat that was astonishing to the participants. He knew what people wanted to hear; he just overshot the target sometimes. On one occasion, Macleod was in council with several important Niisitapi chiefs. The men, regaled in their finery, eloquently spoke and gesticulated as a sign of the importance of their communication. Potts interpreted with a grunt. As the speeches continued with sweeping arms and soaring rhetoric, Potts looked at Macleod and pronounced: "Dey damn glad you're here."

He would do the opposite when interpreting the words of Macleod or other dignitaries of the government to Indigenous leaders, turning a simple question into a drawn-out speech. Long speeches were a sign of respect and importance to Plains people of the time, while eastern dignitaries considered them arrogant or pointless boasting. Potts understood what to supply each side. His diplomatic skills were particularly important in Niisitapi territory where the people had had the

Yale, BC, scene of "McGowan's War": Fears that American armed forces would follow the country's miners into gold territory is a theme that pervades Canada's early history. The bloodless "war" was one incident with the potential to erupt into something larger.

"We don't want you here": Cartoon from 1869 depicts anti-annexation in Canada, with Uncle Sam being kicked out by Young Canada as England's John Bull looks on approvingly.

John A. Macdonald: When he dreamed, he dreamed big. He saw the prosperity generated by railways along the St. Lawrence and imagined a new dominion extending from the Atlantic to the Pacific.

Ottawa's parliament buildings: As they slowly took shape in the 1860s, the social architecture for a new and expanded nation progressed.

Albert Bowman Rogers: American surveyor who discovered two vital railway routes through the mountains.

Survey engineers: Dispatched "into trackless, inhospitable regions, obliged to carry their provisions on their backs over swamps, rocks and barriers ... to do their best to find out all they could, in as short a time as possible."

Donald Alexander Smith: The shadowy force behind the CPR enterprise.

William Cornelius Van Horne: The CPR manager was possessed of a near-herculean work ethic and an all-encompassing knowledge of how to plan, construct and operate railways.

George Monro Grant: A prolific writer and polemicist, he vociferously championed Indigenous rights in British Columbia and denounced restrictions on Chinese immigration.

Amor De Cosmos (the MP formerly known as William Smith): He did not love everyone in the cosmos equally.

To feed their families: Seventeen thousand Chinese men who had sold themselves into servitude ended up in the scarcely populated interior of British Columbia.

Catherine O'Hare Schubert: The only woman among the dozens of Overlanders.

Jerry Potts: The enigmatic Piikuni (Piegan)-Métis war chief and pathfinder had a profound influence on the history of the western prairies.

Mifflin Wistar Gibbs: Angered by discriminatory laws passed in California in 1858, he negotiated the immigration of 500–600 Black pioneers to Victoria, BC.

Chief Crowfoot: The most prominent statesman of the Siksikà (Blackfoot) people in his era.

Mary Macleod: One of the few women to sign as witness to Treaty 7 in Blackfoot Crossing in September 1877.

Big Bear at Fort Pitt, SK: The Cree chief tried to prevent his people from signing Treaty 6 in 1876, believing the terms were unfavorable to his people's interests.

Lower Fraser Valley, BC: "Navvies"—after "navigators," the canal builders of Britain—laying tracks.

Uncooperative terrain: In 1884, the government allowed a steeper-than-regulation grade on the westward drop of the Kicking Horse Pass, known as the "Big Hill."

Cariboo Road: The new railway clung to the cliffs of the Fraser Canyon in BC, suspended like a porch above the foaming waters.

Gabriel Dumont: The Métis leader devoted himself to defeating the Dominion forces to liberate his people.

"The Last Spike": One of the most iconic photographs in Canadian history was staged. The raggedly dressed men who actually built the railway were deemed less presentable.

June 30, 1886: The first train to travel from the Atlantic to the Pacific arrives at Port Arthur, ON.

least contact with European cultures, since they had always stood aloof from the fur trade, and they were disdainful of the Cree, for example, who had been intimately meshed genetically and culturally with the Hudson's Bay Company and the fur trade for many generations.

Potts led Macleod to a good location for an outpost, to be named Fort Macleod, that was wooded and defensible, had a stable water supply and was also nicely situated to stymie the illegal whiskey trade. He also then rode around to many of the Niisitapi bands in the vicinity and essentially distinguished in people's minds the difference between the NWMP and the various American factions in Montana, including the army "long knives" and the various wolfers and whiskey peddlers. In November of 1874, he helped arrange for many of the most prominent of the confederacy's chiefs, including Crowfoot of the Siksiká, Red Crow of the Kainai and Bull Head of the Piikuni, to meet with Macleod. In anticipation, and as part of what he considered an important component of their job in the region, Potts gave the officers a basic introduction to Niisitapi customs and protocol. Within a short time, he established a basic level of acceptance of the NWMP in the territory.

Potts also knew where the whiskey traders were established, the routes they travelled and the places they were likely to try to re-establish themselves once shut out of their original locations. He frequently guided NWMP contingents to these places and basically shut down the trade within a year. The famous Mountie Sam Steele, with whom Potts worked for many years, could never really explain Potts's unerring ability to know where to go and what to do.

> He was the man who had trained the best scouts in the force, and, in the earlier days when the prairie was a track-less waste, there were very few trips or expeditions of importance that were not guided by him or the men to whom he had taught the craft

of the plains. As scout and guide I have never met his equal;
he had none in either the north west or the states to the south.
Many such men have been described in story and their feats
related round many a camp fire, but none whom I have known
or of whom I have read equaled him. In the heat of summer or
in the depth of winter, in rain, storm or shine, with him as guide
one was certain that one would arrive safely at the destination.
It did not matter whether he had been over or in that part of the
country before, it was all the same to Potts, although he never
looked at compass or map.

Potts' influence with the Blackfeet tribes was such that his
presence on many occasions prevented bloodshed. The Mounted
Police and Indians knew his character for tact and pluck and
believed that he would stay with his party to the last moment
no matter how serious the situation might be. . . . It was a great
pleasure to know Potts, for his conduct was always that of a
gentleman, and he possessed most of the virtues and few of the
faults of the races whose blood coursed through his veins.

———

MUCH HAD CHANGED since the not too distant fur trade era, when
Indigenous societies dominated the political and economic landscape.
The period roughly correlating to the creation of Canada was one of
turbulence, chaos, rapid change and disease and the resulting economic disruption. Once proud nations, particularly in the south, were
disintegrating under the forces of disease, social dislocation and the
waning fur trade. Their declining commercial power and success, and
a corresponding poverty, forced a transition to a less confident, subservient status in the evolving milieux. The economic and cultural shift
that began in the mid-nineteenth century undermined their autonomy,

status and pride. By the 1870s, these once numerous and strong peoples were no longer in command of their own destinies. People were dying, their skills and knowledge were no longer valued, and, as if that wasn't enough, their food sources and very survival were at stake.

Against this backdrop, the new Canadian government had sent out agents of empire to negotiate a series of treaties with the various Indigenous peoples—to smooth the way for limited-violence political control, to prevent American expansion, to establish the stability and framework of laws and customs and, naturally, to create a path for the new railway that would be the glue that connected these other objectives. In sum, to establish an administrative structure for the "North-West Territories."

At the time, three main solutions were proposed to the problem of the epic clash of cultures and ways of life happening particularly in the West. These were summarized for readers in George Monro Grant's bestselling book, *Ocean to Ocean*. A thoughtful man, relatively free from the jingoistic prejudices so common to his era, Grant seemed to recognize that the situation was a bit of a conundrum: there was no obvious, pain-free solution to radical change; there would be winners and losers and, in his opinion and that of many others, one way was preferable. One way was also more generally popular in the U.S.: "The first cannot be put more clearly or baldly than it was in a letter dated San Francisco, Sept. 1859, which went the round of the American press, and received very general approval. The writer . . . condemned the Federal Government for not having ordered a large military force to California when they got possession of it, 'with orders to hunt and shoot down all the Indians from the Colorado to the Klamath.' Of course the writer adds that such a method of dealing with the Indians would have been the cheapest, 'and perhaps the most humane.'"

The second commonly discussed way, Grant wrote,

is to insist that there is no Indian question. Assume that the Indian must submit to our ways of living and our laws because they are better than his; and that, as he has made no improvement on the land, and has no legal title-deeds, he can have no right to it that a civilized being is bound to recognize. Let the emigrants, as they pour into the country, shove the old lords of the soil back; hire them if they choose to work; punish them if they break the laws, and treat them as poor whites have to be treated. . . . This course has been practically followed in many parts of America. It has led to frightful atrocities on both sides. . . . It was no wonder that, after a few exchanges of punishment and vengeance, the conviction would become general that the presence of the Indian was inconsistent with public security; that he was a nuisance to be abated; and that it was not wise to scrutinize too closely, what was done by miners who had to look out for themselves, or by the troops who had been called in to protect settlers. The Indians had no newspapers to tell how miners tried their rifles on an unoffending Indian at a distance, for the pleasure of seeing the poor wretch jump when the bullet struck him; or how, if a band had fine horses, a charge was trumped up against them, that the band might be broken up and the horses stolen; or how the innocent were indiscriminately slaughtered with the guilty; or how they were poisoned by traders with bad rum, and cheated till left without gun, horse, or blanket.

The same sentiment was echoed by other travellers and observers. William Francis Butler wrote that "terrible deeds have been wrought out in that western land; terrible heart-sickening deeds of cruelty and rapacious infamy—have been, I say? no, are to this day and hour, and never perhaps more sickening than now in the full blaze of nineteenth-century civilization. . . . The countless deeds of perfidious robbery, of ruthless murder done by white savages out in these Western wilds never find the light of day. The poor red man has no telegraph, no newspaper, no type, to tell his sufferings and his woes."

Grant himself preferred what he called the third way. "The third way, called, sometimes, the paternal, is to . . . explain that, whether they wish it or not, immigrants will come into the country, and that the Government is bound to seek the good of all the races under its sway, and do justly by the white as well as by the red man; offer to make a treaty with them on the principles of allotting to them reserves of land that no one can invade, and that they themselves cannot alienate, giving them an annual sum per family in the shape of useful articles, establishing schools among them and encouraging missionary effort, and prohibiting the sale of intoxicating liquors to them. When thus approached, they are generally reasonable in their demands; and it is the testimony of all competent authorities that, when a treaty is solemnly made with them, that is, according to Indian ideas of solemnity, they keep it sacredly. They only break it when they believe that the other side has broken faith first."

Grant's so-called third way came in the form of official treaties in the Canadian territories. Treaties were a time-honoured and traditional political tool used by multiple Indigenous peoples to settle intertribal alliances, formalize peace agreements, give affirmations of support, or codify trade agreements and the use of shared resources and key locations, such as the Cypress Hills, or the use of key waterways and river systems that crossed or passed through boundary regions of ancestral territories. Treaties were usually heavy on ceremony, speeches and symbolism, and the agreements with the Canadian representatives in the 1870s took on these formalities. There were many who claimed that there was no Indigenous title to the land or that if there was, they could still just be defeated and forcibly removed, but Macdonald and his successor Mackenzie followed the basic premise that the government should at least make an attempt to provide a veneer of legality through formal treaties rather than more brutal means.

Between 1871 and 1877, under Macdonald's Conservative direction until 1874 and then under Mackenzie's Liberal government that replaced Macdonald after the Pacific Scandal, Canadian government officials negotiated and signed seven land treaties with Indigenous peoples in the lands west of Lake Superior and east of the Rocky Mountains. In order to clear the land, agents were sent out to negotiate land settlements to make way for a peaceful transition and change— for the railway and for increased immigration—and to deter American encroachment. The objective was to have the Indigenous people settle in communities and learn to farm and receive an education. After signing they were considered to be under Canada's legal jurisdiction, like all other people in the Dominion. The terms of these seven treaties were similar, with only minor variations, such as Treaty 6, covering a broad swath of central Saskatchewan and Alberta, which contained a provision for greater government assistance in case of famine and disease, and Treaty 7, in southern Alberta, which recognized a desire for ranching rather than farming.

The Cree chief Big Bear tried to prevent his people from signing Treaty 6 in 1876, believing that the terms were not favourable to his people's interests, and he feared losing the power to leverage a good deal in the changing world. But the starvation that came with the disappearance of the bison also contributed to his people's loss of independence. Many reluctantly accepted that military opposition wouldn't lead to success. Chief Mistawasis made the point to several chiefs initially opposed to the treaties: "We are few in numbers compared to former times, by wars and the terrible ravages of smallpox. . . . Even if it were possible to gather all the tribes together, to throw away the hand that is offered to help us, we would be too weak to make our demands heard." The question lingered in everyone's mind: Just how would they survive into the future with the buffalo disappearing and the fur trade in decline? It was clear some sort of change had to happen.

By 1876, all Cree chiefs had signed except for Big Bear. He feared the Canadian government, which had no history on the Plains. He maintained his reluctance even when key Hudson's Bay Company chief factors, whom he had known for years, urged him to sign because the world was changing and the railway was coming. He was a proud and independent man, true to his convictions and respected by his people. "We want none of the Queen's presents: when we set a fox-trap we scatter pieces of meat all around, but when the fox gets into the trap we knock him on the head; we want no bait, let your Chiefs come like men and talk to us," he proclaimed. His people continued to roam the prairies freely for the next seven years, until faced with starvation because of the near extinction of the bison herds and the humiliating reliance on rations provided by the NWMP. When he and his dwindling band signed and moved to a reserve in 1883, they were one of the last major groups to do so.

In general, the treaties promised many small considerations such as farming equipment and livestock, blankets, hunting and fishing tools, food and cash payments, schools if they desired them, farming instruction, the right to hunt and fish on all of the territory in their traditional lands and a designated official "reserve" for their exclusive use. Most wanted to continue to live their traditional way while sharing the land, and also wanted some protection against the powerful global forces that were forcing change upon them. Assistance would theoretically address disease, population decline, the loss of the bison upon which they had depended for generations and the greater numbers of foreigners. Treaties provided for the creation of day schools, upon request, after settling in an area, with the salary of the teacher to be paid by the federal government. The more insidious and infamous residential school network in the West—with its objective of destroying Indigenous

cultures and languages by kidnapping children into often abusive institutions run by churches—was mostly established on a large scale in the
1890s, beginning under the auspices of Macdonald and then expanded
by Prime Minister Wilfrid Laurier into the early twentieth century.

After the signing of Treaty 6, Mackenzie's Liberal government
enacted the Indian Act, which created the Department of Indian
Affairs. The legislation brought under federal control most aspects of
the lives of Indigenous communities on reserves, including deciding
band membership, providing housing and other reserve infrastructure
and services, establishing systems of governance and regulating culture
and education. The act effectively transformed Indigenous peoples into
legal wards of the state. Paternalistic and infantilizing, it removed the
freedom to move about the land as they had always done; sometimes
people could be essentially held captive on their reserve and not allowed
to leave. It also made them subject to the laws of Ottawa, even when
those laws might contradict their own laws and customs. Métis or other
"half-breeds," as they were crudely called at the time, were not given the
same rights, nor the same constraints, as "Indians."

The numbered treaties certainly cleared the land and smoothed the
way for the railway and settlers. They undermined local authority structures and segued over time into policies that seemed designed to create
a fractured and compliant underclass ripe for isolation and exploitation.
Although the concept of the numbered treaties—to provide clarity and
stability in a rapidly changing world—was sound, the haste and tactics
used to get them signed, the ulterior motives, and particularly what
came later, once peoples' independence had shrunk along with the once
mighty buffalo herds, were shameful.

CHAPTER THIRTEEN

THE FINAL PLAINS TREATY

—

The path to extremism rarely starts with black and white but rather with a shade of grey. On a map, the land looks smooth, and big ideas spring to mind. But whereas geographical hurdles could be overcome by technology, grit and determination, the social or human obstacles were not so easy to understand, let alone solve. Maps don't reveal everything, however easy they are to look at on a big table in a government office surrounded by astute politicians with expansive dreams. There were people already living on the land that railway dreamers sought to cross, however diminished in population they were from former times, and they may or may not have shared the same vision of empire or nation conceived along the St. Lawrence. It's not that the St. Lawrence people wanted the Plains people gone; they just wanted their distinct culture and way of life gone, to clear the way for a different model of living, one that was similar to the legal, economic and cultural pattern familiar to them in the eastern colonial settlements along the St. Lawrence and in the Atlantic colonies and provinces.

Many Métis and other mixed-heritage people were already changing their lifestyle to accommodate the new reality, abandoning the fur trade or the commercial bison hunt to engage in other economic activities—trading, transportation, guiding, farming or ranching. It was easier for them, since they had a foot in both worlds. But Indigenous people without long-standing cultural links to the fur trade were becoming culturally isolated and needed to be either brought into the new order or completely isolated from it. The shifting economic opportunities, it was hoped, would take care of the former. The treaty process was designed for the latter. The noose was tightening on their entire way of life, and they were mostly powerless to resist it. The many people flooding west had different ideas about how the world should operate. Many chiefs were astute enough to observe how times were changing, and although reluctant to abandon their heritage and customs, wanted a path for their children to thrive in this new future. Treaties reflected this desire. At a Niisitapi encampment along the Bow River, Chief Crowfoot admitted to Sub-Inspector Cecil Denny of the NWMP, "We all see that the day is coming when the buffalo will all be killed, and we shall have nothing more to live on, and then you will come into our camp and see the poor Blackfeet starving."

People and cultures routinely change. Industrialization had only recently radically transformed western Europe and eastern North America. Many of the bison-hunting Plains peoples had been, in the not too distant past, woodland hunters; horses, and mounted buffalo hunting, had only become ubiquitous by the mid-eighteenth century. But in this case, the difference was that there did not appear to be a path forward for the younger generation; everything seemed to be ending.

Eastern attitudes toward Indigenous peoples had also begun to change. "The North-American Indians are indeed no ordinary race of savages," wrote one traveller to the West in the 1860s, a member of the International Boundary Survey then crossing the prairies. "They exhibit almost all the traits of the worst form of barbarism. They yield unquestioning obedience only to the despotic sway of the chief. They are passionately fond of war, yet are more given to stratagem than to fair fighting. . . . Murder is no crime among these ferocious beings, who stab, shoot, scalp and eat their enemies, with the voracity of their companion wolves." Depicting them as ferocious but inferior raised alarm but not despair and generated a sanctimonious sense of superiority that justified imposing authority over them and taking away their agency, for their own good. It was a tactic of empire that dated back thousands of years. The justification for all imperial control is that it is a benefit brought to the people by a superior people and system. The Romans imposed it on Germanic tribes and many others; the Chinese on surrounding "barbarians" such as the Mongols, Tibetans and Manchus; ancient Egyptians on the Nubians; the Aztecs on the surrounding peoples in Mesoamerica; the Normans on the Saxons in Britain; and the British on the Indian subcontinent.

There was also a widespread belief that Indigenous people were dying out—which was hard to refute given the previous generations of disruption, disease and warfare—couched in the self-serving pseudo-scientific belief in the hierarchy of races derived from social Darwinism, which posited that the fittest races would naturally dominate and the others give way to them. "The lovely valley in which warriors stand forth in their triumphant glory," wrote Duncan George Forbes Macdonald, "in which the young and sprightly listen with throbbing hearts to the chants of other days, in which the mothers fondly play with their tender offspring, will soon know them no more. He will recede before the white man as his fathers have done, and at last yield to the inevitable law which decrees that the inferior races shall vanish from the face of the earth, and that the truculent unimprovable savage shall give place to families capable of higher development."

So it is hardly surprising that in the late nineteenth century, popular opinion increasingly began to view "Indians" as an inferior race facing extinction, and that the empire should extend its benefits to these poor benighted masses, who, although "fiendish," exhibited "the lowest phase of humanity." These ideas were becoming more prevalent and widespread, and were derived from and reflected in much of the writing of the era, particularly obvious in the many Victorian travelogues from the western "frontier."

The travellers of the era—such as Garnet Wolseley; William Francis Butler; William F. Milton (Viscount Milton) and Walter Butler Cheadle; James Carnegie, the Earl of Southesk; Henry Youle Hind; the various men of the Boundary Survey; and other gentleman travellers and missionaries—even while giving a romantic yet stereotypical nod to the idea of the "noble savage" living in harmony with nature, nevertheless promulgated their narrow views based on superficial observations of people and cultures they breezed by, and miraculously found themselves able to proclaim sweeping value judgments and denigrating analyses. Unlike the many generations of fur traders who lived with and frequently married Indigenous women, and who had given rise to the people known as the Métis, this new breed of travellers viewed the land and its politics in a simplistic, superficial manner, with no historical context for how disease and adulterated rotgut liquor and shrinking bison herds had very recently caused havoc and dramatic population decline among Indigenous peoples across the continent. They had no difficulty coming to more or less the same conclusions: the natives were mostly savages unable to govern themselves; they needed civilization and Christianity to show them the truth; the land was underused and lying fallow when it could be producing great crop yields to support large populations; the Indigenous people needed firm management. These views were essentially the foundation of Mackenzie's Indian Act of 1876, which shifted the entire spirit of the treaties from agreements between peoples to enable a peaceful path through the future, to a trust-ward relationship with the state.

The final of these so-called numbered treaties was Treaty 7, signed in 1877 at Blackfoot Crossing, about a two-day boat trip downstream along the Bow River from the newly constructed Fort Calgary. NWMP Commissioner James Macleod and the new lieutenant-governor of the North-West Territories, David Laird, were to be the chief negotiators, and Jerry Potts attended as the official interpreter, along with a contingent of around one hundred Mounted Police dragging two small cannons in a show of pomp, guarding a locked strongbox filled with $60,000 cash. The group included three women, including Macleod's wife, Mary, then pregnant with their first child. Despite the martial reputation of the Niisitapi peoples and their generally fierce appearance and aggressive demeanour, no one anticipated violence or conflict, although the Montana newspapers warned of rumours of violence.

Many hundreds of Kainai, Tsuut'ina, Siksiká and Piikuni, as well as smaller contingents of linguistically and culturally distinct peoples, were to attend. Most of the prominent leaders, including Crowfoot and Red Crow, arrived at the large congregation in mid-September as the leaves turned yellow on the aspen trees and a chill crept into the air at night. The buffalo had been plentiful that summer, and the gathering took on the air of a festive fair as several independent traders set up camp to barter their wares, including Richard Hardisty from the Hudson's Bay Company. Goods included provisions for the NWMP and the treaty negotiables, such as sacks of flour, chests of tea, casks of molasses, sugar and tobacco, and most importantly, crates of ammunition in giant piles under canvas tarps. The spectacular painted lodges of the Indigenous peoples, each one made from twelve to twenty-four buffalo hides, were arrayed on one side of the ceremonial clearing south of the river, while the more mundane standard-issue white tents of the police clustered nearby. On the north bank, the Nakoda congregated with eighty or so lodges, led by their chiefs Chiniki, Bearspaw and Goodstoney; they were supposed to have been part of Treaty 6 but had missed the signing the year before and were invited to participate here. They opted to sign Treaty 7 because it offered better terms for ranching, with greater numbers of cows and bulls to be provided. Many hundreds of horses milled about within rope corrals.

A large bison herd was roaming nearby, and bands of hunters rode out to hunt, while the women lit the cookfires and cleaned and prepared the hides for sale, buffalo robes then being the chief commodity in the region. Smoke drifted through the chill air in the evening, with chanting, drumming and dancing and the neighing of horses and barking of dogs. Soon there was the smell of roasting buffalo, warm saskatoon berries and burning herbs. The women prepared the delicacies, the roasted tongues and the succulent hump, or the always prized boss ribs: the rack of the hump was smoked over a fire to infuse the meat with the tang of the prairie. Then the cooks transferred the rack to a pot, or a leather bag, of boiling water and cooked it with sage and salt. The tender meat, dripping fat and juices, nearly fell off the bones; it was relished beneath the starry sky or inside a lodge while lounging on a buffalo rug in the light of the glowing embers of a dying fire.

One police constable was astonished at the horsemanship and martial prowess on display. "Early the next morning there was quite a stir in the Indian camp. Women were working on horses, which were tied up here and there at their teepees, and parties of two and three warriors kept riding up the hill to the prairie bench above. Then we heard shouting and fierce Indian yells. We all turned and lined the south side of the camp as Indians galloped from the coulee in two and threes, mounted on their painted horses. The riders were all naked except for breechcloths and were painted in the most hideous colours from head to foot. Some had yellow and black spots all over; others, white spots; still others, the body was half black and half white. As they passed us at full gallop, they would lie alongside their horses on the opposite side with just their foreheads showing over the horse's mane. They would shoot off their rifles under the horse's necks right over our heads and after firing they would come to an upright position on the horse . . . as they galloped off, with hand to mouth they would yell out their shrill war cries."

Even a reporter for the Toronto *Globe* was present, for there was still some apprehension about how the treaty proposals would be accepted, as a few minor speeches were made while awaiting the arrival of all the primary chiefs. "All formerly warring elements of a great region were present," wrote a contributor to *Maclean's*, "and no one could tell just what turn events might take. There was no doubt that the Blackfeet were in a position to command the situation." Nevertheless, the concept of a treaty to make peace among themselves, the government and incoming settlers was a powerful impulse in the disruptive era. A small contingent of just over four hundred Cree were present, though their territory was Treaty 6, and they generally kept apart from the Niisitapi despite the tentative peace that had ruled between them for several years since the Battle of Belly River.

CROWFOOT WAS THE MOST PROMINENT statesman for the Siksiká (Blackfoot) people in his era and the chief statesman during these negotiations over Treaty 7. In photographs from later in life, when he was at the height of his powers, his expressive face, deep, far-seeing eyes and unwavering set to his mouth exude wisdom, empathy and perhaps sorrow for his own family, the land he loved and his people, who were being buffeted by forces beyond his control. Born around 1830, Crowfoot grew to manhood during the chaotic period when disease was starting to wreak havoc among Plains people, American whiskey traders were illegally selling poisonous liquor, further fracturing social cohesion, the bison herds were shrinking and the numbers of settlers were increasing. His father was murdered when he was only five. He grew to be a warrior of great renown and prowess, having many gun, lance and knife scars from at least nineteen battles. He rose to prominence for his role as a negotiator, and as he aged, as a powerful orator advocating for peace and stability.

The world was changing, and he sought to find the best way forward for his people. When Sitting Bull of the Lakota Sioux and his people crossed the Medicine Line in 1876 after the Battle of Little Big Horn and proposed a joint offensive against the NWMP and the U.S. Cavalry, Crowfoot demurred: he was generally in favour of the Mounted Police and had a good relationship with Macleod and Potts. Crowfoot had ten wives during his life, and numerous children, but only four of them lived to adulthood. He touched the lives of many other prominent people of his era, including adopting the Cree Poundmaker (Pitikwahanapiwiyin), who in turn became a respected leader of his own people. But of course the Blackfoot Confederacy had a decentralized leadership structure, and although Crowfoot was greatly respected and had enormous influence, many different opinions existed among the affiliated peoples.

On September 19, at noon, with the sun overhead, a cannon fired and an honour guard of fifty policemen escorted Lieutenant-Governor Laird and Macleod to the large pavilion that would give them shade, while the principal negotiators of the Niisitapi, Nakoda and Tsuut'ina congregated in a large semicircle. Many hundreds of others crept closer, near the edge of the camp. A Union Jack snapped in the wind from a tall pole. Potts and the missionary John McDougall, who spoke the Nakoda language, were present. Crowfoot had hired Jean L'Heureux as his personal interpreter. The murmurs went quiet when the tall, dignified Crowfoot arrived. The crowd parted as he approached the council tents, and a robe was placed on the ground for him. He sat and quietly set about filling a stone ceremonial pipe with tobacco, lit it and puffed briefly before passing it to Laird, who likewise solemnly puffed.

At Laird's opening speech, there was a momentary pause and eyes turned to Potts, who stood dumbfounded. Fully fluent in Siksiká and many other languages, he was oddly primitive in his English; he hadn't fully understood the complicated language of Laird's legalistic and ornate introduction, and seemed therefore unlikely to be able to convey the details of the proceedings. "The chief difficulty about his interpretations were that, after he had interpreted from the Blackfoot into the English language, you weren't very much further ahead, for his English was weird," recalled Mounted Police corporal R.G. Matthews.

After some discussion, the famed pathfinder and guide James "Jemmy Jock" Bird was brought forth. The son of a Hudson's Bay Company trader and a Cree mother, Bird had been given a decent education as a boy at York Factory and later at Fort Edmonton. He abandoned the sedentary life, married the daughter of the Piikuni chief Bull Head and spent decades wandering the Niisitapi territories. Now possibly eighty years old and blind, needing a long staff to walk, he was still a handsome man with long, wavy grey hair, and was one of the most respected interpreters in the entire country, understanding perfectly the nuances and symbolic meanings and inferences of at least seven languages and dialects, including English, French, Siksiká, Cree, Nakoda, Dene and Salish. His voice was clear and he spoke without hesitation, turning his sightless eyes back and forth between the orators. "He was a striking, and as it seemed to me, an almost uncanny, figure," wrote one observer of the proceedings.

Throughout the day, there were many speeches by government representatives airily promising such things as one law for all and respect between peoples as well as a list of specific promises. Much has been written about this treaty and the others, debating what was offered, what was understood, whether the oral promises and counter-suggestions were properly entered into the final signed document, whether there was a clear understanding, whether later oral accounts agree with the written accounts and so on. But it does seem clear that the intentions were honourable, even while there were likely some vague misunderstandings as to whether the Niisitapi fully intended to relinquish all future control over their territory and perhaps considered the treaty to be only a peace treaty among the various peoples, or whether the treaty was being signed as a note of respect for Macleod. It is impossible to know for sure. Although Crowfoot was the principal orator and easily commanded the attention of all when he rose to speak, his people did not have a direct hierarchy, and chiefs ruled by persuasion and respect. Thus, although Crowfoot spoke as though able to make decisions on others' behalf, the degree to which his opinion was binding is difficult to ascertain.

Nevertheless, many discussions followed in the days after Laird's initial foray, negotiating, debating and arguing into the night over the best course of action. Always hanging over the negotiations was the anxiety about, and perhaps outright fear of, what was observable to all: that the demise of the bison would become an existential threat in the coming years. Laird even boldly noted this likelihood, to general agreement, though he thought it would take ten years to happen. If it were to happen, what other choice did these people have to save themselves other than to make the best deal possible and hope for the future? Indeed, one of the primary complaints of the Niisitapi, who had seen the buffalo disappear from the northern and southern parts of their territory, was the incursion of Cree and Métis hunters into lands that were far too large for them to patrol, especially with their declining population. They wanted help in preventing these "other" hunters from encroaching upon their territory—a difficult position neither the federal government nor the NWMP could really address.

It was hard to know what to do—no one wanted to give up their nomadic life and the buffalo chase to scratch the land for vegetables. To many of the chiefs, the grand council didn't even seem that important; it didn't offer any meaningful solution to the dilemmas the future presented. How could they even conceive of a life so radically different from the one they knew? What would life be without the buffalo? Or without their free-roaming ways across a land over which they were masters, or had been until very recently? The very idea of being limited to a five-square-mile reserve, that these small patches of land could one day, if the buffalo disappeared, be their permanent homes, was impossible to truly comprehend. These were uncomfortable truths that had to be digested, and many people, including Crowfoot, were already wrestling with these existential questions. But after many days of negotiation and discussion, including nightly inside dozens of lodges, a deal somehow seemed possible.

Crowfoot made one of the speeches that have solidified his legacy as a great orator and diplomat:

> While I speak, be kind and patient. I have to speak for my people, who are numerous, and who rely upon me to follow that course which in the future will tend to their good. The plains are large and wide. We are the children of the plains, it is our home, and the buffalo has been our food always. I hope you look upon the Blackfeet, Bloods and Sarcees as your children now, and that you will be indulgent and charitable to them. They all expect me to speak now for them, and I trust the Great Spirit will put into their breasts to be a good people—into the minds of the men, women and children, and their future generations.
>
> The advice given me and my people has proved to be very good. If the Police had not come to the country, where would we all be now? Bad men and whiskey were killing us so fast that very few, indeed, of us would have been left to-day. The Police have protected us as the feathers of the bird protect it from the frosts of winter. I wish them all good, and trust that all our hearts

will increase in goodness from this time forward. I am satisfied.
I will sign the treaty.

Soon thereafter, on September 22, the other chiefs made speeches or acknowledgements and signed the treaty. The next day, according to one observer, "five or six hundred mounted warriors, stripped with the exception of a blanket round the loins, and in their war paint and feather head-dresses, started a mounted war-dance round our camp." Rifles fired into the air over the heads of onlookers and into the various encampments, with the riders charging in circles, yelling their "unearthly yells."

There was naturally some hesitation, and there was general anxiety for the future, but something had at least been done, a stone cast, a path decided upon. Some tension dissipated, treaty funds were disbursed, and trading with the merchants from the Hudson's Bay Company and the I.G. Baker store representatives began amidst a general, but not too unbridled, celebration.

THE QUESTION OF WHETHER the treaties were good or not has no answer. At the time, they were believed to be the best deal possible for Indigenous groups to save themselves from the vagaries and threats of a changing world. They weren't necessarily bad deals, considering the disasters befalling the people with bewildering speed and force. Similar problems have arisen for other people in the past and could easily arise again today. Consider our modern reliance on cell phones: society now runs on them, yet they are manufactured elsewhere, the materials refined and processed in perhaps a dozen different countries in a complex web of precarious supply lines susceptible to disruption from wars and pandemics. Will that be a problem for people in the future? Who knows? We cannot know the future. And the Indigenous peoples of what became Canada didn't know the future either. The world is always changing, and people respond as best they can.

It also isn't clear what the alternative would have been for the Niisitapi or the signatories of the other treaties—whether they had any ability to walk away from the process over the long term. To not sign would have soon meant starvation and continuous warfare with the encroaching Cree and Métis, who were also pursuing the dwindling bison herds for their own livelihood. But as with the other treaties, the reserves were never intended to be prison boundaries, as they later became, but rather guarantees of exclusive possession, while all the other land was meant to remain open to all, with a central management theoretically ensuring policies for universal prosperity. At the time no one could have envisioned many millions of people living on a land that had never before seen more than a hundred thousand, nor imagined mighty cities and endless farms smothering the formerly wild grasslands. Our modern world was inconceivable. Yet the names on the highway network throughout the modern city of Calgary reflect the importance of the Indigenous peoples and the treaty process in the history and development of the city and its economy: Deerfoot Trail, Blackfoot Trail, Peigan Trail, Stoney Trail, Tsuut'ina Trail, Crowchild Trail, Sarcee Trail, Shaganappi Trail, Métis Trail, and Crowfoot Crossing.

In the circumstances, many Indigenous leaders made the best deals they could. But as is often the case in politics, the deliverables soon fell short of the promises. The worst thing to result from the treaties, from the point of view of the Indigenous signatories, was that not long after they were signed, as soon as the Indigenous people who depended upon the buffalo and the fur trade were at their weakest, they were betrayed by the society and government that had promised them security and a helping hand to transition from a nomadic economy and way of life that had sustained them (with various changes, including the adoption of horses and guns) since time immemorial. Many of the provisions of the original treaties were never adhered to honourably.

Ottawa seemed to take the perspective that, now that the treaties were signed, the land was empty and open for the railway and settlement. People will believe a falsehood if it benefits them, and tolerate it if it doesn't overly inconvenience them or cost them too much. But they will surely see through it quickly if it seems to damage them.

CHAPTER FOURTEEN

LAND OF ROCK AND BOG

—

T he surveyors scouting a route and the engineers designing it along the north shore of Lake Superior faced daunting challenges unusual for railway construction—thousands of kilometres of unavoidable rock and muskeg. Typically, railways were built according to the dictates of geography and common sense rather than political imagining. But in the case of the CPR, there was no other choice—this was the only possible all-Canadian route. The drawbacks and obstacles of this route had become unavoidable after Sandford Fleming scouted and plotted it in 1872. George Grant's popular book about their adventures was more of a travelogue and a polemic on the benefits of Canadian sovereignty than a technical analysis of the hurdles of actual construction of the railway.

"The reader would scarcely be interested in a dry account of the culverts and bridges, built and building, the comparative merits of wooden and iron work, the pile-driving, the dredging, the excavating, the banking and blasting by over 10,000 workmen, scattered along 500 miles of road," wrote Grant when he and Fleming set out to survey the engineering structures then being built for the Intercolonial Railway and then to venture farther west, scouting the route of the CPR. And yet, the logistics involved in such an undertaking at that time of primitive technology and communications in a sparsely populated land is quite interesting.

Precambrian shield forms the northern shore of Lake Superior, the rock coming right to the water. It is a beautiful, rugged landscape that, unfortunately from the point of view of a road or railway, meant levelling and crossing hundreds of kilometres of sloping granite with a thin layer of soil and stunted trees, pockmarked with interminable multitudes of small ponds and lakes. The U.S. side of the lake, to the south, was the opposite, being generally flat and open; good railway country that provided easy access to the prairie landscape west of Lake Superior. Anyone travelling west from Ottawa or Montreal had two choices: they could try to replicate the old voyageur routes—fine for hardened wilderness travellers with plenty of skill and time—or they could enter American territory, a fact not lost on Americans, British or Canadians. By this time, it was easier for the Hudson's Bay Company to get people and news from London through the U.S. than through any territory nominally controlled by the British. It could take two to three weeks to get a letter inland from the Atlantic; telegrams also had to be relayed on U.S. lines that followed U.S. railways, and were certainly not secure, being open to the curious eyes of intelligence agents. The terrain meant that U.S. railways were a safer and more profitable bet, and hence, they already existed. Even Canadians patronized U.S. railways.

And so the work through the unyielding rock and bog continued, albeit at a sluggish pace under the auspices of public infrastructure directed by Ottawa. For anyone awaiting the completion of the first Canadian railway to connect and unify the nation, the Mackenzie years were a fog of dithering and disappointment. After years of criticizing the project as being technically impossible, unrealistic, foolhardy and financially wasteful—not necessarily in that order—the new government couldn't now cheer on the railway's completion, and its delay became a self-fulfilling prophecy. The terms granted to B.C. to join Confederation, Mackenzie believed, were far too generous, far too pricey for the East to shoulder when compared to the possible benefits. Mackenzie wanted the railway to progress cautiously as a government initiative rather than recklessly as a business.

A somewhat plodding but conscientious man, not overly fond of grandiose schemes or of empire building, Mackenzie wanted the railway to be a publicly owned utility for the people. He was not a risk-taker, and his vision for Canada did not extend west of Lake Superior. He assumed greater control over the project after he claimed the Public Works portfolio for himself, the better to keep an eye on it. Moreover, soon after Mackenzie was elected, a continental financial crisis took hold. Government revenues declined and a new caution crept into the construction of the railway. The depression, which was in no small part precipitated by the collapse of the Northern Pacific Railway and the sequence of shadowy and corrupt events of the Pacific Scandal that had elevated him to office in the first place, heralded the end of the great railway boom. In Europe, economic retrenchment was stimulated by the Franco-Prussian War. These events were the final push that resulted in financial and banking collapse, railway collapse and mass unemployment. Transatlantic shipping and grain prices also collapsed, and the lumber industry and American manufacturers dumped their surplus goods into Canada, crushing a nascent local industry. Government revenues soon shrivelled. Moreover, Mackenzie's and the Liberal Party's lack of interest in the West and his repeated denigration of the terms of Confederation were acutely felt in Victoria. Some even called for secession.

In 1874, Mackenzie passed the Canadian Pacific Railway Act, which offered a government subsidy, for every mile of track completed, of $12,000 and twenty thousand acres of land along the main line. But with

the economy in the doldrums there was little interest in railway speculation. The project would be completed piecemeal, without any overarching
coordination or performance objectives.

IT BEGAN WITH THE SEGMENT between Ontario and Manitoba, the
dreaded northern arc around Lake Superior and across the dense Shield
to the prairies. Meanwhile, a lucrative contract was signed with a former
Liberal MP, Joseph Whitehead, to work on a branch line south from
Winnipeg to the U.S. border, covering terrain more favourable to the
practical and economic needs of a railway, and surely more profitable.
Other questionable contracts were awarded to politically connected or
sympathetic parties, political operatives with foreknowledge bought up
valueless land and sold it back to the government at inflated prices, and
there were other insider-related fraudulent schemes in the time-honoured
tradition of government infrastructure projects. The well-known and
influential journalist and later editor of the *Globe* John Willison wrote
that "the Mackenzie Government, like all other Governments in Canada,
had greedy mercenaries hanging upon its skirts, bent upon pillage and
crafty beyond the wit of man in devising means to get at the treasury by
dubious contracts or skilful alienation of the public resources." Although
a friend of future Liberal prime minister Wilfrid Laurier, Willison nevertheless mused, "The fault of the Liberal party was voluble virtue. It
actually believed that it was the 'party of purity'. . . [yet] in the Liberal
party, as in the Conservative party, the forces of interest and plunder are
never asleep and the records of the courts show conclusively that one
party is as good or as bad as the other."

Although Fleming remained engineer-in-chief of the railway survey
throughout the 1870s under different governments, there was a shake-
up in the rest of the survey management team following Mackenzie's
election, with a great many skilled employees dropped and the positions
reassigned to friends and relations and as rewards to Liberal senators,

officials and supporters. The pressure on Fleming to accede to these placements was tremendous even when the people were not well suited to the task. Despite his senior role, Fleming had little control over this corrupt process. Portions of the survey were so poorly done that they later had to be redone and corrected, and superfluous survey work was added as a sort of make-work project to keep the additional men employed, even though many of them had no survey or wilderness skills—and, viewing their appointment as a perk or payoff, were little inclined to overly exert themselves. They had been given their jobs for reasons other than competence, skill or suitability and they saw no reason to grow into their positions, although they were no doubt relieved to have employment during the economic downturn. Owing to the reasons they were hired in the first place, they couldn't easily be fired.

An exchange from the 1880 royal commission looking into the cost overruns and inefficiency of the CPR construction under Mackenzie's public works tenure, wherein Fleming was asked to account for his actions, is illustrative of the extent of the problems faced by competent people dealing with political patronage appointments.

Was that work less or more expensive than it would have been to a private company selecting their own men only with a view to pecuniary results? —It would have made a vast difference if it had been done for a private company instead of the Government.

Do I understand you to say that the work was done at a much greater cost than would have been the case if it had been done for a private company? —In my opinion it would have been done for very much less for a company. . . . Men often had to be employed who were not too efficient. The different sections of the country had to be considered in making the appointments. The men were not employed solely on their merits.

When asked to account for himself, Fleming responded: "I generally felt that those persons employed through political influence had to be kept at their work unless for something notoriously wrong. . . . The patronage had to be respected."

Again, he was questioned: "I wish to get your opinion on this point: whether you believe, from your experience in the management of the Canadian Pacific Railway, that the public interest has suffered on account of the patronage being in the hands of a political party from time to time? —No doubt of it. . . . It was not easy to get inefficient men weeded out when once appointed."

Mackenzie also, to his great frustration and exasperation, became embroiled in what has become known as the Battle of the Routes, according to the pamphlets that vociferously argued their respective cases for the Pacific terminus of the railway. Macdonald had promised the people of Victoria that Esquimalt, the naval harbour just outside of town, would be the terminus of the railway. After all, votes in Victoria were worth more than votes elsewhere at the time (unlike today, when it is votes in the East that are disproportionately represented). Macdonald's rash promise had committed the railway to a route so fantastical and impractical that it raised eyebrows among engineers and surveyors. Making the terminus on Vancouver Island meant the line would cross the mountains of B.C. from the Yellowhead Pass south along the North Thompson River, strike west over Tsilhqot'in terri-tory to the coast at Bute Inlet, proceed along the steep, rocky shore of the inlet more than seventy kilometres west to the Strait of Georgia (the Salish Sea) and then island-hop over forty kilometres across to Vancouver Island, before continuing south along the eastern shore of the island through Nanaimo and on to Victoria. It meant this line would include over ten kilometres of tunnels blasted through granite and cross six channels with 2.4 kilometres of bridges, including spans of a length that had never before been built anywhere. Of the seven to twelve possible alternatives under consideration by Fleming, this route was the most expensive, the most uncertain and the most technically challenging. It was a route determined by the location of votes rather than one based on sound financial or engineering principles. But at least the dynamite companies would have been pleased.

Politics, as usual, reared its ugly head. Mackenzie was not a fan of the Victoria route, for obvious reasons, and he declared that B.C.'s entering Confederation was "a bargain made to be broken." To the people of B.C., however, there were only two routes that excited passion: the ridiculous Bute-Inlet-to-Vancouver-Island scheme was pitted against the old fur trade route down the Fraser River to Burrard Inlet. Each would guarantee the prosperity of the places it went through, and the divisions were bitter: Victoria and the historical Cariboo gold regions on one side versus Kamloops, Yale and the southern Interior on the other. Even the admiralty was consulted for its perspective on the naval defence angle. Multiple naval officers were not favourably disposed toward Bute Inlet and preferred Burrard Inlet, south where the Fraser River disgorges and where the city of Vancouver now lies. Engineer-in-chief Fleming, also for obvious reasons, procrastinated on his final decision. Land speculators placed their bets, buying property in propitious-looking locations. There was much intrigue and backroom dealing behind the public agitations as the factions fought. Who would get the big payoff from knowing in advance where the line would go? There would be general prosperity for all, but there would be greater prosperity for some—a fine example of the cynical observation that while all are equal, some are more equal than others.

Worn out from years of incessant labour and politicking, Fleming took a leave of absence from his job. Temporarily in his place as engineer-in-chief, Marcus Smith, with ties to the Victoria establishment and strong personal opinions, began strenuously advocating for the Bute Inlet route, in contradiction to Mackenzie's unstated wishes. Since

Mackenzie couldn't come out in favour of a route contrary to that of his acting chief engineer without raising the issue of political influence, he promptly recalled Fleming to resume his position and present a more favourable report. Exasperated and annoyed, Fleming produced a detailed report declaring that, based on engineering considerations alone, the terminus should be located in Burrard Inlet and not the contentious but politically palatable (to Victorians, at any rate, who would reap the benefits while the additional cost was borne by others) Bute Inlet. The matter was settled. But Fleming still waffled on which passes through the mountains southwest of Yellowhead Pass would be best. The years dragged on while the bickering continued to shift from region to region, with little momentum.

The CPR would eventually be the biggest railway ever built, but under Mackenzie's public management (some would say mismanagement), this staggering feat of engineering and public policy would not have been built within the lifetimes of the people then working on it.

FLEMING AND HIS SUBORDINATE survey engineers had mapped out most of the route for the CPR in a general way, apart from a few pesky sections north of Lake Superior and a handful of rugged mountainous passes through the Rockies, Selkirks, Monashees, Cascades and Coast Mountains in B.C. and what would later become Alberta. Now the job shifted to the tedious minutiae of the route: exactly which shore of which small lake the rails would travel around, along which small river or creek, around which small uplands. The maps of the time were still too vague to help meaningfully with this work. On-the-ground technical expertise was required. The railway survey hired hundreds of men to work in isolated nomadic camps spread out over thousands of kilometres of land from Ontario to the Pacific. Collectively these workers were called the Canadian Pacific Survey, and their survey work continued throughout the 1870s and early 1880s. Yet with no famous people in charge, no dramatic battles, no stunning episodes of political corruption or gross incompetence to remember them by, their work has gone mostly unacknowledged and unremembered, or at least uncelebrated.

The surveys of the CPS were horrifyingly imprecise by modern standards. They measured distances by pacing and estimating, calculated altitude with primitive field barometers and generally used their imagination to guesstimate the best route suitable for a railway, which cannot have an overly steep grade. They measured canyons for bridges and trestles, assessed rock for tunnels and scrutinized land for possible flooding or avalanches. They searched for the flattest and shortest route with the least number of expensive obstacles. Over six years these unheralded crews covered nearly seventy-one thousand kilometres of terrain in their herculean quest. Axemen followed the scouts, hacking, sawing and chopping a clear "road" through the brush. Chainmen followed the initial blazes, measuring and dividing distances into one-hundred-foot sections marked by poles, after which came transit men, who calculated angles and assessed grade and turnings. Rodmen and levellers followed, leaving their notations along the route at regular intervals, to be interpreted later.

At least thirty-eight members of the survey crews died in the late 1870s doing this gruelling work under primitive conditions. Many more were dismissed for not being physically robust enough for the job or the conditions, patronage be damned. Desertion was also common, particularly from the impenetrable morass of tangled bush in northern Ontario en route to Winnipeg—living in canvas tents in temperatures as low as minus fifty degrees Celsius, eating poor food and outfitted in inadequate clothing, was not to everyone's taste. In British Columbia, the survey work was overseen by Walter Moberly, a former Colony of British Columbia cabinet member and land agent; supplies were brought into the deep interior of British Columbia by horse brigade and a series of small steamboats along the Columbia River and the snaking network of long, narrow lakes of the region, the Arrow Lakes, Kootenay Lake and Shuswap Lake. Through the rambles of the CPS, much of the previously uncharted interior of the southern half of the province was demarcated for the first time, as was a swath of rugged wilderness through northern Ontario.

It couldn't have been money that drove these mostly young men, for the pay was poor. It couldn't have been fame or social recognition, since they were mere supporting actors in the grand show. It couldn't have been for a leisurely sinecure, since their employment was erratic and temporary and wasn't a stepping stone to a more remunerative occupation. Nor was it an easy life: they froze, sometimes to death; some drowned; others burned in forest fires; they sometimes starved or withered away from scurvy and other ailments common to groups of men locked together in close quarters in primitive accommodations in damp, rain, heat or other extreme weather, far from home; and they were swarmed by mosquitoes and blackflies as they stumped through bogs and lowlands. And of course there was social isolation as they spent years scaling mountains, hacking through overgrown alders along rivers and creeks, and sinking into mires and bogs.

"We felt the cold very severely during the night, and mosquito's very troublesome," wrote R.M. Rylatt, one of the surveyors in B.C. "The night was very cold, and as I watched and shivered, I felt very lonely. . . . I made me a blazing fire, and the crackling of the burning wood was at least some company. You in England cannot understand all this. You may think you can, but you cannot." Rylatt's commentary, one of the few first-person accounts of the hardships of this life, conveys a typical sentiment. He had left England in 1871 to join the CPS and traversed the mountains of the West for several years, scouting valleys, rivers, lakes and passes, marvelling at the grandeur and beauty while spending his days scanning for lines suitable for a railway.

In addition to all this hardship, uncertainty and chance of death or misfortune, there were swindling government officials who failed to remit the surveyors' pay back to their families. "Poor deluded fools, it was many months 'ere a dollar was doled out to these suffering families, and even then in trifling amounts," Rylatt complained. "The officials in Victoria threw the blame on the Canadian Government . . . [but] it was found upon investigation the wretch had been withholding just claims not only of the families of the men in their employ, but the merchants generally; and that certain of these sums he had deposited in the bank, the interest thereon appropriating to himself." Bureaucrats also failed to forward personal letters for many months at a time, leaving the field crews with no knowledge of their families, and their families wondering about their husbands and sons. The corruption and incompetence permeated every aspect of the enterprise, as many saw the sloppy management as a trough from which to feed themselves.

In a world where most people seldom ventured far from where they were born—even the nomadic Plains peoples seldom strayed from their (admittedly vast) tribal territories—it must have been wanderlust that inspired them. They surely took the job for the sheer adventure of it, a chance to see something of the world no matter the hardships, risks or inconvenience. "Mighty mountains, towering upwards," wrote Rylatt, expressing a sentiment no doubt shared by many of this seemingly eccentric cohort who threw the comforts of civilization by the wayside in exchange for insight and awe, "their peaks almost in the blue of the sky, so well does their pale snow lines blend into the blue above; then down, far beneath us, their bases buried in gloom, their sides rent and worn by nature's convulsions, and the mad streams ever leaping in foam and tumult from their snowy starting points, gathering force continually, until a river, a huge rolling troubled volume is sent still plunging onwards, forming barriers in the way of puny man. . . . It is impossible to do other than stand and gaze with awe, and sigh as we are reminded of our own littleness."

Another time, when he was left in camp alone one day while the others went ahead, Rylatt scrawled in his notebook to alleviate his loneliness and, perhaps, fear. "In solitude I watched the sun gild the tops of the lofty mountains on the opposite shore of the [Columbia] lakes, watched its bright rays creep down the rugged sides; now below the snow line, lighting up the somber forests of bristling firs which darkened them from the snow to the shores of the lakes, and as at last it threw its silvery sheen over the black waters, my eye swept along to the tiny river, as it stole silently though a swampy valley, and I enjoyed a train of thought none can follow nor appreciate who have not wandered in primitive wildernesses, and through scenes of nature's rudest grandeur."

But whatever their reasons for joining, the crews of the Canadian Pacific Survey over many years in the bush, muskeg and mountains, from the forests east of Lake Superior to the gloomy rainforests of the Pacific slope, created the blueprint, the great linear chart, the travel guide, that would be followed by those who came after—the heavy work crews who graded the path, blasted the tunnels and rock outcroppings, hauled the timber and laid the steel rail tracks by following the blazed path of the surveyors.

But long before the land of rock and bog had been conquered and a railway traversed it, an effective rail link was constructed around it, through the U.S., that finally connected Manitoba and Winnipeg to the East by rail, what passed for rapid transportation in the era. It involved the schemes of the man who was somehow in the shadows of nearly every money-making venture of his era: Donald "Labrador" Smith.

ONE OF SMITH'S EARLIEST INVESTMENTS in western transportation infrastructure was the Red River Transportation Company. The small steamship line was one of the most understated and profitable ventures of the era, despite giving preferential freight discounts to the Hudson's Bay Company on all goods shipped north from St. Paul to the Red River Settlement. Begun by Norman Kittson, a local free trader originally from Lower Canada who had married into Métis society and now dwelt in St. Paul, and James J. Hill, a Canadian-born entrepreneur with whom Smith had shared a tent in 1870 en route to meeting Riel on behalf of the Canadian government, the virtual monopoly churned out dividends to shareholders of up to 80 percent, while charging rates so high it was barely cheaper than a canoe brigade.

Naturally this gusher of cash was threatened by the possibility of a railway, and none of the partners wanted to lose the cash cow that had seen their fortunes soar. In 1876, Hill made the trip to Ottawa and Montreal to meet with Smith to find a way to turn the situation to their mutual advantage. They had their eyes fixed on the moribund and bankrupt First Division of the St. Paul and Pacific Railroad, now in receivership and being reorganized. The main creditors were a group of Dutch investors who were frustrated and anxious over their multi-million-dollar investment; perhaps they would be open to offers. The defunct railway led north from St. Paul toward the Canadian border, trending in the same direction as the Red River Transportation Company steamships. Smith was familiar with the railway; he had travelled on it north from St. Paul years earlier and had seen the prosperity that seemed to seep into the land as far as the tracks led. Now the infrastructure was crumbling, with rotted ties, rusty rails (made of iron rather than steel) and rickety bridges.

But as they say in real estate: location, location, location. Smith and his partners suspected that despite the decrepit infrastructure, the already cleared railbed and, most importantly, the line's location and legal rights-of-way were worth four times what the Dutch investors would be willing to settle for. The land surrounding the railway and its incomplete right-of-way was rapidly being settled by an influx of farmers from the East.

Smith and his partners calculated that the railway's business prospects were rapidly shifting, unbeknownst to the original bondholders, the shareholders or the bankruptcy trustee. The railway also had agreements with the State of Minnesota for additional government grants if the track was extended to certain key locations, and an exclusive right to build a line to the Canadian border, where Smith, now a member of Mackenzie's inner circle, knew that a line south from Winnipeg, which by then had a population of six thousand, was slowly progressing, managed by one of Mackenzie's cronies. In Montreal, Smith turned to his cousin George Stephen, who had become the president of the Bank of Montreal. Stephen perked up when Smith showed him the numbers, and he was soon on a steamship to Amsterdam, where he negotiated a breathtaking discount on the Dutch investors' bonds. The partners then offered to buy out the railway's other creditors. Augmenting their small initial investment of several hundred thousand dollars, Stephen arranged for the Bank of Montreal to furnish them with a $5.5-million loan to complete the transactions, on the condition that he become one of the partners. No one seemed overly concerned about this blatant conflict of interest.

Meanwhile, Smith, Kittson and Hill converted their Red River Transportation Company into stock in the newly minted St. Paul, Minneapolis and Manitoba Railway. The line was running by 1878, connecting to a Canadian branch that, with the Mackenzie government's dubious efficiency, had been slowly wending its bureaucratic way south from Pembina, near Winnipeg, to the border. They of course wanted to link their railway to the Pembina branch and were well placed to do so, considering Smith was one of Mackenzie's loyalists. But the Conservatives detested Smith for his role in toppling them over the Pacific Scandal, and four years later they still hissed and booed whenever he rose to speak in the House of Commons. There was a furious row in the House when Mackenzie tried to push through the deal to grant to Smith, Stephen, Hill and Kittson a decade-long lease on the roadbed of the Pembina branch at favourable rates. Macdonald, now leader of the official Opposition, was indignant at the blatant corruption and conflict of interest (topics with which he was intimately familiar). Mackenzie rammed the lease through, but it was blocked by the Conservative majority in the Senate. So Mackenzie, at Smith's suggestion, merely signed a ten-year agreement to rent him exclusive running rights on the line, a technicality that allowed for the same outcome: huge profits to Smith and his partners. It was the final act of Mackenzie's government before the dissolution of Parliament for the election in 1878.

Smith, Stephen, Hill and Kittson were effectively handed a monopoly on both settlers and manufactured goods travelling west to Winnipeg and the export of grain and other agricultural products to the East. Soon they were earning money enough to make Croesus blush with embarrassment. With an initial investment of a few hundred thousand dollars, the four schemers were set to make hundreds of millions of dollars over the next three decades. In hindsight, their success appeared a foregone conclusion, but the investors did put in several years of challenging, quasi-ethical and stressful work striving to get the financing and meet the construction deadlines in order to claim the government subsidies, including putting most of their personal fortunes on the line. Their eventual success is a fascinating story of determination and vision, a triumph over mediocrity and poor management. One ambitious gamble with an enormous payoff, with the little helping hand of political corruption and insider knowledge.

People like Smith, who have existed throughout history and are still with us today, have an endless preoccupation with status and wealth in a self-affirming cycle, the one continuously begetting the other. They

believe their money is their servant, awaiting a gesture to do their bid-
ding and provide them with whatever they desire. But mostly they are
mistaken. Their fortunes become their masters, consuming their
thoughts and commanding their lives like a shadowy overseer. The
numbers are never enough to satisfy avaricious friendships and the
ever-increasing demands of family. They become consumed with nur-
turing, defending and growing their wealth as if it were a living thing,
a selfish, demanding thing that cannot be put from their mind; a com-
petitive metric to measure against their peers, determining their rank in
a self-imagined hierarchy in which only other people such as themselves found any credence.

THE YEARS HAD TRICKLED BY. Treaties were signed on the prairies,
the American whiskey traders were driven out, the terrifying spectre
of the disappearance of the buffalo shifted a little closer, and Burrard
Inlet was chosen as the Pacific terminus of the railway. Nevertheless,
during Mackenzie's entire term as prime minister, hardly any actual
track was laid, although plenty of surveys were undertaken and huge
tracts of public land were transferred to and between interested and
politically connected parties, often at inflated rates borne by the public treasury. Now, in 1878, it was election time again. The economy was
emerging from its doldrums and Macdonald was in the ascendancy.
His Conservatives won and once again the railway became a priority.
The Conservatives specifically targeted Smith for defeat in his riding
of Selkirk in Manitoba. They fielded Alexander Morris, a former
minister under Macdonald and Manitoba's first chief justice. With
considerable bribes and by paying local Métis families and Hudson's
Bay Company employees to move into his riding and vote for him,
Smith just barely squeaked in—and was immediately charged with
election fraud. Despite considerable additional bribes, his win was

overturned and he was defeated in a by-election. Though for now he was out of politics, his involvement in the CPR was just beginning.

The Macdonald government's soon-introduced National Policy involved tariffs on foreign goods to bolster the creation of a larger internal economy through the settlement of the West—which hastened the need for a railway. He wanted no part in the Liberals' corrupt and inefficient Public-Works-managed project; he preferred an equally corrupt yet presumably more efficient private model. When he cast about for interested parties, his eyes settled on George Stephen, who was the public face of the syndicate that had so successfully turned around the St. Paul, Minneapolis and Manitoba Railway. Imagine his joy at finding a group of successful railroaders and financiers with plenty of capital and strong ties to Montreal. Macdonald wanted the entire railway project to be privatized, but with the proviso that it remain primarily Canadian financed and that the track would be situated entirely within Canadian territory, so that a person could board a train in Halifax and arrive at a terminus on the Pacific without ever having to travel through the United States.

The terms were generous, or seemed to be so. The portions of the line that had been slowly taking shape under Mackenzie's public management—small segments along Lake Superior and in coastal British Columbia—were given over to the new syndicate, as was the barely completed Pembina branch line that, as of 1878, ran to the U.S. border and connected to the St. Paul, Minneapolis and Manitoba Railway. The enterprise was also given $225 million in cash and twenty-five million acres of land, to be chosen at a later date, that were to be "fairly fit for settlement." This was in addition to generous tax breaks and monopoly protection from any branch lines siphoning off traffic to the south to connect to existing American railways. But they would actually have to build a railway within ten years to get most of these payoffs.

The new Canadian Pacific Railway signed an agreement with the government in October 1880, and the deal received royal assent on February 15, 1881. The syndicate comprised the peculiar and scheming George Stephen, still head of the Bank of Montreal; James J. Hill from the St. Paul, Minneapolis and Manitoba Railway; Richard Angus, the Bank of Montreal's general manager and later president; Duncan McIntyre, from the Canadian Central Railway, which ran between Ottawa and North Bay; Sir Stafford Northcote, governor of the Hudson's Bay Company; Norman Kittson; and the New York financier John Kennedy, as a representative of the American and British investors. The shadowy presence of Donald Smith, former head of the HBC and yet another future president of the Bank of Montreal, despised enemy of Macdonald and most of the newly elected government, was kept secret for obvious reasons. Naturally there were howls of outrage from the newly defeated Liberals. Too much land was being given away in the West, the great source of riches for the St. Lawrence people to exploit; too much government money was being shovelled at the project. The Toronto business community was outraged that control of the line, believed to be the key to the prosperity of the nation, was given to Montreal interests instead of to them, despite their competing, and cheaper, bid. But politics, as they say, is politics.

The National Policy of the re-elected Macdonald government called for three things: the completion of the CPR to bind the nation into an interconnected entity; a series of protective tariffs to bolster moribund domestic industry in Ontario and Quebec; and increasing immigration to the West, which would create more Canadian citizens to oppose a feared American influx and would also provide a captive market for these now protected eastern industries. A number of historians have suggested that an unstated fourth plank of this policy was the defeat and emasculation of Indigenous peoples. Whether this needed to be stated as a political objective, it was certainly required as a precursor to successful implementation of the other three policies. The numbered treaties were the diplomatic solution; the widespread starvation, disease and death cycle that was just then taking hold certainly hastened the process and removed any potential opposition. The only question for debate is the extent to which the government in Ottawa could have improved its humanitarian response—and no one comes out looking good. Its behaviour was odious. The episode brings to mind the insight from the ancient Greek fabulist and philosopher Aesop: "We hang the petty thieves and appoint the great ones to public office."

CHAPTER FIFTEEN

THE FIRST TRACK

———

S ir William Cornelius Van Horne was a corpulent, hard-eyed man with a neatly trimmed beard, like a well-groomed cat smug about its place in the world. Ubiquitous cigar dangling from hand or mouth like a talisman, Van Horne exuded an aura of the archetypal capitalist of the era. All he was missing was a top hat and a monocle to complete the caricature. Laconic and direct of speech, he was fond of positive aphorisms such as "Nothing is too small to know, and nothing is too big to attempt." And he certainly attempted and succeeded at big things, despite humble beginnings. By the time he was in his mid-thirties, he had already risen in the ranks of multiple American railways, mastering nearly all aspects of the business, from mechanics to sales to logistics and management, through sheer determination and hard work, aided by a photographic memory, to become one of the top railway executives in a nation that was rapidly covering the land with track.

By the time he was lured north to Montreal in 1881 to speed up the slow progress on the CPR, which was once again a private conglomerate under the auspices of Macdonald's National Policy, Van Horne was possessed of a near-herculean work ethic and an all-encompassing knowledge of how to plan, construct and operate railways. He had previously turned several underperforming enterprises into successful, smoothly oiled, profit-generating machines. Where some cringed at the screech of steel wheels on track and wrinkled their noses at the acrid, penetrating stench of the coal fires that heated the boiler and generated steam, Van Horne heard the music of money being made. He gloried in the smell of success, in the feel of the world changing in a predictable way, the track stretching onward, opening up new possibilities, new places on the map.

Van Horne was born near Chelsea, Illinois, in 1843 to a family of Dutch ancestry who had settled in New York in the 1600s. His father was a lawyer who turned to farming, which led to disaster when fire destroyed everything, and further disaster when his first wife died, leaving young William bereft. Nevertheless, the family recovered, and Van Horne grew up middle-class and began working on railways when he was only fourteen—railways then being new and exciting technology in a growing industry. Van Horne's great insight was that railways should be tethered to communication services, that every rail line should have telegraph lines and express freight service built in tandem as an integrated communication and transportation network. He turned floundering enterprises to profit and was instrumental in speeding up construction through solid logistical planning and management, of people as well as the grand vision. Scheduling, accounting, logistics, repairs, new technology, cost averaging for construction and maintenance of track and bridges and trestles in different terrains, routing, location of repair depots and crews, staffing—he grasped all the interconnecting components that would lead to success and profit.

Difficult to pigeonhole, Van Horne was a talented violinist and painter and had expansive interests in architecture, botany, fossil collecting and cataloguing, and landscape gardening. An avid collector of fine art and a dedicated philanthropist, he donated the equivalent of millions to various causes during his lifetime. A convivial conversationalist with a wide range of knowledge, he could also be a steely-eyed strategist and implacable opponent. He despised drunkenness, sloth and dereliction of duty and had no qualms about firing men on the spot if he detected unsavoury characteristics.

His ambitions were as large as his size; he dwelt in an enormous Montreal mansion noted for expansive rooms and soaring ceilings and filled with pricey art. He was respected in Montreal, serving, among other prestigious ceremonial positions, as governor of McGill University. He later involved the CPR in the sea transport business, connecting the rail line to shipping between Vancouver and Hong Kong in 1891, and also worked to establish the first Cuban railway. He had a grand vision of a mighty integrated transportation network linking the entire country. He pioneered the luxury hotel business connected to the railways, including Château Frontenac in Quebec City and Chateau Lake Louise (both of which he helped to design), and convinced the federal government to create Canada's first national parks to provide a destination and a reason for wealthy travellers to ride the railway across the country. And if that wasn't enough, he also commissioned three ships to be made in Scotland in 1883, which were sailed to Montreal, cut in half and transported to the Great Lakes; there, reconstructed, they became equipment and supply transports for the work along Lake Superior and eventually part of the first-class and immigrant transportation system to get people west to the prairies and the Rocky Mountains.

Van Horne often sat astride a backward chair leaning forward, puffing on his Havana cigar. A man of great appetite, he loved a well-provisioned table, multiple dishes washed down with fine wine, followed by cognac, whiskey and cards into the evening. Yet he was not selfish, and he paid particular attention to ensuring that his workers were also well fed, no matter the remoteness of their work location. If an army was known to march on its stomach, he reasoned, so too would his workers be kept energized and content with a plentiful hot meal to look forward to at the end of each day. Later in life, his face took on a dull, sedentary sag, reflecting years of rich living. He died in 1915 at the age of seventy-two. He was survived by his wife, Lucy Hurd, whom he had married in 1867. They had three children, two of whom survived to adulthood, who were raised in Montreal and became well-established members of the city's commercial and social elite.

Strict on discipline and regulations, especially regarding the perennial railroader's problem of drinking on the job, Van Horne would furiously swear at and lambaste anyone suspected of public drunkenness. But he could also be a jovial and loquacious dinner companion and would spend days marching up and down lengths of track meeting the workers and commenting on their progress, urging everyone on to greater exertion. A colourful, complex, perhaps eccentric man of vast energy and ambition, honourable and respectful of the contributions of others, he defies easy stereotype. What can't be denied is that he had an outsized impact on the development of the CPR, his competence and work ethic likely saving it from ignominious collapse, and hence an outsized influence on Canadian history.

When the CPR conglomerate was finally officially established in February 1881, two managers quickly proved unsuitable for the immense project. It only took a few months for it to became obvious that Alpheus Stickney, general manager, and Thomas Rosser, chief engineer, needed to be replaced right away; progress had been slow and erratic, and the heads of the conglomerate knew that speed was of the essence, since they would soon run out of money: with little or no revenues, the enterprise would be a mighty money sink until it met certain milestones of completion. The thirty-eight-year-old Van Horne soon set things in motion, and under his leadership the line was completed in half the projected time.

He took over the job of general manager in the fall of 1881, after making two tours of the track to assess the progress, riding the rails north to Winnipeg from St. Paul and then west to the newly founded town of Brandon at the western end of track, then east along the partially completed track to Thunder Bay. There would be engineering and logistical problems, he knew, but the land and its challenges could be tackled, and he was impressed with the agricultural potential of the region, which meant the railway would be the catalyst for towns that would in turn generate revenue for the railway—that, in short, it wouldn't be a foundering dud and sink his own career in the process. He also knew that if he could be the one who ensured such a daunting challenge met with success, it would enshrine his own rising star. He moved his family to Montreal. It was a bold gamble for a man in the ascendancy in a growing industry, in a prosperous country, rapidly expanding its rail network. Although Van Horne was offered a very high salary, it was probably the professional challenge of completing such a grandiose project that tipped him into accepting the job.

AT THE START OF 1882, Winnipeg was teeming with new immigrants. The hotels were crammed with many to a room, while less well-heeled patrons flopped on the floors of common rooms. The even less fortunate were housed in hastily constructed "immigrant sheds" during the frigid winter; others somehow survived on the streets. By the summer, more than four thousand men and women were living in tents. The great prairie land boom had attracted them. From barely 250 migrants a year when Manitoba first became a province, in 1870, Winnipeg had emerged as the pre-eminent city on the prairies, the undisputed centre of commercial, social and political activity for the entire region west of Lake Superior and north of the U.S. border. Within ten years it had grown to 8,000. And within five more years it had exploded to over 20,000, on the way to 179,000 by 1921. The city was populated with ramshackle, hastily hammered-together tenements, saloons and hotels, brothels and liquor dens, the streets crammed with horses and wagons. There were even a few stately stone buildings. The raucous din of saws and hammers thundered all day.

The boom had begun the previous summer, when the CPR opened development lots in Brandon, about 160 kilometres west across the flat land where the track now led, and soon spread to other towns and outposts where the CPR was expected to run its line: Portage la Prairie, Prince Albert and the Hudson's Bay Company outpost of Fort Edmonton. Even Port Moody on Burrard Inlet saw real estate speculation. The sheer quantity of raw materials for the construction of the CPR, and the thousands of workers needed to build it, were the main reasons for speculators' sudden interest. They were soon doubling their money, in some cases in a matter of weeks.

Throughout Ontario, community leaders, people of standing, would collect money as if for a lottery, hire representatives to travel west and buy property that was sure to go up in price indefinitely, as the agents began buying and flipping on margin when they arrived and telegraphing the news back home to people eagerly revelling in their rising fortunes. Newspapers promoted get-rich-quick schemes and the coming bonanza. Reporters from eastern Canada and the U.S. rushed to see what the fuss was about, penning glowing portraits of the possibility for real estate riches, some jumping into the fray themselves, so great was the temptation. Lots in Winnipeg were selling for more than similar properties in Chicago, a well-established and well-positioned city on its way to becoming one of America's great urban centres—that alone should have been the tipoff that all was not right.

The speculation was described as a mania, with people caught up in a heady cloud of delusion. Housing lots were doubling in value every few weeks in a frenzy where a form of mass hysteria made people believe they would continue to double their money indefinitely, and that to not get into the market meant they would forever be shut out. It was like the seventeenth century's tulip mania in Holland, where for a brief time rare tulip bulbs could be traded for stately mansions in a speculative bubble that saw the "value" of the bulbs ladder upward simply because people believed they would continue to soar, an extraordinary popular delusion that, when it finally fizzled, altered the social landscape for years. Fortunes were lost overnight, formerly wealthy families reduced to penury, while others, more prescient or lucky, were between trades and hence fabulously wealthy.

Van Horne could sense the insanity and wanted to distance his new company from the growing problem. Soon after he set up his office in the new Bank of Montreal building in downtown Winnipeg, he took the unusual step of taking out ads in local papers informing prospective speculators that the CPR would run its tracks where the company chose, without regard to the interests of property speculators or other outside pressure. No one paid him any heed.

Sam Steele, an officer with the NWMP who had first travelled west in 1874 and had already seen the staggering pace of change in those years, recalled Winnipeg at the height of its real estate bubble when he visited the city on a recruitment drive. "People were ready to buy anything," he wrote. "The hotels did a roaring trade and the bars made profits of hundreds of dollars a day. Every available space was taken up for sleeping accommodation. . . . In the forenoon the speculators were at their writing-tables going through their correspondence; the city was quiet, though crowded with men. At noon there was the usual hearty luncheon; at 3 p.m. the fun began, and was kept up until a late hour. Those who had made money were ready to re-invest it, and the real estate offices were crowded with men ready to buy or sell lots." As there was a shortage of women, "the demand for marriageable females was perfectly wild. The domestics handed over their funds to their employers for investment, and in many cases reaped large returns so that, with the additional advantage of being able to pick and choose from amongst a host of admirers, the best of them obtained good husbands and well-furnished homes of their own."

Hawkers flogged properties in the streets and public auctions drew wild crowds of bidders and bemused onlookers, while in the streets horses and carts loaded with lumber and construction materials pressed through the throngs. Animal dung, cigar smoke and sweat perfumed the air, music flooded out into the streets after dark, whiskey and spirits flowed like water in the evening, and all anyone ever talked about was real estate. Newly minted landlords bathed in Champagne, tossed cigars into the crowds in taverns while, like impresarios, they talked up the next township that was sure to make everyone a fortune as soon as the CPR placed its track. Luxuries and extravagances flooded into town from St. Paul: silverware, grand pianos, crystal goblets, gaudy jewellery and fine clothing. Formerly staid businessmen boasted of their profits in the newspapers, no doubt believing all was due to their acumen and skill, rising in the new social order along with their purported net worth.

Most of the town's exploding population, however, consisted of thousands of footloose young men, primarily from eastern Canada, searching for opportunity and adventure in the "New Eldorado." They dwelt in vast stagnant, unsanitary tent cities on the outskirts of town, eating gruel and stale bread, and were shut out of the grand display of swindles and deals and the frenzy of social jockeying as the game of musical chairs played on, with a perhaps unacknowledged anxiety, waiting for the music's inevitable end. The property ladder, a ladder whose rungs seemed to stretch to infinity into the golden clouds, would never be ascended by most of these young men, who lacked the capital to take even the first step—which was perhaps just as well, as it turned out.

Charles Napier Bell, who had come west from Ontario as a teenager with the Wolseley Expedition during the Red River crisis of 1870, and was working as a customs officer during the real estate boom, later wrote articles describing the outrageous events of the period. One of his stories in particular is illustrative of the heights of the real estate fever and the improbable fickleness of fortune.

One young and promising youth who had been started out of Toronto by a considerate father with $400 to make his fortune in Winnipeg, . . . on arriving in the city with $300 he went on a long spree and one evening brought up at a prominent real estate office. The excitement was at its height, and when he found the people about him shouting out bids for properties put up for sale, he took a turn at it himself and purchased a lot on which he had to make a deposit of $200. On awakening next morning he was sober enough to examine into the state of his finances, and to his dismay found that a single ten dollar bill was all that remained of his cash. A fit of repentance came upon him and he "swore off." With considerable inward trepidation, though with an outward appearance of unconcern, he visited the hotel office to find out the amount of his bill, and was overjoyed when he learned that he had settled up the day before and paid a week's board in advance. He wandered about for a week in great despondency, and at last made up his mind to go to the telegraph office to wire his father asking for money to pay for his passage back home. As the resources of the telegraph line were taxed to their utmost, it was no small undertaking to get off a message, and on entering the office he stood in the line awaiting his turn, revolving in his mind just what he would embody in his message. A wild-eyed, haggard-looking individual entered the office and rushed up to him, exclaiming, "You own lot so-and-so!" It suddenly flashed across the memory of the young fellow that he had in his pocket-book a slip of paper covered with a few hieroglyphics, amongst which lot — were discernible. This he produced and handed to the wild-eyed man, who glanced over it and said: "That's all right; what will you take for it?" The young man asked what he would give, and to his astonishment was told $10,000 for his claim on the property. Hastily abandoning the idea of telegraphing his father he dickered with several men and finally secured $28,000 for the privilege of withdrawing his original deposit of $200 and surrender of the deposit receipt. Being a wise fellow, and concluding that one experience was enough for him, he left for Toronto with a bank certificate in his pocket, and was received into the open arms of his delighted parent.

But all good things must come to an end. In mid-April the craze for building lots had pushed as far across the prairie as Fort Edmonton, nearly 1,200 kilometres to the northwest. Rumours were that the CPR had surveyed the land around the North Saskatchewan River Valley, in the vicinity of the outbuildings clustered about the palisade enclosure. Fort Edmonton was no great urban centre at the time: it could boast mostly some settled older fur traders and their families and some nearby missionaries, rounded out by the temporary encampments of primarily Cree and Niisitapi (Blackfoot) who came to trade. An imminent Eldorado-in-waiting it was not; no railway was even planned in that direction anymore. Nevertheless, Winnipeg speculators barged into the office of the agent Arthur Wellington Ross and snapped up lot deeds for over ten times what they had been slowly selling for the previous fall. Naturally, they anticipated reselling the following day for many hundreds of dollars more to people on the next level of the pyramid, people less astute or bold than themselves. But a strange thing happened. Suddenly, there were no more eager buyers in line.

Then the Red River began to flood, as it usually did in the spring in Winnipeg. But this was no ordinary flood. Water levels slowly rose every day, not cresting until weeks later. People hastily moved their belongings to their second floors, and boats now floated down the main streets. The water even briefly inundated many pricey and supposedly dry "villa lots." Bridges and roads were swept away, the railway link to St. Paul was severed, and commerce ground to a halt. So did food supplies, causing a panic. And when the water receded and the city dried out, everything was left covered with the sheen of stinking mud.

The flood coincided with an anti-speculation policy brought in by the CPR to curb the excesses of human emotion and greed: from then on, anyone buying a lot from the CPR—which had been given the land as part of the government subsidy to create the railway—had to build on it rather than just resell the deed. People seemed to awaken as if from a dream, and, Bell reported, "the effect on the real estate market was sudden and far reaching. Everybody now wished to sell, especially their outside properties [distant lots], but purchasers could not be found." Winnipeg's real estate gasbag, along with that of the northwest generally, had swelled for over a year before it, like all popular delusions, eventually ran up against reality and wheezed away, the stale air hissing as it deflated by the end of 1882. "Real estate advertisements quietly disappeared and the host of boomers struck their tents and silently flitted away to more congenial climes." All those grand fortunes dissipated overnight, leaving the erstwhile investment geniuses without a chair to sit on once the music stopped, wishing they had been just a little less greedy or a little less naive, or had sold a little earlier.

Many now held worthless land deeds—purchased on margin with a small deposit leaving outstanding balances to be paid—in towns that would never thrive, and some that would never even exist except on paper deeds. High flyers were now destitute street dwellers, turfed from their homes along with their now heavily discounted furnishings. Thousands glumly returned east with empty pockets and heavy debts. The excessive money supply caused by easy credit, which had been handed out to anyone—and which had caused the bubble in the first place—suddenly dried up, as no one could pay their debts and no one wanted to lend anything, even to the remaining legitimate settlers and businesses. The ensuing recession was severe, and nearly three-quarters of the region's official businesses were shuttered. The formerly sunny view of the northwest's prospects was now clouded and gloomy, and international financiers frowned at the prospect of any new ventures in the region, extending to the CPR, which would, within a year, face a nearly insurmountable financial crunch.

Construction of the railway continued. Thousands of workers were still needed, and vast mountains of materials were being stockpiled in railyards. But people were no longer flooding into new towns along the railway route as it pushed west. Indeed, the general view of opportunities in the northwest was hamstrung for a generation. But regardless of the real estate bust and the ultimate route of the railway west of Brandon, Winnipeg would be the centre of operations for many years to come, and the undisputed centre of commerce in Canada's northwest—even if it never came close to rivalling Chicago, as the boosters had proclaimed it would.

Van Horne continued with his ambitious job of getting a band of steel tracks pushed west across the prairie and east to Thunder Bay.

IN 1881, THE CPR DIRECTORS decided to change Fleming's original route. The Yellowhead might have been Fleming's preferred pass, but the more southerly Kicking Horse and the as yet undetermined pass west of it had another compelling quality: cost. Everything had been staggeringly expensive around Lake Superior. Land grants and subsidies were based on miles of track laid, and it was slow going in those rocky and boggy lands, draining the CPR's coffers at an unsustainable rate. The directors had to find savings somewhere. The new southern route upon which they agreed was at least one hundred miles shorter, crossing far fewer river valleys, which meant fewer trestles and bridges. Further-more, the route was closer to the valuable coal deposits in southern Saskatchewan and Alberta that would provide fuel for the locomotives and additional revenue from the commodity freight business.

The decision was also based upon recent reports by the NWMP and the treaty negotiation parties, as well as the observations of the bota-nist John Macoun. The southern lands were originally believed to be a northern extension of the Great American Desert, too dry for reliable agriculture. But this was not entirely true. Macoun declared that the basin of the South Saskatchewan River was perfectly good for certain hardy crops and for ranching in the extensive grasslands, an observa-tion proved accurate in the subsequent 150 years. Captain John Palliser and others had seen the land in a very dry phase in the 1850s, but when Macoun travelled the region decades later it was in a wet phase, with plenty of rainfall. Of course these phases switch back and forth, and agriculture proved challenging until the right crops were developed, along with a better understanding of the fluctuating pre-cipitation patterns. Nevertheless, the CPR directors made the gamble on a southern route that hadn't yet been surveyed and hoped that a suitable pass could be located through the Selkirk Mountains. The move was also strategic, to prevent the possibility of any commerce from the southern prairies being diverted to the U.S.; the north, already being geographically isolated from that possibility, could be dealt with later.

But rampant land speculation probably had as great a role in the decision as other considerations. Since Fleming's suggested route had been well known for years, speculators had purchased land from the government once treaties were signed. There was a great deal of corrup-tion and politically connected attempts to obtain insider information. After all, the route of the rail line would determine where communities would rise and who would become rich in the process, and where other—bypassed—communities would wither, so naturally there were bribes, secret deals and (often fraudulent) speculation. Van Horne had already taken steps to deal with leaked proprietary information regarding the company's proposed route; he had fired an entire office division in Winnipeg to staunch the leaks.

The southern route passed through mostly unclaimed land, which would give the company great freedom to place the route and at the same time generate revenue by selling the land. The routing of a railway through land that wasn't already settled would give them complete control over the location of towns. Having control over not only the location of towns but also the street layout around the rail station, which inevitably became the centre of a town, resulted in an appreciation in value of all their government land grants, which they then sold themselves. This one decision drastically altered the course of the economic development of the West, directing agriculture, tourism and the creation of parks to the south.

George Stephen and the other CPR directors were also now discovering an enthusiasm for the unprofitable section north of Lake Superior. The seemingly odd change in perspective arose from a calculation that the CPR could perhaps make a little money shipping timber from the Ottawa Valley to Winnipeg, to support the building boom on the prairies that everyone imagined would follow in the wake of the railway. The sudden enthusiasm was also, at least in part, an attempt to curry favour with Macdonald and to ensure support for the monopoly provisions on transport to and from Winnipeg, a sort of all-or-nothing deal to make sure the entire line was within Canadian territory.

A shifting appreciation of the land led to yet another change in route from the one so assiduously scouted and surveyed by Fleming. Fleming's route, the easiest from an engineering standpoint, crossed the rock-bound Canadian Shield to the north of Lake Nipigon, through a virtual wilderness. Stephen told Macdonald that this route would traverse a region that would never support large-scale settlement, since it was essentially rock and small pools of water. Without the potential to sell land or township sites, the route would be uneconomical. Railway economics of the time assumed that the presence of a completed line generated its own business, transporting provisions, supplies and travellers into new regions and returning with the products of their labours, such that freight was always a two-way income-generating stream. If no settlement was possible, none of this traffic would exist, whatever the ease of engineering design and construction, and it would chalk up only operating losses. The proposed alternative route would cleave to the shore of the lake. It would be longer, but it could be serviced and provisioned easily by water during construction, perhaps cutting in half the time it would take to get it running, and would be closer to possible settlements along the shore. Of course, this opened up the possibility of claims, especially from the Toronto *Globe*, that the company had never intended to build the route at all—the same old issue. The debate seemed never-ending.

DESPITE ALL THESE UNCERTAINTIES, Van Horne entered the Canadian arena to contend with the unique political, economic and engineering challenges of Macdonald's dream. Owing to his generally no-nonsense business approach and his general refusal to entertain corruption, the "Czar of the CPR" earned the enmity of quite a few in Winnipeg who chafed at his brusque manner and his preference for hiring Americans for key jobs rather than British or eastern Canadians. Most of the managers and engineers who built Canada's great national project were actually American, an irony apparently not appreciated at the time, although there was criticism of Van Horne for his apparently misplaced loyalties. Not much escaped Van Horne's attention. He was a shrewd judge of character and would quickly replace underperforming contractors and employees. He was swift to promote and swift to demote, all based on merit, as he saw it, not lineage, patronage or credentials. It was the opposite corporate culture of the survey crews managed by Mackenzie's government in the 1870s.

Of the four segments of track then under construction, Van Horne took complete responsibility for three of them: the prairies west from Winnipeg, the rocky bogs of Lake Superior from Callander to Thunder Bay, and the incomplete sections from Thunder Bay west to Winnipeg. The fourth stretch of track was begun by Andrew Onderdonk, an American engineer contracted to build the line east from near what is now Vancouver towards the Interior, to some as yet undetermined location where the east and west tracks would meet. Onderdonk was left to himself while Van Horne was constantly on the go, rushing back and forth between the company's headquarters in Montreal, where his family now lived, to his drafty office amidst the chaos and effusion in boom-town Winnipeg, to his multiple stops along the track, and south to St. Paul to meet with James Hill and other American contractors to arrange the mighty quantities of supplies, tools and commodities needed for an enterprise of such staggering dimension.

In addition to his day job, Van Horne was also a master poker player and routinely pulled all-nighters, sipping whiskey and smoking cigars, before heading off to work the next morning. The politics and psychology of the CPR was like a giant game of poker, with huge gambles, bluffing and stone-faced boastful claims based on aspiration and desire that he sometimes instinctively knew were falsehoods. A great deal of his job was managing the expectations of politicians and their endless need to persuade or mislead the public, passive-aggressive engineers, grumpy workers, pestering speculators and impatient and skittish investors and financiers. If he was a juggler, he would have had ten balls in the air.

His primary goal throughout 1882 was to build momentum that had been sorely lacking in the project so far, to prevent it from getting

mired in hopelessness at the enormity of the task and all of the challenges—technical, logistical and of course weather-related. Indeed, in
March a bout of storms blocked the track, hindered workers and
delayed the arrival of needed supplies. Without a sense of possibility
and optimism, Van Horne feared, the project would become moribund,
progressing sluggishly through a fog of hesitancy; after all, a murkiness
of purpose without animating enthusiasm had caused it to flounder as
a government project. He needed to energize it with a spark of pride,
and in this he was remarkably successful. In 1882, Van Horne brashly
promised to build over five hundred miles of track in a single year on
the prairies alone.

AS VAN HORNE MARSHALLED the forces of his CPR army, urging
them on to greater exertion; as the line under his management ground
through the hair-pulling problems of the northern Ontario geography;
and as the work took flight across the easier prairie landscape, the final
route of the line farther west toward the Rockies was still being final-
ized, after Fleming's original route through the Yellowhead Pass had
been abandoned.

The mountains were a maze of rocky peaks, glacier-plugged passes
and raging river torrents. Hundreds of heavily forested valleys led to
dead ends or grades too steep for a railway to traverse, or veered in the
wrong direction—each twist of direction or blockage by canyon cliffs
potentially adding millions to the construction costs or requiring dangerous compromises on grade and angles, and ultimately the safety of
the eventual construction workers and the even more eventual passengers. There just wasn't an obvious or easy transportation route through
this tortuous topography. The directors had optimistically assumed that
a feasible route could be found, that one had to exist somewhere south
of the Yellowhead and yet not too close to the U.S. border, where it
might be easily captured in some future conflict.

The farther Van Horne and the track crept west, the more financially committed the enterprise became to a southern route. Without a suitable pass, the company would be stuck with a gargantuan logistical and financial nightmare that would require a massive retrenchment, the decommissioning of hundreds of kilometres of track and the redeployment of hundreds of thousands of rail ties and steel rails, the abandonment of completed and partially completed bridges and trestles, and a demoralizing blow to public sentiment upon which future government support rested. The loss of money, and just as importantly and perhaps even more so, the loss of time, and the crushing of morale and momentum could easily be enough to swamp the financially precarious enterprise, put a stake in the heart of the careers of the upper managers and financiers and perhaps even sabotage the final stage in the formation of the Canadian empire.

CHAPTER SIXTEEN

MR. OATMEAL AND
THE KICKING HORSE

———

In 1881, the executives of the CPR syndicate sent Major Albert Bowman Rogers, an experienced American surveyor, to scout for a new southern pass through the Rockies and the Selkirk Mountains. Rogers was a hard and grumpy man, driven and stubborn, known for feeding his men a diet of oatmeal after long hours spent bushwhacking through the wilderness.

Rogers's assignment was to discover a hitherto unknown pass that would satisfy the unyielding demands both of his employers and of physics. The commonly used footpaths or canoe routes were useless for a railway, where an easily engineered gentle grade and overall distance translated directly into money. There were four potential southern passes through the Rockies that had not been investigated by Fleming's survey: Kicking Horse, Vermilion, Howse and Kootenay. Once he settled on one of these, Rogers would move on west to the Selkirk Range to locate a way through the tangled corridors of steep, heavily forested mountains where no suitable pass had ever been found. Good thing he was stubborn.

Rogers is famously known as the surveyor who discovered two vital railway routes through the mountains, the Rogers Pass in Montana and the even more daunting Rogers Pass in British Columbia. His route in B.C., now also the route of the Trans-Canada Highway, follows the Beaver River west and up and then descends from the height of land along the Illecillewaet River to the south-flowing branch of the Columbia River, near present-day Revelstoke. He had become driven to discover the elusive southern pass after the CPR promised him a cheque for $5,000 and that the pass would be named after him, thereby bestowing upon him, at least in the obsessive tunnel of his mind, an essence of immortality.

Small and wiry, Rogers was a proud, determined and fierce-looking man with dirty, patched coveralls and enormous mutton-chop whiskers that gave him the aura of an Old Testament prophet. His eyes "seemed to look at and see through everything at once," yet this seeming prescience was incongruously balanced by a predilection for chewing tobacco such that "every few moments a stream of tobacco juice erupted from between his sideburns." Known for frequent furious bursts of invective, he was often rude, insulting, denigrating and belligerent, and his employees generally despised working under him. "Hell's Bells" Rogers cared not a whit about their safety, comfort or food. "He had no mercy on horses or men," recalled guide Tom Wilson, "he had none on himself. The labourers hated him for the way he drove them and the packers for the way he abused the horses." Many recalled the harsh conditions and near starvation they endured under his leadership.

To save money and time, Rogers ordered his exhausted, hard-driven work crew to be fed oatmeal, bacon and beans every day, fare apparently to his liking, but when anyone complained he became insulting and mocking, calling them effeminate gourmets or accusing them of wasting resources. "Give Rogers six plugs of chewing tobacco and five bacon rinds, and he will travel for two weeks," someone ruefully recalled. And he was reprimanded for this more than once, especially by Van Horne, a man with the opposite view of how labourers should be fed at the end of a hard day. "We must take no chances on this season's work," Van Horne gently chided him in 1883, "because any failure to reach the desired results and have the line ready to put under contract will be very serious if not disastrous. . . . It is also exceedingly important that an ample supply of good food be provided and that the quantity be beyond the possibility of a doubt."

Van Horne continued, but with a diplomatic undercurrent of frustration: "Very serious reports have been made to the Government and in other quarters about the inadequacy of the supplies provided last year and a good many other reports have been made tending to discredit our work. . . . We cannot expect to get good men for that work at as low or lower rates than are paid further East and we must feed the men properly in order to get good service. It will be cheaper for the Company to pay for twice the amount of supplies actually necessary than to lose a day's work for the lack of any." "The Old Geyser," as Rogers had unaffectionately come to be known, no doubt grumbled about the added expense—even his parsimonious employer wanted him to loosen the purse strings.

On another occasion, after receiving even more complaints, Van Horne tried to explain away the major's peccadilloes in a letter laced with euphemisms. "There has been a good deal of feeling among some of the Canadian Engineers particularly those who have been accustomed to the Government Service against Major Rogers, partly from natural jealousy of one who is looked upon as an outsider, partly from his lively treatment of those whom he looks upon as shirkers or 'tender feet' and partly from his somewhat peculiar methods of securing economy. . . . He is something of an enthusiast and is disposed to undertake himself and to put upon his men more severe duties than most engineers are accustomed to and I have reason to believe that in his anxiety to economize in every possible way he has gone too far in some cases and that a good deal of unnecessary discomfort, although no suffering, has resulted from it." In other words, the old major was stingy, even when an expense wasn't his to pay. Taking no great pleasure in food himself, he felt that others didn't or shouldn't either. Nor did his insulting diatribes and profanity endear him to others.

But not all his subordinates viewed him with such distaste. Tom Wilson, a young packer of Irish descent from near Toronto who would go on to become one of the most recognized Rocky Mountain guides in later years and the "discoverer" of Lake Louise, had a fond recollection of his time with the crusty old major, claiming the rough exterior was a shield for a sensitive inner soul driven by staggering ambition and self-doubt. "Very few men ever learned to understand him, yet he had a generous heart and a real affection for many. He cultivated a gruff manner to conceal the emotions that he seemed ashamed to let anyone sense. His driving ambition was to have his name handed down in history; for that he faced unknown dangers and suffered privations. To have the key-pass of the Selkirks bear his name was the ambition he fought to realize." This naturally was of little concern to the suffering men he employed, whose names have not been appended to famous mountain passes despite their own privations and hardships.

Born in Massachusetts in 1829, Rogers apprenticed as a ship's carpenter but made only a single voyage before turning his back on the sea and enrolling in Brown University's engineering program, before moving on to Yale. After he graduated he joined the engineering department of the Erie Canal, then under construction. By the late 1850s, he had moved to Minnesota, where he was commissioned major by the governor during the conflict with the Sioux in 1862. He then devoted the remainder of his career to the survey and engineering of railways, including the Milwaukee and St. Paul railway, the Minneapolis and St. Louis line and the Hastings and Dakota line.

A renowned location engineer with an unparalleled eye for unconventional routes and construction insights, Rogers came to the attention of James J. Hill, of the Canadian Pacific Railway syndicate, who was also then in the process of hiring Van Horne. Hill recruited the fifty-two-year-old to be in charge of the difficult and challenging Mountain Division, tasked with plotting the shortest route between Moose Jaw and Savona's Ferry near Fort Kamloops, a job that would involve scouting and assessing two new passes.

In 1881, Rogers departed St. Paul and travelled by rail to San Francisco and then by steamer to Victoria before heading inland to Fort Kamloops. It was still a two-week journey of daily travel. He had arranged for a large survey crew to proceed by paddlewheeler up the Missouri River to Fort Benton and then by wagon and horseback north to the Bow River Gap, where the Bow River exited the Rocky Mountains west of Fort Calgary. The team consisted of five engineering outfits of twenty-five men each, with a year's worth of supplies, and their formidable job was to begin clearing a route west toward the Kicking Horse Pass, which descended to the Columbia River. Rogers's plan was to travel east from Fort Kamloops along a previously undiscovered route and meet his own survey parties as they progressed through the Kicking Horse Pass, and to do so by July 1.

From his close reading of the survey notes from earlier railway survey parties, Rogers learned that Walter Moberly had noted, fifteen years earlier, that a surveyor had travelled up the Illecillewaet River. Although he didn't venture far enough east to see the Great Divide, he had observed "a low, wide valley as far as he went," but he was not convinced that it would pass through rather than just end in a rock wall. Moberly considered the failure to go farther east a "disappointment." Of course, it was very difficult country to travel through, covered in massive fallen trees, riddled with swampy depressions and blanketed in thick undergrowth, including the infamous bane of explorers, the devil's club, leafy spine-covered shrubs that ripped at clothes and skin. This region intrigued Rogers, and it became the focus of his attention. In fact, he had a lot riding on its success, since few other options seemed viable.

At Fort Kamloops in April 1881, Rogers and his nephew Albert spent time collecting supplies and equipment for the journey, calculating rations and "trying to find out how far an Indian can travel between suns with one hundred pounds on his back and no trail, how little food he would require to do it." Rogers visited Chief Louis of the Secwépemc (Shuswap) Band and hired "ten strapping Indians on rather an ironclad contract:—their services would be ours without grumbling until discharged, and if any came back without a letter of good report, his wages were to go to the church, and the chief was to lay one hundred lashes on the bare back of the offender."

Pleased with this unconscionable employment arrangement and the money it would save, Rogers set off with his new indentured charges. The supplies included "2 rifles, 200 rounds ammunition, 8 pairs blankets, 2 axes, 50 feet ⅜-inch rope," six small tents, some cutlery, utensils and cooking paraphernalia, "800 lbs. of flour, 337 lbs. bacon, 25 lbs. baking powder, 25 lbs. salt, 10 lbs. tea, 1 tin of matches." A small steamer took them to the mouth of the Eagle River on Shuswap Lake and thence they struggled on across the Gold Range to the Columbia River, where they built a cedar-log raft and loaded the supplies. Rogers and his nephew climbed aboard, while the Secwépemc porter-guides swam nearby as the contraption floated to the Illecillewaet River. Rogers, true to form, observed the meagre supplies dwindle and enacted "a strict ration," which "caused much discontent among the Indians, as the work was extremely hard." Once ashore, they soon found themselves "picking our way over mudflats, scaling perpendicular rock-points, wading through beaver swamps dense with underbrush and the villainous devil's clubs, all the time balancing one hundred pounds on the back of the neck, [which] made life anything but a pleasant dream, and I am convinced, but for the fear of the penalty of returning without their letters of good report, our Indians would have deserted us."

For five days, the party of twelve struggled ever upward through dense, damp forest and persistent snow patches several feet deep, across avalanche chutes that were so powerful they had "crush[ed] the timber into match wood for several hundred feet," and balancing on several snow bridges over raging ice-cold torrents, "which were one hundred and fifty feet above the river's bed." By the end of May, they came upon a fork in the river, while above them towered "the back-bone or main range of the Selkirks." Either stream could be the long-sought elusive pass that would make Rogers, at least in his own eyes, immortal. Everyone else was just hungry.

They kept on, occasionally spying an enormous blue glacier peeking through the dense forest. (The Illecillewaet Glacier was soon to become one of the CPR's premier tourist attractions, boasting an elegant hotel with fountains and tennis courts and hiking guides to lead well-heeled Europeans and Americans to view the spectacular scenery before their evening repast of imported luxuries.) The party began travelling at night, once the sun had set and the snow hardened enough to hold their weight, setting up camp again in the morning when the sun turned everything into slush. "The terrible travelling with our heavy loads, soaked to the skin by rain and wet brush, wading in snow and ice-water, and sleeping in but one-half pair of blankets to each man had begun to show on all our faces." They cached food and supplies for the return trip, noting how the food was being eaten more quickly than Rogers had anticipated, despite the near-starvation diet, as they ascended a summit for a better view.

They started up to the peak in a single-file line, trudging silently while cringing at the frequent bouts of "rumbling thunder" of avalanches tearing down the slopes. At the top, Rogers observed water melting away and flowing both east and west, the height of land of the pass.

Since the dense, congested cedars and firs blocked all sightlines, the next morning they decided to ascend the south side of the pass to get a better, overarching view; they followed a line of trees that demarcated two avalanche chutes. They were now "gaunt as greyhounds" from not enough food. "We crawled along the ledges," Albert recalled, "getting a toe-hole here and a finger-hole there, keeping in the shade as much as possible and kicking toe-holes in the snow crust." Once above the treeline, they followed a ridge. Four of the Secwépemc men tied themselves together and began crawling slowly to the ledge above. One slipped backward, dragging the three others off and over in an instant, plunging ever downward along the steepness of the slope. "They fell some thirty feet straight down, striking upon a very steep incline" and continued slipping and rolling through the slushy snow, tangling up in the straps and ropes before plunging over another ledge. Fear and shock and stunned silence gripped the remaining climbers. What would they do if the men were injured? How would they proceed in a forced march through the dense forest with no food, carrying injured companions? They descended until, to everyone's relief, they spied four moving specks far below.

Leaving them for now, Rogers, Albert and six Secwépemc continued onward to the summit, arriving in late evening, exhausted. "Such a view! Never to be forgotten! Our eyesight caromed from one bold peak to another for miles in all directions. The wind blew fiercely across the ridge and scuddy clouds were whirled in the eddies behind the great towering peaks of bare rocks. Everything was covered with a shroud of white, giving the whole landscape the appearance of snow-clad desolation." With no wood for a fire, no boughs to make sleeping platforms, only a few nibbles of dried meat and bannock for a repast, soaking with perspiration and stuffing down mouthfuls of snow to quench their thirst, they took turns slumbering and whipping each other with pack straps to "keep up circulation." Was it worth it? Apparently it was. "The grandeur of the view, sublime beyond conception, crowded out all thoughts of our discomforts." But despite their exertions they were unable to continue east of the pass to see whether it connected to where Rogers hoped it did. The Major had not brought enough food and they could go no farther.

After a mostly sleepless and miserable night, they raced down as soon as the sky showed the faintest lightening, sliding through the snow until they came upon the junction where their food was cached. They were delighted to discover that the four who had fallen the day before had managed to kill a caribou and were now lounging about a large fire roasting and smoking it.

There is no record of anyone ever having travelled over this pass before; Rogers gained the historical credit, but Albert and the ten unnamed Secwépemc are equally co-discoverers, given the hardships and dangers, and there is no chance any of them would have completed the mission without the support of the entire group. They descended back to the Columbia, where Rogers discharged eight of the men to return home, presumably with their letters to avoid being whipped and having their wages stolen by the local priest. He and Albert and the remaining two continued south to Fort Colville in Washington Territory, where they too were discharged to return home via the old fur trade routes.

Albert and Rogers continued to Spokane, where they bought horses and supplies, hired two men and rushed east, crossing back into Canada via northern Idaho along the Moyie River. They hired two more Secwépemc guides to take them farther north, where they ascended the Kootenay River and then descended the eastern leg of the Columbia and pressed on through Kananaskis Pass to the Bow River. There they met with a camp of railway surveyors and engineers on July 15, a mere two weeks after Rogers had promised to do so. One of the crew was the footloose youth Tom Wilson.

When he had heard of the recruitment drive for the exploratory survey crews for the CPR, the adventure-seeking Wilson sought a discharge from the NWMP at Fort Walsh, where he had been a recruit, and set off for Fort Benton, where Rogers had decreed the survey corps should congregate. He knew horses and was promptly hired as a packer. The *Benton Weekly Record* recorded on June 2, "The British flag was flying to-day, and as the sun shone upon the twenty odd new tents pitched upon the beautiful green flat, the scene was rather attractive. . . . Many of the party are young gentlemen of education from Toronto, Ontario and Winnipeg, while a number come from Minnesota and other parts of the United States." The trading firm I.G. Baker was, not surprisingly, outfitting the entire operation, which soon set off across the prairie in a dusty cavalcade of horses, wagons and marching people. They trundled northward and "without trouble or incident" arrived in Lethbridge, then called Coal Banks, a tiny settlement that consisted of a ferry and a small coal export operation. Since the sudden disappearance of the buffalo, incoming freight wagons had been leaving empty instead of piled with hides. The returning wagons needed some ballast weight to run smoothly, and so a demand developed in Montana for coal, being easy to mine from the hillside and easy to load. It was the beginning of the resource-extraction economy in the West.

The survey outfit continued across the prairie, unhitching the pack horses and freight horses to swim across the Oldman River, which was running high in the spring flood, while the wagons were wrapped in canvas and floated across, pulled by ropemen on each bank. The Highwood River, at the trading outpost of High River, was especially dangerous and frequently flooded, as its name suggests. A month later, on July 3, they forded the Bow River and hauled in, dusty and weary, at Fort Calgary, which at that time consisted of four log buildings—the NWMP fort, a mission, the Hudson's Bay Company post and the I.G. Baker premises. From there the surveyors proceeded west to Morley and then along what Wilson described as "a narrow Indian path" to the site of Old Bow Fort, up and down steep hills that made hauling wagons a dangerous and exhausting undertaking. When they were about six miles east of Bow River Gap, they stopped to construct a permanent base of operations and await Rogers. The only thing that concerned Wilson along the month-long journey was that on the expanse of grassland around Fort Macleod the "Blackfeet, Peigans and Bloods, while not displaying any serious hostility, worried us somewhat. They prowled around the camp at night and carried on petty thieving, particularly of tobacco, of which we had a good supply."

The once formidable Niisitapi were now merely "prowlers," looking in at the survey camp as the men sat around campfires, but unable to penetrate the community or economy of that new enterprise. They had no contact point or method of entry into the new economy taking shape around them. Wilson's campfire image, with the shadowy people looking in from the fringes, was a prescient metaphor for their exclusion from the changing world; unlike in the fur and hide trade, there was no role for them. These were the only Indigenous people whom the survey party encountered during their month-long journey across the Plains, yet a mere generation earlier mounted horsemen numbered in the tens of thousands, and no traveller from Fort Benton to Fort Calgary could expect to cross the land without encountering both buffalo and the buffalo hunters.

Although the rail crews did not witness it, the disappearance of the buffalo and the concomitant waves of disease, amplified by malnutrition and despondency, were then devastating most of the Indigenous communities across the prairies. One crew of surveyors returning south to Fort Benton at the end of the season was waylaid near the Highwood River by a band of warriors led by Crowfoot (Isapo-Muxika), and "the chief was in an ugly mood." The governor general of Canada, the Marquis of Lorne, had recently toured the prairies and held a ceremony at Fort Macleod. Crowfoot's belief was that the visiting dignitary had promised him certain presents that had not been received, so he demanded restitution from the survey party. When, not surprisingly, the surveyors couldn't produce the promised items, the chief and his warriors plundered their supplies. It was just one small incident indicative of the growing hardship and discontent that would soon culminate in a violent uprising.

AS HE TRAVELLED EAST to meet the survey crew, Rogers had tasked his nephew Albert with leading a pack train along the Columbia River to the mouth of the Kicking Horse River to ascend it east to the summit—a challenging task for a twenty-one-year-old whose first mountain foray had been earlier that summer with his uncle. The narrow, rocky gorge was deemed by most too treacherous for horses. Albert's party travelled high on the canyon walls, through "thick timber where we could not see a yard ahead . . . [and] stretches of deep deceptive moss that in places hid dangerous crevices and holes," across "rock and gravel slides that needed but a slight movement to start them rolling . . . [and] over huge boulders, where one pushed the other up, then was in turn pulled up." The route was so rocky, dangerous and convoluted that Albert and his two "Indians" became mired and lost, ran out of provisions and were on the verge of starvation when they met a party sent out to find them near the mouth of the Yoho River. They were a sorry sight, bedraggled and forlorn, having eaten nothing but a porcupine in two days.

The first thing the three weary men did was feast on a meal of "tea, bannock and boiled salt pork of the variety commonly known as sowbelly." Rogers came rushing down the trail, in a state of agitation over his nephew's well-being. "He was plainly choked with emotion," recalled Wilson, "then, as his face hardened again, he took an extra-vicious tobacco juice shot at the nearest tree and almost snarled . . . 'Well, you did get here, did you? You damn little cuss' following [*sic*] another juice eruption, he swung on his heel and shot over his shoulder, 'You're alright, are you? You damn little cuss.'" The others were shocked, but Albert knew his uncle. And "during the rest of the walk to camp, the furious activity of his uncle's jaws and the double-speed juice shots aimed at the vegetation indicated our leader's almost uncontrollable emotions."

The next spring Rogers, his nephew and six others returned to the region of the previous year's adventures, this time making their way up to the pass from east to west along the Beaver River. Once again Rogers had packed too little food and starvation loomed as a possibility should someone become injured or lost. They were forced to ignominiously retreat and try again in July, finally making the summit of the Selkirks, completing the circuit and observing the peak they had ascended the previous year. The trek was, as might be supposed, not an easy jaunt. The forest was thick and overgrown, the view entirely blocked, and the travel slow and dangerous, barely two miles a day on some days as they scrambled over numerous chutes where avalanches had pulverized the mighty trees. Beneath the brooding glaciers in what would later be called Glacier National Park, on July 24 they stood in a small meadow coloured with blooming wildflowers and named it, just as he had dreamed, Rogers Pass.

Later that same summer, young Tom Wilson, then clearing the route to Kicking Horse Pass, had his own adventures. While warding off the damp, huddled around a crackling campfire in the lodgepole pine forest along the Bow River, waiting out a rainstorm with a band of Stoney travellers and guides, he heard a thunderous rumble but could not see where it originated. One of the Stoney guides, Edwin Hunter (who also had the name Gold-Seeker because he had earlier guided a prospector to a promising copper deposit), told him that the rumbling came from one of the mighty glaciers that loomed above the "the lake of the little fishes." Hunter offered to take Wilson there, and the two men struggled through the forest on their horses until they emerged onto the shore of a magnificent turquoise lake set in an amphitheatre of rock and ice. "For some time," Wilson recalled, "we sat and smoked and gazed at the gem of beauty beneath the glacier. [Hunter] told me that higher up were two smaller lakes, one of which his people called the 'goat's looking glass,' as the goats came down to it to use as a mirror while they combed their beards."

Wilson immediately renamed the sublime lake Emerald Lake, considering it more apt than Little Fishes. It was later imperially named Lake Louise by the Geographical Society, after Princess Louise (Louisa Caroline Alberta), one of Queen Victoria's daughters, who was married to the governor general. (An unconventional aristocrat, in her role as viceregal consort she promoted the arts, higher education and women's rights. Having disliked Ottawa, she returned to England in 1881, and when her name was bestowed upon the province of Alberta in 1905, perhaps she infused the new province with some of her disapproving spirit.) Today "the lake of the little fishes" (such a pleasing name) is one of the most well-known tourist destinations in North America, with a spectacular château on the shore, and numerous breathtaking hiking trails, one of which ascends to Mirror Lake, and a world-famous ski resort nearby.

The next day, Rogers rode into their camp. "Blue Jesus!" he roared when he saw Wilson had returned for another season. "I knew you'd be back. You'll never leave these mountains again as long as you live. They've got you now." Rogers was mostly correct. Wilson set up a guiding and packing business in Morley in 1885 and later moved to Banff, the same year he married Minnie McDougall from Owen Sound, Ontario. They raised six children, and he was one of the most prominent guides in the region for decades thereafter.

In camp that night, Rogers confessed to Wilson that he still harboured doubts about the viability of Kicking Horse Pass and wondered about Howse Pass as an alternative. Moberly, of the 1860s survey crews, had claimed the better route was through Howse Pass, a little farther north. Anyone who has hiked Howse Pass can attest that it certainly seems easier to traverse than the treacherous grades and canyons of the Kicking Horse. Rogers and Wilson set off with some pack animals to investigate it themselves, to make sure of the situation so that Rogers wouldn't have the eternal shame of being responsible for a poor decision. They followed the Bow River as it turned north to its headwaters, and then pressed on to the intersection with the Saskatchewan River, with the intention to follow it west and up, over the height of land. But the track was tangled with deadfall, swampy, rocky and infused with pestering clouds of mosquitoes and blackflies. "Blue Jesus!" Rogers erupted one day. "We won't get through here to the Columbia in two weeks at this rate. A man carrying a pack on his back could travel twice as fast as we are doing. I'll give you a fifty dollar bonus if you'll go through alone on foot," he said to Wilson. "You ought to do it in ten days easy." The Major told Wilson that he would backtrack to the main crew and work his way around to meet Wilson by the Blaeberry River, which descends from Howse Pass to the Columbia Valley. Without the pack horses, Wilson was alone in the vast wilderness of what is now central western Banff National Park.

It proved to be "a hard road" of scrambling over deadfall, rocks and swollen rivers. Wilson spent days finding his bearings in the dense forest. The descent from the summit of Howse Pass "was even more difficult than the Kicking Horse. There were times when I could travel a mile in an hour. There were miles of deadfall six to eight feet in depth to be scrambled over and in traversing them one had to be very careful almost to feel one's way a foot at a time for a rolling log or breaking rotten one could easily have resulted in disaster for me." He feared that he would break a bone amidst the rockslides, canyons and gorges and then starve. But he eventually stumbled upon the Blaeberry River and travel became easier. By this time, his rations had dwindled to a single daily piece of bannock, so he tightened his belt and continued on to where he had agreed to meet Rogers, who would presumably have more food, or at least some oatmeal. When he did finally come upon a big campfire with Rogers and two others resting around it, Wilson just wanted to eat. Rogers had earlier been worried and was cursing that Wilson hadn't shown up on time: "If that boy don't show up what in hell will I do? No one but a fool would send a lad on such a trip alone, and no one but a fool would try to make it alone." Wilson's unfavourable report of Howse Pass put Rogers's mind at ease; his preferred route would pass through both Kicking Horse Pass and Rogers Pass. The Major rushed back to Montreal to deliver his enthusiastic news to Van Horne and George Stephen in person.

But Van Horne still had reservations despite Rogers's boasting; Rogers was a peculiar little man with foibles and peccadilloes that did not lend credibility to his claims. While Van Horne didn't doubt that a pass existed, and that Rogers had traversed it, he still wondered whether the man's rough wilderness eyeballing of the mountains would prove practicable for a railway or be more suitable as a pack-horse trail. Railways had specific requirements when it came to grade and obstructions, and Van Horne wanted to ensure, before millions of dollars were spent, that Rogers wasn't just being optimistic or prideful, since these characteristics had been evident in his character on other occasions. He decided to send out several survey engineers to verify Rogers's work, to get a second opinion before it was too late and the enterprise would be committed to. Two of these chosen individuals were Charles Shaw and James Hogg, who were prickly and inflexible, with high opinions of themselves, and they got into arguments with the intemperate Rogers, Wilson and others during the 1883 season.

That same season, Fleming and George Grant became travel companions again, twelve years after their first journey. They were also sent to verify a part of the route and to give a second opinion of the viability of Kicking Horse Pass and Rogers Pass before the expensive work of the railway proceeded beyond the point of no return. Fleming's book *England and Canada: A Summer Tour between Old and New Westminster*, published in 1884, is a detailed account of their journey along the route that the railway now follows. By then there existed a roughly cut wagon road west from Fort Calgary that followed the Bow River for a while before degenerating into a pack trail suitable for loaded horses, and finally into an old Indigenous trail that veered off over Kicking Horse Pass and down the Kicking Horse River to the Columbia River. There were markings on the trees, however, and teams of workers were busy sawing, hauling and clearing brush. Fleming and Grant were now middle-aged explorers, no longer as robust as they had been on their first survey trip. Fleming had been recuperating from stress-induced exhaustion in Europe for the past three years, and now, at fifty-six, although still in good shape, he was no longer so indomitable. Grant was now principal of Queen's University in Kingston and possessed a physical appearance that reflected his sedentary life.

Nevertheless, the descriptions of the route are revealing. The Kicking Horse trail wound "down and up gorges, hundreds of feet deep, amongst rocky masses, where the poor horses had to clamber as best they could amid sharp points and deep crevices, running the constant risk of a broken leg.... A series of precipices run sheer up from the boiling current to form a contracted canyon.... To look down [from the narrow, treacherous trail] gives one an uncomfortable dizziness, to make the head swim and the view unsteady, even to men of tried nerve." The steep Kicking Horse Pass was a dangerous obstacle; there was no way for engineers to construct a route with a grade that was safe for railways.

Farther west along the chosen route, ascending Rogers Pass, the trees dwarfed those in other regions—cedars four feet in diameter amazed the crew, while the "the rain continue[d] falling incessantly." Hauling heavy loads on their backs, made heavier by the water that soaked into them, left them "completely disheartened." The trail was littered with rotting fallen giants, slurping mulchy sections and skunk cabbage bogs, mist and flies. "The walking is dreadful, we climb over and creep under fallen trees of good size, and the men show that they feel the weight of their burdens. Their halts for rest are frequent. It is hot work for us all. The dropping rain from the bush and branches saturates us from above. Tall ferns, sometimes reaching to the shoulder, and devil's club, through which we had to climb our way, make us feel as if dragged through a horsepond, and our perspiration is that of a Turkish bath. We meet with obstacles of every description. The devil's club may be numbered by millions and they are perpetually wounding us with their spikes." But they weren't alone in their misery. During the summer of 1883, there were now dozens of men in camps clearing the route and occasionally revealing sections of land that would require expensive feats of engineering.

Fleming and Grant made a final observation of Howse Pass, pronouncing that Wilson's and Rogers's assessment was accurate and that the increased distance of about thirty miles would not compensate for the slightly gentler grade, especially since the route was committed to head west along the Bow River rather than farther north along the Saskatchewan River.

So even in the fall of 1883, as the tracks raced across the prairies toward the mountains, the final route was only determined at the last moment, after nearly two decades of exploring, surveying, travelling, near starvation, reversals, reinspections, several major reroutings and much political anguish, stress and gushers of money flowing into the ditch. And still not much of it had actually been built.

PART FOUR

THE CONSTRUCTION

CHAPTER SEVENTEEN

THEY WORKED UPON
THE RAILWAY

—

A s Rogers and the other surveyors—egos primed for battle, eyes with a downward hint of calculation as they grasped at posterity—quibbled and quarrelled over the exact and final placement of the route through the mountain passes, the construction of the track across the prairies progressed at an incredible rate, aided by a small army of labourers, some blessedly railway-friendly terrain and Van Horne's logistical genius.

Van Horne was anxious to complete the prairie section fast to earn government subsidies on this comparatively cheap and easy segment, so that the revenues could be used to fund the work on the more expensive and technically challenging zones around Lake Superior and through the Rockies. The CPR needed to avoid having its limited capital tied up in non-revenue-producing activities until the end. There was no possible way to generate revenue along the virtually uninhabited 1,500-kilometre stretch north of Lake Superior through the rugged Canadian Shield; there was no agricultural or settlement potential at

the time, and therefore no real estate potential. Railways feasted or
starved on volume—of people, of goods needing to get to them and
of the surplus products of those people's labour needing to be transported to distant markets. To aid efficiency in earning the government performance grants, Van Horne even employed a "flying wing"
of mobile rail workers under his direct command whom he dispatched
to challenging sections to get them completed during each year's
work season.

The logistics of the immense undertaking were tangled and complex.
Steel from New York and New Orleans was shipped by rail through
St. Paul. Timber for ties came from distant regions that had bigger,
easily accessible trees. Quarried stone for bridges was barged to rail
depots. Food for a small army of men and animals, clothing, materials
for temporary accommodations, coal, tools, survey equipment and
other miscellaneous items were all brought in from the U.S., since the
St. Lawrence was still frozen in the early season and gave no access to
the lands of the northwest. The "end of track," as its leading edge was
called, was a mobile town, buzzing with activity and noise; grading
crews, tracklayers and carpenters toiled amidst mountains of crates,
rails, ties, spikes, pyramids of gravel, wood pilings, square timber and
food. "End of Track," remembered railway worker P. Turner Bone in
1883, "was something more than just the point to which track had been
laid. It was a real live community, a hive of industry, in which teamsters,
tracklayers, blacksmiths, carpenters, executive officers, and other trades
and professions all had a part. They had their quarters on a train com-
posed of cars loaded with rails and other track material, followed by
large boarding-cars for the workmen, and by sundry smaller cars for the
executives. This train was pushed ahead as track-laying proceeded; and
at the end of a day's work, it might be three or four miles from where
it was on the morning."

One incredibly productive day near present-day Strathmore, Alberta, saw 6.4 miles, or nearly ten kilometres, of track laid in a single day. By the end of the 1883 season, Van Horne had orchestrated the track to cover the entire prairie section from Winnipeg to west of Fort Calgary, along the Bow River into the mountains. The sheer length of new track was staggering; it had required perhaps ten million cubic yards of dirt and thousands of timber posts and pilings used for building bridges, culverts and other structures in the roadbed to be constantly shuffled ahead of the end of track. Building the line came in stages: once the surveyors demarcated the precise line to minimize the grade and the need for bridges and trestles, unskilled Irish immigrants, called navvies, cleared the trees and brush from the railway route. They were followed by grading crews, who controlled horse teams dragging scrapers with plows. They in turn were followed by men with shovels who elevated the roadbed slightly above grade and filled in hollows.

Tracklayers laid wooden railway ties across the graded roadbed approximately two feet apart. Across these, labourers placed heavy steel rails around thirty-nine feet (twelve metres) long. Others then pounded spikes in place with mighty sledges. More labourers shovelled gravel around the structure to help keep it stable. Later crews installed telegraph lines, signals, sidings and switches. It was back-breaking physical labour with picks, shovels and wheelbarrows. Like convoys of ants, horse and mule carts trundled back and forth as the end of track moved west. Van Horne was frequently seen marching along the track, puffing away on his cigar, his substantial girth no apparent impediment to his endurance and frenetic energy. Yet he caused much grumbling among the sub-managers, whom he constantly harassed in colourful language to increase the speed of construction. Nevertheless, he ensured that good, if simple, food in abundant quantity was something to look forward to at the end of a workday, when the activity quieted, campfires were lit and men relaxed into the starry evening, often too exhausted for any other activity.

The work was done quickly and roughly, the prime motive being to get as much done as possible, no matter the initial quality, to trigger the promised government grants, to keep up enthusiasm and momentum and to engender the feeling that the workers were part of something momentous and that they would see it completed in the not too distant future, rather than a nebulous concept of nation building whose completion would be for the next generation to celebrate. The speed of completed track across the prairies was indeed impressive, beyond the imagining of nearly everyone except Van Horne. But as a consequence of the rush, actually riding on a train over these early tracks was an adventure in itself. "We had planned to do some office work on the way," wrote P. Turner Bone, "but—as the track had not as yet been ballasted— the train rolled like a ship in a choppy sea, so that it was impossible to do any draughting; and we had just to pass the time as best we could. At times, following a clatter which sounded like broken dishes, as the car gave an extra roll, we could hear a burst of strong language coming from the cook. Thus we were not without entertainment on the way."

As fall slowly turned to winter in 1883, the aspen leaves yellow and the peaks snow-dusted in October, the end of track approached the summit of Kicking Horse Pass, where the hard and challenging work would begin. One of the advance brush gangs clearing the path for graders inadvertently set a fire. Young CPR track-preparation surveyor Charles Aeneas Shaw was in the vanguard nearing the summit when the fire disrupted his routine.

> It had been a very dry season, and there were piles of brush and timber all along the line; the whole valley was soon in a blaze. Our camp was in a small open spot near the Bow River, which at this point was quite wide and had a small island in it. So we

made a raft and ferried over our blankets, some supplies and cooking utensils. Everything else at the camp site we piled in a heap, with wet tents and some earth on top. Then we swam to the island.

The fire burned for days. It was pretty hot, and the smoke was bad for a time, but we, our camp outfit and supplies came through safely, also our horses, which we had driven to a small meadow close to the river. But some of the men and teams working on the line were burned.

That fall also saw some of the first signs of problems on the prairies with the hunger among Indigenous peoples, now that the buffalo were nearly extinct. East of Blackfoot Crossing the Niisitapi demanded rations that at first the work crews were unable to supply. In retaliation, they allegedly began removing survey stakes and scattering them over the prairie, or making off with the workhorses and then offering to help find them for a reward of food—manufacturing a need for their services in a desperate attempt to insert themselves into the economic order. Tea and beef were the items in greatest demand. Later that fall, Van Horne enacted a policy of increasing food distribution to maintain good relations, even if the Canadian government seemed unconcerned or even deliberately obstructive.

RAILWAY WORKERS WERE OFTEN CALLED navvies, a shortened form of "navigators," after the canal builders in England. As the work similarly relied on great numbers of physical labourers using hand tools and domestic animals to dig ditches, make mounds and level ground, the term was soon applied to the railway workers constructing the initial lines, often far removed from any towns or services. Work conditions were almost always worse under contractors than under the CPR itself, and didn't improve until well into the twentieth century. Many accounts have been written of the harsh conditions, foul food and abusive labour practices common in the work camps, where men lived in canvas tents or crowded into hastily constructed, unventilated, windowless bunkhouses infested with lice and rats. "I wish you could have seen those men," wrote Anglican missionary J. Burgon Bickersteth at the time. "They came in covered with mud from head to foot, and proceeded to divest themselves of their wet boots and socks and overalls, which they hung up from every conceivable corner. Some put on dry socks, but most stayed with bare feet. The floor was soon as muddy as it was outside, with men coming in and out, and, of course, everyone spat where they wished." Everyone slept in their clothes, and usually the men could wash only once a week, on Sunday, so rashes and infections were common complaints. Nor was there any running water, and the only facilities were poorly dug pit toilets.

Food, unless Van Horne was around, was monotonous but plentiful, but also unbalanced, consisting in large part, especially during shoulder seasons, of beans, bread, hard cheese and partially spoiled meat. "There must have been 200 of us and more [crammed in the cookhouse]," according to one worker. "There was plenty of food on the table, but unless one was very hungry it would be difficult to eat a good meal, because the conditions under which it is served are distinctly unattractive. One man sticks his fork into the potatoes, another puts the spoon he has just had in his mouth into the sugar, or dumps a dirty plate right down on to the cake. Everyone eats as if his life depended on it, only raising his head to ask a neighbour to pass something else."

"I suppose, dear reader," wrote an early twentieth-century prairie homesteader who also worked as a navvy, "you think we were a lot of brutes driving other brutes (horses and mules) and I suppose we were, but by such practices was the west opened up and developed. There was a saying about 60 years ago that in every mile of the grade of the old CPR was the grave of a working stiff. The bad water on the prairie took a heavy toll of life." The navvy's life was particularly harsh, demeaning and dangerous for those who didn't speak English, which was a considerable portion of the workforce. Another worker described the death of a young Russian man, who spoke no English, on the Grand Trunk Pacific Railway as it pressed into the foothills en route to Jasper in the early twentieth century. "So there we left him [on the bank of the Athabasca River], and another is added to the number of those who never return. It is a tragedy which is enacted over and over again out here. Pioneer work demands its toll; and nowhere a heavier one than in railway construction."

And yet, despite the hardships, the human spirit rose to find joy in even the bleakest of situations. "We were a strange gathering at night-time," Morley Roberts wrote of his time on the work crews. "We sang at times strange melancholy unknown ditties of love in the forests, songs of Michigan or Wisconsin redolent of pine odour . . . or some other English sea-songs. Then we would tell each other stories or yarns."

One prescient move by Van Horne that probably saved countless lives and sped the rate of construction immeasurably was his insistence from the outset that alcohol be completely prohibited in labour camps. Given the nature of the workforce and the living and working conditions, drinking could have been a problem of staggering dimension. Bored, exhausted men would have sought out hard liquor to ease their discomfort and relieve the tedium. Not only would they have squandered their wages, but the lingering effects of a night's spree, perhaps even drinking on the job, would have led to accidents, fights and groggy men right when precision teamwork was required. Of course, smugglers rose to meet the demand for booze. Cans of vegetables were drained and filled with whiskey, as were nitroglycerine and kerosine canisters. One woman smuggler pretended late-stage pregnancy, the soon-to-be-born bambino being in reality a rubber sack of hooch. Doubtless much booze made its way to the work camps and was eagerly consumed, but for the few years of rapid construction, enough of it was blockaded that the worst of the consequences were averted.

WHILE VAN HORNE PERSONALLY supervised the construction of the railway across the prairies and through the northern forests along Lake Superior as it pushed west across the country, the track west of the mountains that began at the coast and worked eastward was managed by Andrew Onderdonk, a thirty-seven-year-old engineer and construction contractor who had recently completed the San Francisco seawall and parts of the first subway tunnels under New York's East River, among other projects. Beginning in 1879, Onderdonk and a group of American financiers had won four major contracts to push the railway from Port Moody east to Yale, the head of navigation on the Fraser River, then through the Fraser Canyon and Thompson River Canyon approximately two hundred kilometres northeast into the Interior, to Savona's Ferry on the western shore of Kamloops Lake. Onderdonk won the initial contracts from the Canadian government, and later contracts directly from the CPR, primarily because he was the head of a well-financed coalition of American backers. Unfortunately for them, the initial contracts inherited from the government were $1.5 million below even his own estimates of the cost. How he would complete his proposed work was an open question.

Onderdonk moved his family north to Yale and managed the challenging work until 1885. Like Van Horne, he was a master of logistics and planning. He was tall, impeccably dressed even when in the field, and handsomely well groomed, with a drooping moustache that would have made Jerry Potts envious. He was an even-tempered, collegial, blandly genial man of eastern establishment pedigree, from a Dutch-Anglo family dating back two centuries with a distinguished presence in commerce, government and medicine. Unlike many of his peers in the railway business he was not a colourful personality, preferring a quiet life of social respectability. An engineer by training, he knew his business and had, by his mid-thirties, already earned a reputation for competence and trustworthy, dependable opinions. He took on challenging projects once he had assessed their feasibility, not before, and as a result he had strong financial backing.

A man like Onderdonk was exactly what the CPR needed to bolster its credibility and stabilize its skittish lenders. So naturally Charles Tupper, minister of public works in Macdonald's government, bent the rules a little to secure his participation. His was not the lowest bid but he was the one they believed could actually complete the job. As the railway engineer Henry Cambie noted succinctly, "No such mountain work had ever been attempted in Canada before, and we were confronted by new problems almost every day." But Onderdonk was an engineering contractor who won the bid to design and build the track according to an agreed-upon set of criteria; he was not directly employed by the CPR or the federal government. And unlike Van Horne, his job would be over once the track was constructed, and he would move on to other projects, with no role in managing the operational railway.

While Van Horne was pushing the track west across the prairie at a rapid pace—an astonishing 1,450 kilometres in under a year and a half—and somewhat more slowly around the northern bulge of Lake Superior, it barely progressed at all east of Yale in the Fraser Canyon. The terrain was ridiculously challenging for a railway. Onderdonk faced four mighty tunnels just out of town, followed by twenty-three more tunnels within thirty kilometres, one of them nearly 480 metres long. The rock was granite, and despite using compressed-air drills for boreholes and dynamite from a factory in Yale—which Onderdonk had had built for the purpose—the thunderous explosions cleared rock at a rate of barely two metres a day. It took a year and a half of continuous dynamite explosions to blast the first handful of tunnels before a significant length of track could be laid. In addition, the Fraser Canyon had steep sides with precipitous drops to the foaming water below. Mountains rose to nearly 2,500 metres on each side. The line clung to the cliffs, roughly following the route of the Cariboo Highway, built decades earlier during the gold rush and still the only viable commercial transportation route to the interior of the province. Just this one section northeast of Yale would eventually require six hundred trestles, bridges and retaining walls, totalling around forty million board feet of lumber.

One of Onderdonk's most competent assistants was Michael James Haney. Born in Ireland, his family had immigrated to New York State when he was a boy, and he eventually drew on his love of mathematics to become a railway engineer. He worked his way west and north, becoming a senior construction foreman responsible for rivers, gorges and cliffs and anything else challenging or unconventional. Once he saw the terrain, he knew from experience that no railway was ever going to run the Fraser without a lot of infrastructure, all of which in those days had to be built with wood. One of his first actions was to construct a steam-powered sawmill, specially configured to process the large timbers needed for trestles. Rather than trying to produce the materials for each section of the project on-site, he set up a sort of prefab construction facility that could turn out custom woodwork according to detailed measurements submitted by field crews, to be shipped out to them for installation. Such logistical improvements vastly improved the operation's efficiency.

The old Cariboo Road could not be shut down, of course. It was in constant use by mule trains, stagecoaches and horses, all while dynamite explosions were sending enormous rockslides crashing into the canyon. The new railway also would cling to the cliffs of the canyon, suspended like a porch above the foaming waters below. Not surprisingly, there were numerous accidents along narrow sections where passing was impossible for the huge teams of horses hauling supplies and equipment from the mines, or passengers in stagecoaches. Even while blasting continued, men dangled from the cliffs above the Fraser, hammering together wooden beams that were lowered on pulley systems, and drilling holes, setting explosives and scampering up to escape the blast. This was downright foolhardy from a safety point of view. Apparently the Indigenous workers were near fearless in their embrace of this rock work, as were the Chinese. There were many deaths and maimings. Demand for speed was so great that there was sometimes no time to transform the nitroglycerine into dynamite, resulting in many unplanned explosions.

"The difficulty of keeping this road open can only be appreciated by people who have seen prairie schooners," Cambie recalled. "These usually consisted of two wagons, coupled together and drawn by nine yoke of oxen or teams of mules, the whole well over 100 feet long. It should not be difficult to realize what these meant going round curves. I remember upon one occasion near old Spuzzum suspension bridge that a blast had been fired, filling all the road. A fine old fellow named Dave McBeth, who was well known in British Columbia and who died in Vancouver a few years ago, was foreman. He got the slide partly cleared away when a coach came along. . . . Among the loose stuff a rock, of which Dave was unaware, had been left, and the coach, in which happened to be Judge McCreight, upset. The judge was irritated and told Dave, much to the amusement of the other passengers, that if he was ever brought before him he would have no compunction in condemning him to be hanged for his carelessness in allowing such an accident to happen."

The work was so dangerous that within the first six months of his contract, Onderdonk, facing an overflowing hospital in Yale, commissioned an expansion to accommodate the influx of injuries, mostly from falling boulders crushing people, but also from the usual round of construction accidents inherent to large numbers of men in imperfect work conditions dealing with large draft animals, heavy tools and explosives on unstable ground.

———

THE MOUNTAINOUS LAND covered in giant trees that he beheld from the deck of the creaking sailing ship had long loomed large in the imagination of his people. Dukesang Wong was one of hundreds of thousands who had made the dangerous month-long voyage east across the vast Pacific Ocean, in search of opportunity and to escape the chaos, war, poverty and famine that racked China in the mid-nineteenth century. Now his ship, a small Christian missionary vessel, was lying in quarantine until the crowded passengers, filthy and weary and malnourished, could disembark. He railed against this apparently futile health measure with his characteristic logic and defiance: "We, who hold cleanliness so high and propriety so dear, to have the kinds of diseases that those white authorities say—it is totally unworthy of them. Left here in the squalor of this deck as if we are animals, even less than dogs!" In truth, he had little knowledge of infectious disease, like nearly everyone else at the time. Quarantine was the only health measure that was routinely enacted, just as the Irish had been kept quarantined in Montreal not too many years earlier.

A philosophical and contemplative man, Wong was much at odds with his fellow passengers, all young men whom he called "the working peasantry," who were illiterate, unlike himself, one of the few educated people aboard the ship. They were from different regions of China and spoke various dialects. "The poor labourers sit on deck and sing," he wrote, "expressing more of their sorrows in their untrained wailing voices. They express their emotions so much: it is shameful for them and for me to hear them."

Wong faced his future with stoicism, optimistic about his prospects. It was during the maddening lockdown of quarantine that he had time to truly contemplate his predicament. Before he had boarded the ship in Canton, he had mused: "It has been said that the land to which I am now headed is wild and uncivilized, and that people kill each other daily . . . there surely must be some areas where it is not so barbaric." But as he waited on the deck with time on his hands and barely contained anxiety, he pondered the rumours that he had heard during the voyage. "We hear tales of wild and crazy events outside town. I doubt the truth of these tales," he naively assured himself.

Soon, however, he realized that Portland, Oregon, was not the place of comfort and prosperity that many imagined. "The misery I see daily disturbs my thoughts, and I find it difficult to think about anything except my companions' suffering in this new land to which we all so desired to come." There was not enough work nearby, the food was poor, and it was freezing cold by the winter of 1881. Wong and his compatriots huddled around fires for warmth and dreamed of escaping the "degrading treatment of the white people in the town." Portland was wild and lawless, a part of the American frontier with few regulations and many wanderers and itinerant labourers. One evening he witnessed "a man being violently beaten by another of his own kind," and was astonished that no one stepped in to stop it. "I could not believe what my eyes were seeing. There were white people standing around and not one of them moved to stop the beater. Surely there are no manners and rules here."

"Our people would talk through differences and hear each other, no matter how grave the problem," he told himself, "but those white people fight and die in disorganized combat. Such is their law and order, such is their barbaric justice. A man near me said that it was their way and only fair, the honor code of their traditions. . . . It is like the tales of the sages, when settling of differences was done in ancient China by survival of physical strength and not by an arbitrator." But while the new land was proving to be a shock and a disappointment, Wong had plenty of time to brood over his own less than ideal past that had brought him there at the age of thirty-five. His homeland had a veneer of civility that concealed an equally brutal system.

Wong had been born into privileged Mandarin aristocratic ease, with an apparently delightful childhood until the fateful day when his life's path—of personal advancement and a lofty place in the social order— was derailed by tragedy. His father was a magistrate, and in a particular land dispute he decided in favour of one family over another. There were accusations of corruption. At the public banquet hosted by the benefiting family, a servant was bribed to put poison in the magistrate's food, and he agonizingly expired over a period of a few hours, his fingernails displaying the telltale black of arsenic. "I must continually remember only him," Wong wrote of his father, "but I can only remember the black nails of his fingers and they torment my sleep."

The local families turned against the Wongs, destroying their honour and status. Their properties and entitlements were forfeited, while no action was taken against the poisoner. Within the year, Wong's mother had committed suicide, his sisters were married off beneath their station, and young Dukesang was cast adrift, spending the next decade as an itinerant tutor of the Confucian classics, a job considered far beneath his station in the hierarchical society. All his petitions to restore his father's, and hence his family's, honour were rebuffed by the imperial court. The humiliation was unbearable. He concluded that his prospects would never improve and so chose to "venture to that country they call 'the Land of the Golden Mountains.'"

Mid- to late nineteenth-century China was beset by turmoil. The Opium Wars and the Taiping Rebellion caused tens of millions of deaths. With a growing population and not enough farmland to provide sufficient food, disruptions in imports of manufactured goods such as cloth, as well as floods, sea pirates and bandits in the countryside making travel and commerce riskier, the declining social stability resulted in staggering levels of poverty and starvation. Taxes and land rents rose, and vast numbers of displaced peasants migrated to Canton, one of the country's largest cities, to search for work. Competition for jobs amid the crumbling economy and political instability was so fierce that many, like Wong, turned to labour brokers and sold themselves into servitude. Some left to work in the gold rushes, some to guano mines in Peru, some to coal mines or farms. They especially were sent to build railways in Canada, the U.S., Australia and New Zealand.

In return for their passage overseas, or a lump-sum payment to their families, they found themselves toiling in low-paid, low-skilled jobs, hoping to earn enough money to build a better life for themselves and their families. The labour brokers typically took a cut of their salary. Many planned to bring over their wives and families once they were established. Wong contracted for a young wife before he departed; Lin was a child when he left, and he reasoned he had plenty of time to make a home before arranging for her journey across the ocean. Such workers tended to keep to themselves. They did not speak the language and, owing to the hostile welcome they often received, they had no easy way to learn it or the local customs.

Wong was offered employment farther north, in a place the Chinese immigrants called Saltwater City. New Westminster was then a chaotic boom town of wooden buildings and boardwalks over muddy streets that boasted about 1,200 people. It had sprung up during the gold rush and was now flourishing again with the rush of railway construction. Wong was one of approximately 17,000 Chinese men who were labour-ers in the scarcely populated interior of British Columbia between 1881 and 1884, most dwelling in ragged shantytowns along the rail lines. It certainly wasn't the land of great opportunity they had imagined, but they persevered and struggled to make a life for themselves—a lonely, hard life with few prospects to advance their situation. They were often met with hostility and ill treatment, and, lacking English, they were at the mercy of sometimes unscrupulous employers and merchants.

There was already a significant Chinese community in B.C., par-ticularly in Victoria, dating to the 1850s gold rush. In those years and immediately afterward, reception of the Chinese had been less hostile. But racism had increased in the intervening years. There were people of many backgrounds kicking about B.C. by the 1880s, yet the Chinese seemed too alien even to others of disparate backgrounds—in language, in dress, their hair in a braid, or queue, and eating unusual foods. Some of the stigma attaching to the new Chinese migrants stemmed from their backgrounds as semi-indentured servants and their lack of English; many never bothered to learn the language. They also worked for lower wages, as sometimes negotiated by local representatives of the labour brokers back in China, which inflamed the fear that they would take jobs and reduce wages for everyone, angering the unions and politicians like Amor De Cosmos.

Wong was quickly singled out for his education and his English skills—though he admitted that "English is hard to speak"—and was elected to be the spokesman for his railway work crew. But the people he worked with and was supposed to represent spoke in their "village language," which he also found "hard to understand." Not at home in either world, he must have led a lonely life. Only the hope for a better future could have propelled him on.

Nevertheless, when Wong first set eyes on the terrain through which he and his countrymen were supposed to build a railway, the Fraser River Canyon northeast of Yale, he was staggered with disbelief. "The people working with me are good, strong men. There are many of us working here, but the laying of the railroad progresses very slowly. It seems we move two stones a day! And they want this railroad built across these high mountains, some two thousand miles! Even over the plains of our homeland, such railways took over a generation to build, so I can imagine these white people will face failed dreams."

CHAPTER EIGHTEEN

GOLD MOUNTAIN

———

When Onderdonk first disembarked from a ship in Victoria harbour in the spring of 1880, he was welcomed ashore by a delegation from the Anti-Chinese Association. They were concerned that his plan to construct the railway would involve bringing in Chinese labourers, whom they feared, rightly as it turned out, would be paid less than the prevailing rates paid to white workers. The Workingmen's Protective Association, the province's first union, had formed two years earlier, in 1878, and had focused most of its efforts toward expelling the Chinese from what they believed to be their land, and they weren't above intimidating prospective employers. In 1879, Noah Shakespeare, a future mayor of Victoria and member of the legislative assembly, had founded the Anti-Chinese Association as a group with the same objective. They wanted instead to import British railway workers and have them settle in the province afterward, since they considered them more culturally compatible with the existing population. But workers from Britain would demand salaries that

Onderdonk knew would make impossible completion of the railway under the terms imagined by the federal government.

Nonetheless, before he had even started work in Yale, Onderdonk had promised to first employ white labourers from British Columbia, then somehow transport some French Canadian workers from eastern Canada, then look to the U.S. before searching for Indigenous workers, and only as a last resort would he contract with labour brokers to import Chinese workers. Who knows what he was actually thinking, but the Anti-Chinese Association was at least temporarily mollified. At the time, there were fewer than forty thousand white people, of either European or North American descent or birth, living in the entire province. Almost all of them, of course, were themselves immigrants. The labourers who worked on the railway were almost exclusively male, and there were simply not enough young men to build the railway even if Onderdonk could hire them from every other industry, such as gold and coal mining, fishing and fish canning, and the merchants supplying them. White workers brought in from the U.S. didn't stay long because of middling wages and the harsh conditions in remote locales. Many, if not most, young Indigenous men in the region, the Sto:lo, or Lower Fraser River Salish, also worked laying the rails, doing masonry or supplying timber, but they were not universally enthusiastic and wouldn't solve the labour shortage either.

Onderdonk knew that Chinese workers would be necessary, since he estimated he might need many thousands of labourers to complete the job. There already were several thousand Chinese in B.C., men who had crossed the Pacific during the mid-century gold rushes in California, the Fraser River and the Cariboo. In May 1882, Macdonald informed the House of Commons, after yet another request from Amor De Cosmos to restrict Chinese immigration, "If you wish to have the railway finished within any reasonable time, there must be no such step against Chinese labor. . . . At present it is simply a question of alternatives—either you must have this labor or you cannot have the railway." But Macdonald, who strongly identified as culturally British, also bowed to public pressure and declared the Chinese to be "an alien race in every sense, that would not and could not be expected to assimilate with our Arian population."

The anti-Chinese sentiment arose principally from the downward pressure on wages, economic competition that correlated to an identifiable group. Most Chinese immigrants at the time did not initially plan to remain in Gold Mountain and so devoted little effort to changing their dress or customs to adapt to the local cultural norms or to learn English. This in turn emphasized their distinctiveness and rendered them easier to exploit, since they did not understand the local traditions, laws and customs. During the gold rush, Victoria, and B.C. generally, hosted a bewildering array of customs and traditions, but by the 1870s and 1880s there was a shift toward a European, and particularly English-speaking, identity. What began as an economic conflict soon morphed into a cultural one, or, as is common, the cultural element was added to provide morally sanctimonious cover for a formerly bread-and-butter issue, which then became a self-fulfilling prophecy of racist condescension.

Newspaper editorials sneered at the cultural differences in an almost comical manner, depicting Chinese in a sinister, mocking caricature with slanting eyes, exaggerated braids, cringing posture and coarsely distorted features. Eventually this culminated in the "yellow peril" propaganda of the later nineteenth century throughout North America, associating Chinese with crime, gambling and opium. The vote in B.C. elections was barred to Chinese and Indigenous people in 1872, and after 1878 Chinese were prohibited from working on government projects, cutting out a large source of often higher-paying work. In contrast, Chinese people could vote in elections in Manitoba and could also practise as doctors.

But Onderdonk had hired and worked with thousands of Chinese labourers when constructing the Central Pacific Railroad in the United States. They were good, reliable workers and he never had any problems with them as a group. He also knew that they worked for $1 a day while white labourers were paid $1.50. The math was incontrovertible. Chinese work camps were also more agile and could decamp and move on to the next segment of construction in less than half the time it took other workers, and with little fuss. They generally supplied their own cooks and paid for their own food. Onderdonk did hire several thousand white workers and an unknown number of Indigenous men (who were superior rock and timber workers but were inconsistent in their loyalty and tended to leave when it suited them rather than when the work was complete), but he also brought in Chinese railway workers from the U.S. And he requested permission from the federal government to import workers directly from southern China.

Since there was still a labour shortage, the government allowed the CPR to contact labour brokers in China and arrange for the importation of labourers, similar to today's temporary foreign workers who power Canada's agricultural sector. Starting in 1882, the first of ten shiploads of men arrived, bringing about six thousand immigrants in all, who were unloaded in Victoria and sent up the Fraser River to Yale on smaller boats. Over the next five years many thousands more Chinese came to B.C., perhaps seventeen thousand in total, at any given time making up perhaps two-thirds of the railway workforce in the province. To impoverished men who had barely been able to earn two dollars a month in China, a dollar for a day's labour, even though a third less than the going rate for non-Chinese labour in B.C., seemed like a good opportunity—not that most of them had any choice in the matter. Nevertheless, some money was frequently sent back home to support their families during the turbulent times of poverty and starvation.

Exporting the labour of peasants was a well-established practice in China, and the men who signed up paid forty dollars and 2.5 per cent of their wages to the brokers, who had local agents in B.C. and elsewhere. The brokers promised to look after the welfare of the men they enlisted but never truly fulfilled their obligations once the men were on-site, leaving them to fend for themselves in a world for which they were wholly unprepared. They had no idea what to expect, what the climate would be or where they would live and work. It must have been a frightening prospect, but it puts into perspective how bad life must have been for them in China.

If the work was brutal, hard and dangerous for the navvies, it was even worse for the Chinese workers, who were called coolies. The Chinese were given the most dangerous tasks, involving dynamite, tunnelling and cliff work. It would be illegal for anyone to work or live like that today, but because the economy was poor and governments had no resources or infrastructure for social programs, there was little option for many of these people. Technology was primitive, food production inefficient and distribution hampered by the fact that, ironically, a railway hadn't yet been completed.

At least six hundred Chinese were killed working on the railway in B.C. alone, and many others were injured in blasting accidents or died from diseases, including scurvy. Unlike their fellow railway workers, the Chinese supplied their own clothing and transportation to and from the job sites and provided their own, mostly inadequate, medical services and food. Representatives of the Chinese labour contractors organized the men into work divisions of around three dozen each, which included two cooks and a bookkeeper. A white, English-speaking foreman or boss directed their daily labours and communicated with the general contractors.

Despite their second-class status, the Chinese workers were not always docile. When they were shortchanged on pay, they stopped work until every penny was paid. Petty interference with their customs, including tea drinking, was met with a stony refusal to work. There were occasionally conflicts between them and agitators who harassed them.

When a Chinese worker was injured or died, often in explosive accidents or crushed by rocks, no compensation was paid. Often their families in China were not even notified. To the railway magnates, board of directors, dreamers and financiers, these accidents were distant things that affected other, lesser people. Decisions were made. Instructions were issued. And people suffered and died. These orders were not given by immoral men necessarily, but by absentee ones. This is a problem whenever decision making occurs far from the physical work, where the bonds of humanity are weakened not only by social distance but by geographical distance as well; where the effects of one's decisions are not directly observed or felt and the balance sheet tells the only tale they hear. Other times the need to get the work done before financial collapse meant safety was secondary. Sometimes the technology didn't exist to do things more safely; it was an era when people died early from all sorts of ailments, from disease to infection, that are now easily treated with modern medicine, and it was still routine for women to die in childbirth and for men to die in all manner of farming and industrial accidents. Although accident and death rates were significantly higher for Chinese workers, they were often excluded from the official calculations and reports, almost as if they didn't exist, in order to keep the official tally of death and dismemberment down to an acceptable level.

Medical issues were not merely a minor concern. The *Yale Sentinel* reported in 1883: "Here in British Columbia along the line of the railway, the Chinese workmen are fast disappearing under the ground. No Medical attention is furnished nor apparently much interest felt for these poor creatures. We understand that Mr. Onderdonk declines interfering, while the Lee Chuck Co., that brought the Chinamen from their native land, refused . . . to become responsible for doctors and medicine."

The Chinese railway camps were characterized by squalor, with dilapidated tents or leaky cabins to shelter them from the elements, their food cooked over open fires, their meagre diet of rice and dried salmon enlivened by hot tea. Food was frequently poor for most in this era, without electricity or refrigeration or distribution systems to get imports into remote regions, especially in the winter. There were no fresh fruits or vegetables at the work sites, and this proved particularly harsh for the Chinese, who could afford little. Because they frequently moved camp, at their own expense, they had difficulty obtaining or consuming sufficient calories with so little time for gardening. Many tried to grow small portable gardens with some familiar vegetables like bok choy, but scurvy was still common. Hundreds died in the work camps every year from diseases and malnutrition, the malnutrition making them more susceptible to the diseases, especially in cold, wet winters. The Chinese labour agents provided no meaningful assistance, and neither did the railway management under Onderdonk. In fact, during the three winter months each year when the weather made work impossible, the Chinese, and the others too, were often discharged where they were, leaving them to live in destitution, panning for gold or trying to find jobs in tiny villages that had no real economy. Many could barely exist on the meagre wages once taxes, food, clothing, footwear, shelter, equipment, medicine and doctors' fees were accounted for, yet they still remitted sums to families back in China.

WONG TRAVELLED THIS LONELY, dangerous path following the railway for many years, enduring the brutality, hardships, indignities and snubs, the poor diet, freezing winters and brutal, back-breaking work. His diary records his experience in clear, simple prose. "My soul cries out. I wish I had never experienced such bad days as those in which we now live. Many of our people have been so very ill for such a long time, and there has been no medicine nor good food to give them. Even the strongest of us are weak without medicine to fight against these diseases, which spread very rapidly. It is such a sorrowful sight. The white doctor has told us the illnesses come from lack of fresh food, but we cannot grow any fresh food, as all of us, including the white people, are moving constantly . . . The good doctor has gone to the larger town in search of better food for the very ill, but I am afraid that the medicines will not arrive here to these poor gutter-shelters. . . . These are troubled times for us Chinese. There has been word among the employing company that we are not good workers and do not work enough for the schedules and plans of the railway owners. How does one work when so ill?"

Contrary to Wong's worries, the Chinese were by all accounts exemplary workers. According to the contractors who dealt with them, they put in long hours, performed the most dangerous jobs generally without complaint, took care of their own injured and their own cooking and were scrupulously honest.

According to Wong, many Chinese workers became so disillusioned and broken by the experience that they turned to "spending their days in the opium shacks, with little food and even less strength. This is a bad omen. . . . So many of us Chinese suffered and died recently; I cannot recount them all." Another time he observed, "There is some fresh food for us and enough fish to fill our stomachs. So many have suffered from diseases and have been working their skin off, appearing more like skeletons, so sick without food and rest. Even the fresh food here will have little effect on some of the poor frail bodies, but all of us are greatly relieved."

On one occasion Wong recalled a theft. "Today Hsin Wun Ming resisted a young white man's attempt to rob him of his mother's newest jade piece, a beautiful stone. Hsin Wun Ming resorted to hitting the thief. When the young robber awoke, it amused us all how he stared at us in response to the offer of some chicken congee. The white man is always afraid of our food. The young devil rushed away as if we were offering him poison . . . it was laughable to see him scurry away."

Matthew Baillie Begbie, the itinerant judge from the gold rush era and the first justice of the Supreme Court of British Columbia, still patrolled the Interior, trying to keep the peace as best he could in a land that continued to change chaotically even decades after the first gold rush. He was frequently aghast at the ill treatment of the Chinese, the taunting, pranks, semi-organized mob beatings and attacks on their rudimentary work camps, which were set apart from the camps of the white workers whom they greatly outnumbered. He contended with denials, perjury and the difficulty in communication, which made it nearly impossible to prosecute the agitators.

To distant eastern economic interests, many of whom had never visited a work site and certainly not one thousands of kilometres away in the wilds of the mountainous frontier, the Chinese workmen were just commodities, inputs and outputs to be purchased, deployed and discarded, cheap to obtain and easily distributed, their lives line items in the expense column. Only what they hauled around, blasted apart or sawed and hammed together had any value. Conditions were so bad for Chinese labourers that it almost seems like a form of slavery, with the veneer of a contract and free will. Many thousands worked hard, long days to build Canada's first transcontinental railway, under conditions that would be illegal today, but it was upon the backs of the Chinese labourers on the most challenging and dangerous sections, the canyons and steep mountains of British Columbia, that the greatest burden was placed. It would not have been completed without their herculean work ethic and stoic suffering and endurance.

Yet years of labouring on the railway did not earn them any sympathy from the majority population. The Chinese continued to face discrimination and lack basic civic rights and respect. An opinion from the *Port Moody Gazette* of April 12, 1884, is a good example: "WARNING: The Chinese are beginning to encroach upon property in Port Moody, which should be kept free from them. If they obtain a foothold in the central part of the city, that neighbourhood will be rendered uninhabitable for white people, and property will decrease in value. Necessity compels us to tolerate a few Mongolians in the community, but let them herd themselves and not attempt to mix in with the whites. There is no affinity between the races, nor ever can there be, in spite of all that is preached about the universal brotherhood of man."

There were, however, observers who noted the injustice and boldly wrote about it—usually to little avail. George Monro Grant wrote, "It is not enough for us to allow Chinamen to come to our shores merely that, while living, they may do our rough work cheaply, repelled the while from us by systematic injustice and insult, and that when dead a Company may clear money by carrying their bodies back to their own land. A nation to be great must have great thoughts; must be inspired with lofty ideals." This more aspirational view of what the nation of Canada could be was certainly sidelined for many people during the era of Macdonald and Laurier, and indeed for much of the twentieth century.

No sooner was the railway completed in 1885 than the federal government, under pressure from the government of British Columbia, imposed a tax on Chinese immigrants. The $50 so-called head tax was not a general entrance fee for all newcomers but applied only to Chinese. The government that had imported them now strove to get rid of them. After Macdonald died in 1891, rather than remove the head tax, in 1903 Laurier increased it to $500, making it a true hardship for a general worker to pay. But when even that outrageous sum proved insufficient to keep people from fleeing the wars and calamitous natural disasters that continued to plague China in the early twentieth century, in 1923 the government of Mackenzie King introduced the Chinese Immigration

Act, effectively squelching all immigration from China apart from small numbers of students and officials. It remained in force until 1947.

Any country can set immigration quotas as it sees fit, of course. Canada, having banned Ukrainians and incarcerated them in labour camps during the First World War, allowed them to immigrate again only in 1923. But the Canadian head tax and eventual exclusion during peacetime applied only to the Chinese, despite their outsized contribution to the construction of the single most important piece of civic infrastructure that enabled the country to exist independently from the United States. Upon hearing news of the tax, Wong plaintively wrote in his diary, "The leaders of the white people demand money—our poor savings—taken from we who have so little, given to those who are not so taxed." He was incredulous, given the need he saw for more workers, all the unfinished business and all the opportunities in a generally sparsely populated land. "There is much work to be done and not enough people to labour at it," he wrote. "But the Western people will not allow us to land here any longer, while they scold us for not working enough. How these acts wear my soul down to nothing. . . . I cannot understand why. The work is great, and there aren't enough labourers."

After this entry, in which his weariness with government policy is apparent and his exhaustion from fighting conformity and the sneering condescension that pressed down on him and his people, smothering them under the burden of a politically astute yet incompetent leadership, is abundantly clear, he offered a timeless observation that captures the essence of the great problems of the late nineteenth century, and, in different contexts, the same foolish squandering of opportunity that shackles Canada today: "These mighty lands are great to gaze upon," he wrote, "but the laws made here are so small."

COINCIDING WITH THE NEW ANTI-CHINESE taxes and restrictions, the CPR significantly shrunk its work crews. Many, especially Chinese workers, were left destitute, living in caves or in tents, turning to itinerant gold panning or sporadic labour to survive. Coal mining was added to the industries where Chinese were forbidden to be employed, exacerbating their poverty and marginalization. Some went into the laundry business, and others took up small-scale agriculture and sold produce at impromptu farm markets. Justice Begbie even commented, "I do not see how people would get on here at all without Chinamen. . . . They are the model market gardeners of the province, and produce the greater part of the vegetables grown here."

Many actually starved, some to death, others to near skeletons subsisting on inadequate government relief. "We have been burying some of the people who died over the hard, foodless days," Wong recorded, "but the sight of those dead is hard." Some chose to leave the country, though many others remained despite the indignities, oppression and attacks. Most of the Chinese diaspora initially was located in Victoria and along the lower Fraser River, but many soon drifted east to settle in the new towns of the prairies, Calgary, Edmonton and Winnipeg, where they organized cultural and community associations. Several years after the completion of the railway, more than ten thousand Chinese remained in Canada.

Many stayed on with the CPR or took other jobs to make new lives in Gold Mountain—fool's gold it may have been to many, but still they came. Wong kept working for the railway even after the last spike was driven, repairing the line, improving bridges and adding spur lines. "I have pondered this fresh new land," he wrote, "yet it is a land already full of sadness." Yet he was also dreaming of the time when he could bring over the young woman he had contracted to be his wife. He had been saving his earnings the entire time. "I desire material things sufficient for my living," he remarked, "and to bring Lin to an established house. The glitter of gold will not bring her to me. It would be only too easily robbed from me, so I labour onward, being called foolish by some people. Is it a fool's dream to want to establish myself, to be well respected and a full man?" By 1887, he had had enough of the railway life. Now forty-one years old, he went into business as a tailor with a man from his hometown, sailed back to China for a visit and, upon returning to Canada, became moderately successful as a tailor and a teacher in the Saltwater City, New Westminster, before moving to Vancouver.

Wong continued to be smarter and luckier than most. He was able to save enough money to bring Lin over in the 1890s, and they eventually had eight children together over the course of a thirty-five-year marriage. Wong's final diary entry was a paean to the future as he and Lin welcomed a daughter to their family after having seven sons. "It is still the feast of the full moon," he remembered. "My fate now has provided a daughter, a precious eighth child, a great joy for all this house! Her brothers will know this goodness and take care of her, loving her. She has come in my old age, a joyous sign, and she will be able to bring me pride, I know! It is good. Her brothers are men now, so she will be assured a good life. She will look after Lin when I leave these lands for the final journey homeward." Dukesang Wong died in Vancouver in 1931.

It might be, as is sometimes said, that the world heals itself by forgetting. But it can also heal by remembering.

CHAPTER NINETEEN

BETRAYAL

———

The Plains were black and alive with buffalo, dust clouds revealing their location on the horizon. Beneath the sun and stars,
the coulees and valleys, filled with cottonwoods and aspen,
were populated with antelope, elk, deer, black and grizzly bears, packs of
wolves and innumerable birds and other smaller creatures. The sky was
big overhead. It was hot, dry and sunny in summer; cold, dry and sunny
in winter, until the chinook wind howled over the mountains from the
west, bringing warm weather, fresh coastal air and a brief respite from
winter's bite.

The spirits were alive in this world—animals talked to people, giving
advice or portending the future in visions. Mystical ceremonies bound
men and women to epic journeys or quests, leading them into danger
and adventure. Wise women and mystics announced omens and interpreted dreams, making pronouncements on where to find buffalo, what
ritual would ensure victory and how to propitiate the vengeful or malev-
olent spirits that sought to lead them astray. Medicine bundles and

spirit-infused talismans offered protection, luck or insight into the mysteries and vagaries of the world. An aborted Sun Dance festival, interrupted by nearby enemies, could mean a dangerous return to disputed territory to complete the ceremony the following year; the timing of a grassfire or the unexpected power of a storm was cause for reflection. An unusually large murder of crows or ravens was a significant portent, depending upon its direction of flight. The timing of wolves howling or the colour of the setting sun meant things of import not to be ignored, things that directed behaviour, changed the course of lives. When people died, their spirits drifted off to the east, to the Sand Hills, where ghost people lived in ghost villages and hunted ghostly buffalo.

The spiritual and cultural world of the peoples of the Niisitapi confederacy, and all the Plains people in general, was a world as mystical, vivid, tactile and violent as the world depicted in ancient Viking sagas, replete with tales of personal bravery, honour, betrayal, victory, love, revenge, epic journeys and legendary undertakings; the unfathomable cycling of life and its churning beneath the moon and sun.

Campfires smouldered, smoking and drying buffalo meat for storage; scrounging dogs barked, warning of visitors. Secret societies convened and made their decisions; children collected firewood; women tanned hides, mended lodges and painted them to tell stories and myths and to reveal visions of the world. Buffalo tongues slowly roasted over coals and savoury stews burbled with the scent of sage and wild onions, enlivened by the sweet tang of prickly pear cactus in the summer and ripe saskatoon berries in the fall. Boys played at war in preparation for their life as warriors—the people were surrounded by enemies and constantly on the search for intruders, defending their hunting grounds from encroachment and honing their skills stealing horses from rival tribes.

In winter storms they huddled in the valleys, gathered around fires under buffalo robes while the wind whined outside. The Elders perhaps smoked a pipe, quietly drummed or chanted before launching into tales of the heroes of the past, the making of the world and the trickery of spirits, and other legends passed down through the ages—such as the adventures of the young man who travelled to the ethereal villages of the Sand Hills to retrieve his wife, who had journeyed there by mistake and became trapped, or the deeds of those who called upon mysterious forces to bestow upon them the ability to conceal themselves from enemies or give them strength in battle.

Other tales were more prosaic, such as the tale of Running Eagle, the most well-known Kainai (Blood) warrior woman, *awau-katsik-saki* or "manly-hearted woman." She'd been born with the name Empty Valley, but her husband was killed in battle against their habitual enemy, the Crows (Absoraka) from the southeast. While in mourning she had a vision. The Sun spirit told her that she could have her revenge under strict conditions: "I will give you great power in war, but if you have intercourse with any other man, you will be killed." Empty Valley quickly earned renown as a raider of daring escapades, capturing many enemy horses and racing off with them at night, wounding and killing, until she was honoured with the male name Running Eagle and became a leader of a band. Some called her the Queen of the Plains, and on at least one occasion she was at the head of a thousand-person army bent on some matter of honour or retribution along the Saskatchewan River. Before raids in the darkness, she gathered her band and chanted an inspiring ode to her own prowess (which no doubt rolls better off the tongue in its original language): "Be all brave and do your best / It's a good thing to hear each other say / I have good luck in battle."

She charged in wearing a woman's dress but men's leggings, Hudson's Bay blanket draped over her shoulders, yowling her battle cry. Between raids, she reputedly refused to abandon her duties as a woman, not disdainful of them but proud as she cooked and repaired clothing. When some of the men suggested that she shouldn't bother with menial women's work, she replied that it wasn't menial and said, "I am a woman.

Men don't know how to sew." Over time her reputation grew such that many sought to earn renown and revenge by killing her. Inevitably, one night on a raid, she was spied by a guard near the band's horses. He challenged her as she slowly backed away, hoping to fade into the night. But she wasn't quick enough and the man shot her, only later discovering that he had brought down the infamous Running Eagle.

Even in its golden age, this life was hard and often short, the people worn down by hardship, injury and the weight of events. But there was pride in the struggle, doomed though it was, just as there is for all who contend with time and nature. By the 1870s, however, this world had been in decline for years.

IT HAS BEEN SAID THAT NOTHING is beautiful unless it can be lost or destroyed. The mighty buffalo herds of the North American Plains were one of the most beautiful of living phenomena, and their disappearance seemed impossible. But—in the apocryphal manner that a rich person goes bankrupt—they began a slow decline in the nineteenth century, such that it was nearly unnoticeable over the generations. Then suddenly, within a single lifespan, somewhere between thirty and fifty million of the shaggy ruminants were just gone. Destroyed. Never to return in such numbers.

The 1870s saw the first stuttering gaps in what had been an unlimited food source for countless generations of Plains peoples. In former times, herds were so large that days could pass while they migrated. Their range stretched from northern Texas to Kansas and up to the aspen parkland of the central northern Canadian prairies. Photographs and sketches from the era show seemingly endless herds extending to the horizon while bewildered onlookers stared and perhaps shot some for entertainment or dinner. One American chronicler touring the western Plains wrote in 1858: "Of buffalo we saw millions, and very near the same number of antelope. For nine days of our travel we passed through one continuous herd of buffalo: The whole country was literally blackened with them as far as the eye could reach daily. We had to surround our camp with fires at night, to keep from being over run by mighty herds of this wonderful animal."

Their numbers began slowly decreasing throughout the nineteenth century after guns and horses made their way to Indigenous peoples a century earlier, prompting many groups to abandon their woodland lifestyles and embrace the buffalo hunt. Buffalo could be hunted on horseback using rifles instead of the labour-intensive and risky exercise of herding them over cliffs or into paddocks.

The Métis had been organizing semi-industrial bison hunts for generations since the early nineteenth century, Red River carts trundling across the prairie loaded with dried meat and hides. With the widespread adoption of guns and with hunting by more commercial operations to feed workers in the far-flung supply chains of the fur trade, which by the 1830s stretched to the Far North and crossed the Rockies to the Pacific, bison herds began to dwindle. By the late 1860s, Métis hunters had begun to travel farther west from Winnipeg in search of them, and the herds were noticeably smaller.

In 1866, the Methodist missionary George McDougall stole the Manitou Stone, *pahpamiyhaw asiniy*, from its prominent location on a hilltop overlooking the Iron River, near the present-day Alberta-Saskatchewan border, fearing that it competed with his own efforts to introduce Christianity. The stone, an ancient 145-kilogram meteorite, was venerated by the Plains peoples. It was believed to have great spiritual power to protect the buffalo herds, and was a pilgrimage site for all the peoples in the region. McDougall first took it to his nearby mission, where he hoped it would draw crowds, and then the Methodists removed it from the land altogether and took it east to Ontario. (It eventually came to rest in the Royal Alberta Museum in Edmonton, and plans are afoot to return it to a dedicated centre near its original location.) The loss of the Manitou Stone was a devastating psychological blow, and many prophesied that sickness, war and the death of the buffalo were sure to follow.

Soon came a period of particular upheaval, with a seemingly endless cycle of raids, violence and retaliation between all the Plains peoples and waves of white refugees from the East, intent on wresting something from an unsympathetic world, in endless conflict with the original inhabitants of the land, with their bewilderingly different ways of life. The declining buffalo made everything more difficult, more uncertain; old territorial understandings were necessarily violated, peace treaties were short-lived, and war proliferated. People died regularly, shot, scalped and left to the elements. Disease and toxic whiskey were both the cause and the effect of this erratic, unstable world. Disagreements became more frequent and deadly in the pressure of competition over dwindling resources.

The construction of the railways in the U.S., particularly after the Civil War ended, increased the number of people who were migrating west, and the work crews themselves needed food. In the 1870s in the U.S., trains could be stuck on the tracks, unable to move as they were engulfed by meandering herds of buffalo, passengers atop the cars firing away with rifles for sport. Migrants became settlers and the non-Indigenous population increased. The expanding numbers of farmers viewed buffalo as a pest more than anything else. A single migrating herd could trample and destroy vast swaths of farmers' crops, flatten the fences that kept domestic animals enclosed and turn water sources into a muddy mess. This herd behaviour posed no threat to nomadic equestrian peoples, who could just gallop away and observe the destruction from a distance, but it was a disaster for settlers whose livelihood and shelter and means of food production were fixed in one place and maintained with considerable labour. Bison didn't understand railway tracks and the need for them to be kept clear, nor did they understand the distinction between domestic crops and wild grass. Herd behaviour was, simply, incompatible with the changing times. Wild roaming buffalo herds could not coexist with domestic farming and ranching.

By around 1870, an estimated two million buffalo were being killed on the southern Plains each year, and the industrial-scale predation accelerated dramatically throughout the decade. The famous "Buffalo Bill" Cody was one of many hundreds of contract hunters sent out to basically exterminate them for the Kansas Pacific Railway. In one eighteen-month span, he alone reputedly shot 4,300 of the majestic shaggy beasts. His team of hide strippers worked overtime at their grisly task of skinning the carcasses and preparing the hides for shipment east to feed the new fashion for buffalo coats and to be turned into machine belts to feed the Industrial Revolution. People shot them for fun from the roofs of railway cars or the decks of steamboats plying the Missouri River, leaving them to rot or be scavenged by the ever-expanding wolf populations, which were in turn shot for their pelts. The tender tongue, which was a delicacy, and a few cuts from the hump and hindquarters were eaten, but the rest, once skinned, was left as rotting blobs covering the prairie. The bleached bones that littered the land were collected to be shipped back east and ground into fertilizer.

The extermination of the buffalo was even pursued as a tactic in the U.S. Army's warfare against Indigenous peoples. "Let them kill, skin, and sell until the buffaloes are exterminated, as it is the only way to bring lasting peace and allow civilization to advance," famously proclaimed General Philip Sheridan, addressing officials in Texas. The buffalo hunters, he said, "have done more to settle the vexed Indian question than the entire regular army has done in the last thirty years." He praised the great kill-off as a brilliant tactic, because "they are destroying the Indians' commissary. . . . Send them powder and lead, if you will . . . Then your prairies can be covered with speckled cattle, and the festive cowboy, who follows the hunter as the second forerunner of an advanced civilization." Gangs of men also began setting fire to the prairie mid-season to destroy the forage that the herds needed. Although most of the wanton killing took place in the American territory, buffalo roamed back and forth across the border, and in Canada, the dwindling herds and the associated problems that would present themselves were becoming clear to all by the 1870s.

By 1887, buffalo were all but extinct, with barely a thousand known to be living. Although they have made a slow comeback on managed ranches, nearly all of their natural habitat has been turned into farmland or is used for cattle ranching instead. But by then buffalo had long ceased to be the primary food source for the many tens of thousands of Plains people who relied upon them. The great Canadian buffalo famine was fiendish and devastating, and in Canada it remains the worst environmental and humanitarian disaster the country has ever faced. Buffalo were the primary food source for the entire Plains, and neither the local people nor the Canadian government was prepared for how quickly the change came about. People grew weaker, becoming skeletal, glassy-eyed and unable to walk properly. Their immune systems became weak and infectious disease took hold. And although there were other animals to hunt and fish to catch, these never had been the bulk of the diet. Soon, people had no clothing and no shelter, since these too were supplied by the buffalo. The human population declined along with the buffalo in a furious vortex of mortality that sucked the life out of the land as nature sought some new balance. This dramatic and disastrous turn of events happened just after the signing of the seven numbered Plains treaties.

The whole region no longer produced enough food to feed the people living there, and supply lines from the East were primitive at best. There was no way to send food, or anything else, in great quantity to the prairies except by the small-scale canoe and boat network, or by travelling along the U.S. rail system and the steamboat network along the Missouri River. And yet food staples produced elsewhere and brought in at great expense from distant locations were the only short-term solution to the problem. If the railway had been built a few years earlier, it could have changed the situation significantly.

When, in the experience of anyone in Canada, had tens of thousands of people suddenly found themselves without any of their usual food sources? (At the time, the horrors of the Irish potato famine of decades earlier were for the most part unappreciated by non-Irish people.) As they say about any disaster, it's never just a single disruption that collapses a system but the confluence of several disruptions. In the 1880s, there was also a drought that reduced water levels on smaller rivers to such low levels that the paddlewheelers couldn't navigate them easily. And there were years of early frosts and generally poor growing seasons, damaging the first attempts to grow wheat and other crops. Even when farms were productive, with no easy means to get the grain to market or even to a mill to grind it, farmers sometimes had to travel a hundred-kilometre journey each way to do so. The government generally failed to provide the proper tools, equipment and training to make subsistence agriculture viable. The breeds of cattle that were initially imported to replace the buffalo were unsuited to the climate and perished in the winter, or they became diseased with tuberculosis, in turn poisoning the people who ate them. In addition, there was overfishing everywhere by increasing numbers of peoples, and with no buffalo to hunt, people turned to hunting anything and everything else, hastening the decline of other species too.

At Fort Edmonton, a federal Indian agent wrote in distress: "I have never seen anything like it since my long residence in this country. It was not only the want of buffalo, but everything else seemed to have deserted the country; even fish were scarce. . . . The poor people were naked, and the cold was intense, and remained so during the whole winter; under these circumstances they behaved well, and no raids were made on anything here. They ate many of their horses, and all the dogs were destroyed for food." Similar scenes played out across the prairies, to the horror of some and the indifference of others.

None of the government people making key decisions about the prairies had ever been there, and to them the original inhabitants of the frontier were just a shrinking demographic appendage to the lofty ambitions of empire builders. In the coming years, federal government policy, or neglect, proved to be the beginning of our own homegrown potato famine, or more accurately, buffalo famine, a combination of natural disaster and political indifference, incompetence and general hostility. It was clear that the people running the empire didn't care equally about all the subjects under their dominion.

While the Hudson's Bay Company had, throughout the nineteenth century, used its network of communication routes and forts to distribute smallpox vaccines to its employees and their often Indigenous or Métis families and customers, the Canadian government was less involved with this remedy in the handful of years after Confederation. The political establishment wanted to claim the land as a valuable addition to the expanding country, and to control the people who lived there, but it didn't want the sudden responsibility of caring for them or dealing with any of their problems.

The government also had no idea what to do logistically during the smallpox epidemic of 1870, which killed so many people that it was not possible for the remainder to procure enough provisions for the sick, which, in a vicious cycle, resulted in more famine, which weakened people further, making them in turn more susceptible to disease. "Thousands (and there are not many thousands, all told) had perished on the great sandy plains that lie between the Saskatchewan and the Missouri," wrote William Francis Butler at the time, around when Fleming and Grant and the first railway survey parties were crossing

the land. "Why this most terrible of diseases should prey with espe-
cial fury upon the poor red man of America has never been accounted
for by medical authority; but that it does prey upon him with a violence nowhere else to be found is an undoubted fact. . . . The history
of its annihilating progress is written in too legible characters on the
desolate expanses of untenanted wilds, where the Indian graves are
the sole traces of the red man's former domination. Beneath this
awful scourge whole tribes have disappeared." With the belated distribution of smallpox vaccines, the incidence of that particular disease
declined, but it was soon supplanted by the rise of tuberculosis,
another great killer, perhaps triggered initially by malnourished and
weakened people eating tainted bison or cattle.

Barely were the numbered treaties signed than the balance of power
shifted dramatically away from the Indigenous peoples. They were
now forced to rely on the government to honour its proclaimed com-
mitment to provide aid in times of hardship or a "national famine."
But the response was lackadaisical. Government flour rations were
often delayed by poor shipping and distribution networks. Nothing on
that scale had ever been organized or implemented before, and the
Hudson's Bay Company's river networks were inadequate for transporting enough bulk supplies to feed the tens of thousands of people
in remote locations who were suddenly without sustenance. In fact,
the famine was partly tamed by the Hudson's Bay Company to the
extent that its limited resources could help, but its employees, families
and contract workers also relied on these same so-called country foods
for their own survival.

Alleviating the humanitarian disaster would have taken a dedicated
effort by the people and government in the East, with attention paid to
logistical and fiscal efficiency. But instead, for political reasons, most of
the food was purchased in Montreal, loaded on trains south across the
border and sent west through Wisconsin and Minnesota, before being

transferred onto steam paddlewheelers. At Fort Benton, the provisions were loaded onto ox carts and trundled north across the prairie into a region without roads, railways or any other efficient means of transportation or travel. Alternatively, some paddlewheelers chuffed north along the Red River and dispersed goods throughout the rivers of that network. To say this supply chain was long, complicated and subject to delay and disruption is an understatement. Moreover, the food coming up from Fort Benton in the U.S., organized by the I.G. Baker Company, was poor quality, with musty flour and old, mouldering beef. There was limited surplus food in the region, but what rations did arrive were wielded as a tool of oppression, sometimes allowed to rot under guard rather than being distributed.

By the 1880s, the government was distributing supplies only to those people who were living on reserves and not to people who still travelled the land—and soon the nomadic life itself was impossible in a meaningful way, since the horses that enabled it had been eaten out of necessity. There was also no longer an economic reason for this nomadic lifestyle, since the bison had disappeared everywhere. Because the buffalo had provided everything, when they were gone, the people were left with nothing. There was no longer any material for clothes, lodges or sleeping robes, and nothing to trade for other necessities of life such as guns and ammunition. In a few short years, Plains peoples went from being self-sufficient, confident and proud to destitute, impoverished and, worse, dependent. They suddenly found themselves economically and politically irrelevant in their own land.

For those in the East, it was easy to dismiss the reports of starvation as things happening to people in some distant land, or surely not as bad as it was said. Even comprehending the problem was a challenge at first in a technologically primitive society. Many people along the St. Lawrence were illiterate farmers scrabbling to make a living themselves. There was not much surplus food within the system. At the time, Canada was basically a Third World country, not economically or socially advanced by the standards of the era, and the prairies were essentially isolated from regions of the country that might have been better positioned to manage such a dire situation. Most of the people along the St. Lawrence had never been to the West and knew nothing about those regions or the people who lived there, and so they were reluctant to shoulder any expense to deal with the problems.

This confluence of disasters was compounded by the government's incompetence and indifference, sprinkled with a dose of hostility. Both parties in Ottawa displayed a collective callous disregard of the situation. In their limited defence, there were no methods of communication that in any way could depict the horror that was unfolding on the Plains, but there were plenty of reports and letters and complaints attesting to these horrors, however inadequate words on paper were to convey the true situation. James Macleod of the NWMP was so disgusted with the government's failure to honour its obligations to the Indigenous people, despite his having provided it with a clear and detailed assessment of the situation, that he resigned as commissioner.

Much of the responsibility for the mismanagement and foul political decisions in the 1880s lay at the feet of Edgar Dewdney, an English-born former land surveyor and politician representing ridings in British Columbia, whom Macdonald had appointed as lieutenant-governor of the North-West Territories in 1881. Dewdney was also the Indian commissioner in an era that had no democratic representation. He used the famine as a tool of social and political control to compel the Indigenous peoples who had recently signed treaties to permanently relocate to official reserves, where the government would then send farming implements and teachers—although the tools, seeds and equipment were never sufficiently provided, to the great frustration of many, and the teachers were often ill-informed brutes with no stake in the success of the endeavour. Dewdney's callous mismanagement and general downplaying of reports of suffering from starvation or disease resulted in untold death and misery.

Dewdney was also fond of feathering his own nest, so to speak. Since he was given the choice of where to situate the new capital of the North-West Territories, why not allow for a little self-interest to direct his decision, he reasoned. There were several obvious options, such as Fort Qu'Appelle, or even keeping it where it was initially located, at Battleford. But Dewdney had speculated in land in a region where the CPR line was likely to be placed, a dry, undistinguished patch of prairie, not even on a lake or river, known to the Cree as Pile of Bones, after of its most distinguishing feature. So in 1882 he renamed it Regina and commenced the construction of government buildings, pleased with the increase in value of his land.

The Macdonald government, which was naturally inclined to be stingy, was hammered by the Liberal Opposition—not for its weak response to the humanitarian disaster, however academic it was in the eyes of people reading reports in a distant city, but for spending even as much as it did, which was deemed a waste of public funds. Regardless of the technical capacity of the government to entirely solve these massive problems, it is the callousness of the discussion by key figures who knew what was happening that is so disturbing. Debates in the House of Commons saw the Opposition accusing the government of wasting money, spending too much by increasing the yearly expenditure on food rations for the West, so the government promised in response to be more parsimonious. One line of reasoning was that, since the people were depending upon the charity of the government, they had no right to complain about insufficient rations or poor-quality ones such as rancid pork, diseased cattle or damp, mouldy flour. To be so clinical and calculating in the face of horrifying suffering and death—people dying from hunger and disease, children among them—is inexcusable. Such circumstances should never have been seen as a vehicle to advance a political agenda. And yet, as is often the case, the political squabbling proved mightier than the common good.

These were not the debates of a society deciding what to do when stuck between a rock and a hard place, but a situation where one group was doing all the suffering while another chose to provide only minimal support, despite having just signed treaties promising to protect them and treat them as citizens of a new political entity. If Ottawa wanted the benefits of political jurisdiction over the land, it was obliged to assume responsibility for the problems as well—particularly as it had very recently promised to do just that. And yet in some quarters the starvation was viewed instead in a vaguely positive light; by weakening the Indigenous population's independence and increasing their subjugation, it would be easier to establish government control. People were essentially offered a choice: accept this control by moving to reserves, where some meagre low-quality food would be provided (with an attendant corrupt bureaucracy to perpetuate abuses upon the people), or starve to death.

There is no way to describe what happened other than as a betrayal—a legal betrayal, a moral betrayal and a technical betrayal that was and remains a stain upon the nation's honour. To be fair, the sudden disappearance of the buffalo and the concomitant starvation was a problem that was never going to be entirely solved by some government people thousands of kilometres away, with no road, railway or river connecting them to the region. But they certainly could have done more to alleviate the suffering, provided more competent and effective education and equipment for a transition to an agricultural economy, weeded out the corrupt Indian agents and curbed the excesses of the churches. An editorial in the *Saskatchewan Herald* in the spring of 1885 pointed out the incompetence and failure of the government policy: "Everyone here knows that almost all of the Indians in the district suffer from scrofula and dyspepsia. . . . Their policy seems to be comprised in these six words: feed one day, starve the next."

The litany of downright disgusting conduct, including the sexual exploitation of women and girls by immoral, abusive and sadistic politically appointed agents, suggests a staggering level of incompetence or a nearly psychopathic lack of empathy. One example out of many stands as the symbolic apogee of the demeaning cruelty that in the worst cases passed as government distribution of food aid. Starving people were called to the ration house by the Indian sub-agent with the promise of food, only to be told it was an April Fool's joke and sent away hungry with their crying children.

And it should be noted that the famine dovetailed neatly into the overarching objective of smoothing the path for the railway to meet the political plan of Confederation. Ironically, had the railway been completed by then, the distribution of humanitarian relief would have been a much simpler mission.

THE LAND WAS ALSO NOW BEING JABBED by a new prong of empire: missionaries, set on converting the free tribes and binding them to the new spiritual truth. Part of clearing the land was clearing the old culture as well. The stereotype of the preacher, arms gesticulating wildly, clawing at the heavens, eyes popping with certainty and wild with passion, exhorting obedience, promising salvation and threatening eternal damnation is a well-established trope. In truth many were far more subtle and not nearly so "fire and brimstone" in their approach or ambition. Many were creating ways for Indigenous languages to be written with new symbols and structure. These people, like many today who wield interpretations of science or the claims of select experts to silence debate, were enveloped in the armour of certainty and gloriously free from self-doubt, even while proclaiming others to be frauds. Their official goal was to help, as they saw it, the Indigenous peoples to adopt a foreign belief system and way of life. Some form of change was inevitable, and many Indigenous leaders knew it, but the offer of aid in the transition was tied to their abandoning non-compliant customs and beliefs.

From the perspective of people of a different faith or belief system, the simplified argument went something like this: There is a powerful sorcerer in the sky who created and controls everything. For some reason we know about him and you don't. If you do what he wants, as determined by his earthly representatives, you get rewarded. If not, you get horribly punished in a fiery world of torture for eternity, unless you pay some form of penance or confess to his self-declared representatives and change your way of life—in which case you will be fine.

Many Indigenous peoples found it difficult to believe that everything they had been taught by their spiritual leaders was wrong and these newcomers had all the answers to life's greatest mysteries. This Victorian-era activism wanted to bring progressive enlightenment to the "poor benighted savages" who were in need of salvation and help on the road to civilization. And withholding food supplies until they submitted was one effective tactic in this noble (as they saw it) struggle.

In dealing with Indigenous peoples, or, indeed, with anyone with different perspectives, the missionaries of this era suffered from a lack of imagination. They were distracted by the apparent material poverty of the villages—detritus strewn about, hides, carcasses, dirt and so on—and failed to see their complex and rich internal world. As outsiders they were blind to the subtleties and nuances of Indigenous cultures. Images from the time invariably show the missionary standing while the Indigenous converts are crouched or sitting subserviently, eyes downcast. In any case, it is well known by missionaries, even if only subconsciously, that destruction is a necessary part of their job. Construction and destruction cannot exist without each other. You must destroy one world before you can create a new one, erect a new mental scaffolding upon which to hang ideas, motivations and under-standing, a new set of boundaries beyond which most people's thoughts seldom venture.

Perhaps this seems villainous. But villains don't always know they are villains. Sometimes people are cruel without intention. They go to bed with a clear conscience, fully believing they are right and that their actions are for the greater good. Or perhaps at least the lesser evil. That is the reasoning behind all totalitarian impulses, efforts to stifle debate and opposition or dissenting opinions because those opinions are passionately believed to be wrong and in need of correction. The irony is that in failing to allow ideas to be tempered and strengthened by exposure to challenge and altercation, flaws, sometimes egregious ones, are left unnoticed and unexamined, lying in wait for unforeseen events to expose them and lead to unintended consequences. Some missionaries merely wanted to help relieve the suffering they perceived but were boxed in by their own worldview and the misguided confla-tion of industrial material success with spiritual conformity.

Indian agents and missionaries were merely different prongs of the same fork, representatives, most of whom were idealogues or patronage appointees, with little knowledge, understanding or interest in their responsibilities or their charges. They weren't all abusive as individuals, but the very nature of their job was abusive. Consider the type of person interested in such a position of intrusive power over others, who would be drawn to it, similar to those drawn to run residential schools later when they were created under Macdonald and then vastly expanded under Laurier throughout the 1890s and into the early twentieth cen-tury, and especially after school attendance was made compulsory in 1894. It's not a wholesome position to have over others, and there were no checks on their power and no accountability, owing to the remote locations of the schools, the primitive state of travel and communica-tion, the moral sanctimony sweeping the land, and the righteous mindset and firm belief of those in control that they were right and these "savages" needed to be corrected.

Many Indigenous leaders were clear-eyed about the clouded future that emerged in the wake of the declining buffalo in the era of the treaties. They observed the world changing. They wanted a path for their children in the new order, new skills to help them succeed and thrive, just as any parent wants. What they didn't want was for this schooling to be run by foreign religious sects, with the ulterior motive of indoctrination and cultural replacement, using harsh and damaging tactics to achieve those goals. Or for their people to be ground down by the depredations of sexual predators and psychopaths in the role of government officials.

The powerful forces of disease and economic destruction, combined with the more subtle and corrosive forces of missionaries, Indian agents and the residential school system, undermined Indigenous peoples' confidence in their worldview and conspired to break them so they could be remade in a different form. But how long can people live in a world that just keeps taking from them?

EACH GENERATION IS BORN ANEW, seeing the land fresh as it is, as it has become. For older generations, new realities caused dissent and bewilderment as the world changed rapidly around them and they were powerless to stop the forces that were propelling everyone and everything toward an unknown and unsettling destiny. For many Indigenous people, the former days of trade and peace and plenty were now mere tales of a golden age, derided and perhaps disbelieved by younger generations, old people's unreal remembrances of the world as it seemed in the flourishing of their youth. But for those who bore witness to the changes, where once the land was an explosion of vitality, a kaleidoscope of cacophonous life swirling with the seasons, now there was just wind hissing through the grasses, great piles of bleached bones, and thin and hungry people wondering what the future held for them.

It bears repeating: each generation sees the world anew. Years later, when newcomers from a distant continent rode the new railway en masse onto the prairies, they saw nothing of the proud warrior societies that had dominated the vast sea of grass, master equestrians and unflinching hunters arrayed in their buffalo robes, crowns adorned with exotic feathers, furs and talismans, tall and vigorous, whose legendary exploits against enemies and struggles against the urges of capricious spirits were sung of around fires beneath the stars. Instead, what they saw were cringing, emaciated wretches dressed in rags, unable even to feed their own children, eyes downcast in defeat. Seldom do a people fall so far and so quickly, and seldom does a betrayal run so deep. In the years after the railway was completed, the glory, complexity and mystery of this world was but a memory, and for many not even that. For the newcomers it had never existed, except in scarcely creditable accounts of a heroic age.

The distemper of the era boiled throughout the early 1880s as the railway took shape across the land. The growing discontent and intolerable conditions drove the land's original inhabitants to seek succour in a leader who promised them a chance to fight back against the intolerance, injustice and degradation; a chance perhaps to regain control of lives that fluttered in the wind.

CHAPTER TWENTY

TEETERING
ON THE BRINK

———

B y the spring of 1883, only the prairie section of the great railway was complete, a stretch of steel track that now led nearly 1,500 kilometres from Fort William, the old fur trade depot at the western edge of Lake Superior, through all the mushrooming tent cities along the line to within sight of the Rocky Mountains. The track was quickly pushing into the mountains, although the sections over the Kicking Horse Pass and Rogers Pass were hardly even properly surveyed. Meanwhile, Onderdonk's western section was still a collection of piecemeal clearings, graded road and partially constructed bridges and trestles. But the most problematic part was between Fort William and Lake Nipissing to the east, where the Canada Central Railway had recently completed its end-of-track terminus that would link to the ever expanding network of railways spidering throughout Ontario and Quebec.

While Van Horne urged on the crews on the prairies to staggering speed and efficiency, and Onderdonk blasted away at the canyons of the Fraser River with the backing of his imported Chinese labour, the section of track cutting north of Lake Superior was bogged down—literally. The land was peppered with swamps, ponds, lakes and stunted spruce forests, interspersed with uprisings of granite, one of the hardest rocks in the world. It is an understatement to say that pushing a railway through this land proved more of a challenge than the surveyors had anticipated. Challenge translated into extra expense, causing a great sigh of frustration in the offices in Montreal, which as time and money dwindled, morphed into eye-popping incredulity and hand-wringing, and then perhaps into the occasional extra splash of whiskey as insolvency loomed over the directors like a shadow.

Van Horne described the route, particularly the section that clung to the shoreline along the north of Lake Superior, as "two hundred miles of engineering impossibilities." The bogs sucked in money just as they did timber, track, gravel fill and even locomotives. One particularly nasty stretch of muskeg, barely ten kilometres across, was undetectable until crews placed anything heavy atop the latticework of waterlogged timber and scrub growth, and then everything slowly sunk under the murky surface. Engineers were stressed and resigned in disgrace; contractors' egos deflated as their dreamed-of profits were transformed into gravel for the bogs. Work was delayed by years as nature sought to tame the hubris of contractors, engineers, politicians and hapless immigrant labourers, many from Ireland, others from Italy and the Canadas.

Even the work camps along this remote stretch were in a shambles. Illegal whiskey was rampant in the construction camps, impossible to keep out, as had been managed on the prairies, and in some cases controlled by gangs that ruled some of the towns and camps, bringing in rotgut liquor to the workers through bribery or intimidation of local officials. The labourers dwelt in shantytowns of canvas tents with dirt floors, or sometimes in mobile train cars that were dragged along portions of the track as it progressed. The food would have brought a smile to Major Rogers's crinkly face: oatmeal, pork, beans and bannock.

The work was nearly as dangerous and back-breaking as that being done far to the west in B.C. Dynamite couldn't be manufactured as quickly and cheaply as pure nitroglycerine, and the railway's end of track along Lake Superior was far from any cities with dynamite factories. Since it was cheaper and more expedient to skip the process of transforming nitroglycerine into safer dynamite, sometimes the more volatile substance was used, resulting in accidental explosions and ghastly deaths as the crews cracked their way through the nearly impenetrable granite of the Canadian Shield. Hands, arms and legs were blown off from imprudent handling. As well, other accidents, disease, exposure and malnutrition took their toll on the workforce. The need for speed was so paramount that the quality of construction began to decline as the directors sought to tame the beast that was devouring capital at an unsustainable rate. Stonemasonry and steel trestles and bridges were being quickly and more cheaply replaced with softwood chopped from the nearby forests; fill for levelling the terrain was not given time to properly settle; culverts for drainage were bypassed; longer curved go-arounds that would slow speeds were substituted for rocky, bog-riddled sections; grades became steeper. These and innumerable other shortcuts caused future problems, and it wasn't uncommon for work to be redone even before the line was ever heavily used.

The construction scene was a constant hive of activity, which stopped only for the most dangerous or inhospitable weather. Following the graders, men hauled and manoeuvred steel rails using ox and horse carts and hand-drawn pulleys, sledgehammering all day long. Mosquitoes, blackflies and gnats stung and bit so that men's faces were often swollen and puffy with poison; camp life was a lurch back to medieval times, by far the worst along the entire route. Making matters worse was that rumours of the foul conditions discouraged men from hiring on, not wanting to be taken to the wilds of the bush where they would effectively be held hostage to the company and its increasingly uncomfortable, if not horrifying, work conditions. If a person decided to quit, they had to keep paying board until the company got around to transporting them out, that transportation also being at their own expense if they hadn't completed their contract. If they complained they were fired, and the few times they tried to strike, the work action was quickly suppressed; where would strikers get food in such remote locations if it wasn't provided by the company?

Still, despite the obvious power imbalance, wage inflation soared at the moment when new expenses were crippling the operation. Workers were paid just over a dollar a day in Ottawa and other urbanized centres of Canada. Labourers in B.C. were paid up to $1.50 for a long, hard day. Along the track of northern Lake Superior, the daily rate rose to $1.75, which included board, the quality of which varied widely depending on who was in charge.

The railway in this section was a money pit. But at the same time it was, literally and figuratively, a morale-sapping mess at once too big to fail and yet too big to proceed, a chaotic churn of innumerable setbacks that was sucking dry the coffers and leeching away the optimism that had once animated management to push on with Macdonald's great dream.

In the 1884 season, along the track north of Lake Superior alone, the CPR had nearly twelve thousand workers, a huge number considering the nation's population, along with two thousand horses and twelve steamers on the lake. In addition there were the crews in the West who by now had moved into the mountains and were slogging their way over the Kicking Horse and Rogers Passes, nearly insurmountable technical and engineering obstacles mitigated only by their relatively short distances. But the rock and bog of the Shield north of Superior had no easy sections. It was just days, weeks, months of constant blasting and filling. Van Horne soon had three proprietary dynamite factories, each producing a ton of explosives a day and shipping it on railcars to the end of track, where it was deployed clearing the rock—the thunderous explosions were endless. Every kilometre of track had to be clawed forward painstakingly slowly and at staggering expense—blasting, removing and clearing rubble, levelling the track bed, piling the rock into bogs—before a single wooden tie was laid or a single steel rail spiked. Those government grants, the ones that had seemed so lavish a few short years ago, now seemed puny and had long been spent.

With the entire nation focused on this single objective—the need for speed being the key animating spark that kept everything buzzing—the commercial work being directed to the railway was unparalleled in the country, the economic activity generating private and public capital and investment simultaneously. The hope was that all this work would generate a grand economic payoff for the workers and the investors and the government afterward, and provide the means for new immigrants to reach the hinterland of the young nation. But in the daily grind, not everyone was enjoying the road to this soon-to-be-glorious future. As with the Chinese in B.C., many thousands paid a high price for all this so-called progress.

The detractors had said that the Lake Superior portion of track could not or should not be built, yet this was the section that politically had to be built. Of course, the land the rail was being pushed through was generally believed to be worthless—frozen and wind-lashed in winter; boiling, humid and insect-infested in summer; nearly no good farmland or river or lake access. But it was only a few years before the value of all that exposed rock, tainted with the oxides of copper, nickel and iron, was sniffed out by canny travellers and speculators, who cheaply bought up vast sections of land that later proved to be a veritable treasure mine of mineral wealth, which in time provided more business for the railway, helping to push it to profitability. The Lake Superior section of the line did eventually pay off. But at the time it looked thoroughly bleak to the investors, despite the government subsidies and loans.

Meanwhile in Montreal, George Stephen, Donald Smith and the others responsible for financing the CPR were starting to sweat. Scrutinizing the documents led them to an unavoidable conclusion: the CPR would go bust long before it could be completed and begin generating any significant revenue. The terrain was just too rocky, convoluted, steep, remote and unforgiving, not to mention the vast distance from Montreal to the Pacific, particularly since the line could not go directly but wound circuitously around innumerable unavoidable geographical obstacles. With bleak resignation, they approached Macdonald in early 1884 and barely persuaded him to brave the wrath of his caucus and the Opposition to supply another $30 million. But that too ran dry in less than six months. They needed a further $22.5 million to guarantee the dividend payments, which provoked the Liberal Opposition in the House to go apoplectic, predicting the route would be a snowbound, underused link to nowhere that would surely destroy the country.

The financiers, meanwhile, had sunk everything they owned into the CPR and had negotiated loans for even more; if it went down, they would go down with it. Even Van Horne, while technically a salaried manager and executive, had invested nearly all of his personal financial resources into CPR stock. These men couldn't let it fail or they would be personally ruined, along with their families and many friends, their reputations tarnished beyond repair. And as Macdonald feared, failure might precipitate a financial crisis for the new country as banks, investors and contractors, unable to meet their obligations, tumbled into insolvency. The CPR had become the tail that was wagging the dog.

THE CONSTRUCTION FAR TO THE WEST in the mountains, while not as dreary and unremittingly difficult, had two large sections that were nearly as problematic to survey and build, and they also caused some rising blood pressure and hand-wringing in far-off offices. For the men on the ground, it no doubt produced florid bursts of cussing and praying to accompany the broken bones, sicknesses and miserable camp life. The line pushing west through the Bow Valley and past the Lake of the Little Fishes had neared the summit of Kicking Horse Pass before the snow closed in for the winter. In the spring of 1884, the headquarters of the Mountain Division moved to a spot below the lake that would become known as Laggan Station, the present-day hamlet of Lake Louise.

By early summer, up to twelve thousand navvies were flooding the region on packed railcars, ready for the big push over and down from the pass to the Columbia flats, then up again to the infamous Rogers Pass. Forest fires burned the mountainsides, steam engines squealed, hundreds of draft animals grunted, men yelled and hammers rang out. The canvas work camps were filled, yet many of the new recruits were unsuited for ten-hour days of hard labour, having been drawn west by adventure and money. "I saw the primaeval forest torn down, cut and hewed and hacked, pine and cedar and hemlock," wrote Morley Roberts, one such newcomer. "Here and there lay piles of ties, and near them, closely stacked, thousands of rails. The brute power of man's organised civilisation had fought with Nature and had for the time vanquished her. Here lay the trophies of the battle." It was no longer the peaceful, quiet forested valley surrounded by majestic snow-covered peaks that it had been just a few years earlier, when surveyors like Tom Wilson relished the tranquility and beauty.

All the blasting of rock cliffs and tunnels with dynamite caused avalanches to tear down from summits, crossing the valley and rising up the far side, smashing a corridor of mangled trees. The mighty gangs of men continuously hacked and hammered to clear, hoist and haul debris away in wheelbarrows and horse carts and replace it with ties and rails, a seemingly endless churn as the corridor pressed west. Van Horne, here as he had along Lake Superior, gave in to the forces of economics and politics and ordered that all stonemasonry work was to be replaced with easily available wood to save time and money. Soon there were fantastic wooden latticework bridges hanging off the cliffsides. It would all have to be replaced in the not too distant future, but for the present anything that could get a train through would serve. The line, for example, crossed the Kicking Horse Gorge eight times on precarious scaffolding and unsecured wooden planks, zigzagging back and forth over the river during construction.

Once the crews began the descent into Kicking Horse Canyon, some of the problems that were overlooked in Rogers's initial feasibility survey became apparent. In short, the terrain made it impossible to keep the overall grade within the limits then acceptable for locomotives. The natural grade was too steep, and the narrow canyon left no room for wider turns to level it out. Suddenly the longer distance of the dismissed Howse Pass route didn't look like such a disadvantage after all.

In 1884, the government agreed to allow for a steeper than regulation grade on the westward side of the pass, known as the Big Hill. When complete it dropped four and a half feet for every hundred feet of distance, a 4.5 per cent grade. It was a temporary measure until an engineering solution could be devised that wouldn't delay the opening of the railway. The Big Hill required specially built heavy-duty locomotives, which slowly crept up or down the pass with three stopping platforms where brakes were inspected. For this section of the route, trains were split into smaller lengths and were ferried up and down before being reconnected. Sometimes, to get a single train through, five steaming locomotives slowly plodded up or down the hill multiple times an hour. The cumbersome arrangement resulted in huge time delays and additional fuel and manpower costs. There were many tales of runaway trains surging down the final stretch onto the flats, but thankfully expensive, deadly accidents were few. The Big Hill was eventually replaced, in 1909, by the famous Spiral Tunnels, engineering marvels designed by John Schwitzer. Two tunnels were bored into each side of the narrow valley, giving room for trains to snake back and forth on switchbacks deep within the bowels of the mountains, which reduced the grade to a more reliable, and much safer, 2.2 per cent.

By September 1884, the line had descended the length of the Kicking Horse River to its junction with the Columbia River, and then through the fall it followed the Columbia for around twenty-seven kilometres before crossing the flats to ascend the Beaver River to the summit of Rogers Pass in the Selkirk Mountains, the final great obstacle in the mighty line. Van Horne knew that he could have run the line northwest and south again in a giant loop following the Columbia Valley, but it would have added 125 kilometres of expensive track and hours of additional travel time once completed. It may have been the better choice, though—Rogers Pass was an ogre of an obstacle.

In early 1885, over a thousand men geared up for the push up, over and down the other side to meet up with the track being pushed west from Kamloops by Onderdonk's crews. The right-of-way had been cleared, the tunnels mostly blasted, and everything was a hive of buzzing activity and the constant noise of men and animals and tools banging and saws cutting timber, toiling away in the rain and the muck, skunk cabbage and devil's club that had so agitated and frustrated Rogers and his survey team the year before. All the while, above them hunkered millions of tons of snow awaiting a trigger to embrace gravity. Precipitation is heavy in the Selkirk Range, which is sometimes known today as the interior rain belt. The high peaks obstruct the heavily laden clouds moving east from the coast. The clouds first drop their moisture on the Coast Range, where the Fraser River turns north along the infamous gorge that was claiming so many Chinese lives. After lightening their load, the clouds float over the arid Interior before dropping more precipitation around Revelstoke, at the bottom of the western side of Rogers Pass. Portions of the pass can receive up to an astonishing ten metres of snow a year.

During the winter of 1885, the dynamite blasting set off awe-inspiring avalanches unlike any the workers had seen elsewhere. Ominous rumbling preceded great swaths of the mountainside sloughing off, rolling down to the valley of the pass, smashing construction materials, scattering men and leaving a path of mangled trees and debris plugging the valley. "Glaciers which had never left their rocky beds above the clouds," wrote Sam Steele, "under the shocks of the blasting operations broke away and came crashing down, cutting pathways from a quarter to half a mile wide through the forest below. One avalanche, which came at the summit of the pass 20 miles from the Beaver camp, descended 5,000 feet with such velocity that it went across the valley and up the opposite side for 800 feet."

On February 10, 1885, after several days of heavy snow, another avalanche thundered down the Selkirk Mountains, taking an advance construction party by surprise, burying five men and killing one instantly, while sweeping away all their provisions. Another man was mangled by debris. The injured were slowly taken downhill to a field hospital, where they joined other injured men who had slipped on snow, plummeted off ledges, fallen through ice, been mangled by their draft animals or had their fingers or toes crushed by primitive tools or machinery. Some portions of track were hastily redesigned to avoid particularly avalanche-prone areas, but it wasn't until years later that thirty-one snowsheds were constructed to shelter a total of 6.5 kilometres of track, at last protecting trains from routinely being swept off the track and destroyed.

The CPR still hadn't settled on a Pacific terminus, the cause of so much acrimonious conflict and argument over the decades, starting with the Chilcotin War of the 1860s, and so Van Horne set off on a great cross-country inspection tour. He was by now becoming ever more corpulent, his time spent mostly at his Montreal office, where his fondness for rich food and his sedentary idiosyncratic pursuits, such as painting and architecture and tending his collections of Japanese porcelain and French Impressionist art (before it was expensive and celebrated), consumed what little time he had that wasn't devoted to the CPR and the incessant worries over finances and logistics. His peccadilloes continued to amuse him, however. Around this time, he was known to hand people a cheap cigar with a premium brand's band affixed to it, then nod at their expressions and exclamations affirming his good taste in cigars. He would occasionally sign his own paintings with the name of a well-known contemporary artist and likewise privately chuckle at proclamations of his good taste in art. Despite his position on the upper rungs of Montreal society, it seems he was a deeply unpretentious man who saw through the snobbish façade of cultural superiority and was fond of secretly mocking his social peers for their falsity and slavish devotion to fashion. He preferred the company of railway workers along the line, which he personally inspected whenever possible, and was known to spend time with them in the evening, where he seemed to be at ease and genuinely enjoy himself drinking whiskey, smoking cigars, playing cards and telling tales.

Van Horne had been putting off his western tour for some time, for political reasons. But late in 1884 he was forced to make a journey over the Rockies himself to assess the progress and make some decisions. The line needed a terminus for its completion. Port Moody, at the western end of Burrard Inlet, was the frontrunner, but Van Horne wasn't convinced. He made his way west through the U.S. and stopped in Victoria for some meetings before sailing east and up the Burrard Inlet through the mighty temperate rainforest of the Lower Mainland, which was being frenetically sawed down for railway ties, roof shingles and raw logs for export. He noted that Port Moody had virtually no space for a new city to develop—the land demands of the CPR alone would consume most of the available flat terrain. He returned west and his eyes fell on Gastown, or Granville, much closer to the ocean. He planned to name the place Vancouver, after the island across the Georgia Strait, to provide a geographically familiar association with a place people already knew. The dreams of the Port Moody boosters were shattered instantly, the imagined grand swelling of their land value deflating as all speculative bubbles eventually do. They protested, naturally, but in vain. The provincial government agreed to subsidize continuation of the line farther west to this more suitable location. One city declined while another rose.

While he was in British Columbia, Van Horne took the opportunity to inspect the progress of Onderdonk's work. Onderdonk was under contract to the government, which would then turn over the built track to the CPR. Because Onderdonk never would have the responsibility of running a railway over his portion of track, Van Horne worried that he might be tempted to cut corners. He was right to be concerned.

Onderdonk was in such a rush to complete his section, and the terrain and remoteness of his work so extreme, that it was hardly surprising the standards of the line for which he had responsibility were revealed to be deficient compared with the quality of construction on most of the eastern sections of track. At one time the expenses were so large— hundreds of thousands of dollars over budget—that he was arrested for not paying his debts to contractors, until the railway arranged for him to be released. It would cost even more money in the coming years and require a continuous but much diminished labour force to rework and improve many sections of the line, just as the sections around Thunder Bay that were built by the government during the Mackenzie years rather than by the CPR itself were also deficient. The tunnels were small and rough, the bridges were slapdash and in some cases unstable, and the levelling was imperfect. Sections sagged, others wobbled, others fell into disrepair quickly. There were landslides, bridge collapses and track washouts. Van Horne was not impressed.

The log trusses were the worst Van Horne had ever seen in all his railroading years, erratically patched and shored up to make them stable, while debris and rocks were continually tumbling down onto the track. To avoid ever more expensive and time-consuming tunnelling, the track had been built with hundreds of long curves that made travel time longer and maintenance far more expensive; much of it had to be repaired or redone in the coming years. And there were to be great battles between the CPR and the minister of railways, Charles Tupper, who was then succeeded by John Henry Pope, over whether the quality of the rail structures that the government handed over to the CPR met the standard implicit in the contract. The dispute wasn't settled until 1891, partially vindicating the CPR but not enough to satisfy them that they hadn't been handed merely a "temporary road."

BY 1885, THE CPR HAD BEEN nearly bankrupted by the unimaginable cost of blasting and constructing through the Canadian Shield around Lake Superior and in the mountains and gorges of British Columbia. But they could not slow or stop the work; if they did, their highly specialized workforce would disperse, and it would cost a fortune to start the whole operation up again, build the momentum and lure workers back. As with a contemporary pipeline, the expense of starting and stopping work, with thousands of labourers on standby, not working but still drawing pay, results in staggering cost overruns. If the workers drifted away to find other opportunities, the project would die. The directors knew they could not temporarily pause the project until they could build up their finances to pay for the final stretches. It must be done now or never.

Soon the workers' pay became erratic or delayed. In one instance, in March 1885, at a major construction camp near the town of Golden, B.C., the pay car was delayed for months, and the workers went on strike. Major Sam Steele, who was frequently touring the line as part of the NWMP's attempt to maintain order and stamp out booze and smuggling in the isolated work camps, warned Macdonald and railway officials that they were creating a dangerously volatile environment by not paying these men on time, particularly when their life was so hard and their entitlement so meagre. More than three hundred men formed a mob to march on a nearby camp and claim restitution or ransack it to claim their pay, but they were talked down by a mere eight Mounties and the heartfelt promise of the local manager that their pay was en route. But how could the CPR get pay out to the workers, or the contractors, or the suppliers, when they didn't have sufficient cash flow to do so—or at least to be able to do so for all the workers at once? No easy answers presented themselves. Directors James J. Hill, John Kennedy and Duncan McIntyre abandoned the CPR, believing it would go under. By then, only three of the original investors remained: George Stephen, Donald Smith and Richard Angus.

Even the Bank of Montreal, hitherto so compliant, owing to Stephen's (who was also still the president of the CPR) and Smith's prominence on its board of directors, balked at further outlays and risk. The whole unwieldy contraption of the CPR was now teetering under its own weight—leveraged to the hilt, like a line of dominoes ready for toppling, the directors desperately trying to scrape up another million to keep it going for another month. In a meeting in Montreal, Smith sighed and reputedly said despondently to Stephen that they had two choices: go cap in hand to the government or face criminal prosecution. But the government was no longer an option. John Henry Pope, Macdonald's most influential cabinet minister, had already persuaded him once, arguing, "You will have to loan them the money because the day the CPR busts, the Conservative party busts the day after."

Macdonald could see no political way forward. Many in his government had threatened to resign if he asked for more funds for the CPR.

Rumours were swirling, and the company's stock was dropping as Stephen engaged in ever more creative methods to persuade investors to loosen their purse strings. The line was actually making money on its completed sections, but it lacked capital for the final construction to earn the government track-dependent subsidies and unlock its true value by connecting the St. Lawrence to the Pacific—and to earn enough money to service or pay back its loans and the interest on its bonds. When Van Horne returned east, he did so along the CPR route—by train where possible, by horse, boat or cart when not. The signs of economic activity were everywhere. Indeed, all along the line across the prairies, giant mounds of buffalo bones were being loaded onto railcars for shipment to St. Paul, where they would be ground up into fertilizer. The skeleton of the old economy was literally being hauled away by the railway to clear the way for the new one.

Stephen made three voyages to London in 1884 to raise funds. Van Horne was paying workers in the bush north of Lake Superior with Bank of Montreal cheques instead of cash—being isolated at work camps all winter, although fed and housed, the men would be unable to cash them until spring, by which time he hoped the funds would be available. Stephen and Smith had steadfastly sunk all their assets and credit into the venture. Now, contemplating receivership, they had appraisers go through their Montreal mansions, itemizing *objets d'art*, silver cutlery, hand-crafted furniture, imported carpets and other accoutrements of wealth. Perhaps they could keep the thousands of men working another month if they sold off their personal possessions.

As the increasingly desperate and nearly bankrupt CPR stumbled along its victory lap, one final obstacle suddenly placed itself in the way—a shocking threat to Canada's existence that proved to be the catalyst for the CPR's second wind: the return of Louis Riel.

CHAPTER TWENTY-ONE

RIEL'S LAST SPIKE

————

In the 1880s, Canada absorbed well over a hundred thousand immigrants each year, mostly impoverished rural workers from Ireland and Scotland or refugees from the congested urban slums of industrializing England. As the decade progressed, so did the number of immigrants crossing the Atlantic, crammed into the fetid holds of wooden sailing ships, lured by the exaggerated promise of good times, free or cheap land and the opportunity to make a better life for themselves. By 1883, thousands of the new arrivals were finding their way west to the prairies along the long, circuitous, partially completed segments of the CPR, or along U.S. railways. Once at Winnipeg, it was cheap and easy to be carted farther west, and locomotives pulling the ubiquitous "colonist cars" were hauling several thousand settlers every week farther along the line. They soon started busting the sod and transforming the endless grasslands, now empty of buffalo, into sod houses and homestead farms. Some of the settlers brought with them seeds, tools and livestock such as oxen, cattle, chickens and sheep.

The government was giving away quarter sections of land, provided it was worked for three years, which meant ripping up the grassland and replacing it with grains and other hardy crops. Even land adjacent to the railway went cheap, purchased from the CPR along their right-of-way; most of the cost was then rebated by the government if the settlers planted crops and built buildings. New towns began to pop up like weeds wherever the railway had a scheduled stop. People concentrated their farms there, along with services such as newspapers and flimsy hotels with bunkbeds and cookhouses, wooden façades and canvas walls. These tent cities went by names now familiar: Brandon, Regina, Moose Jaw, Swift Current, Medicine Hat and Calgary. The NWMP had constables and officers patrolling the new settlements, trying to keep the peace and, like Justice Begbie in B.C. decades earlier, maintain some semblance of order and official presence so that anarchy didn't arise among so many disparate people vying for land and opportunity. The courtroom was an ever-moving canvas tent or even the back of a flatbed ox cart.

Trains kept trundling west loaded with steel rails, mountains of timber for ties and crates of spikes, along with food, tools and other construction equipment. Once the track had been laid, another group of specialized workers followed: the telegraph construction teams. They erected poles along the tracks and strung telegraph wires between them. The telegraph was revolutionary: suddenly people could send and receive news immediately, instead of after months of riding a horse, dogsled or canoe to deliver handwritten missives. The Canadian prairies were now part of the expanding information network, which made it much easier for law enforcement to keep the peace, as it received information from Winnipeg and St. Paul, and for the railway to manage equipment and supplies or report progress, as well as for new arrivals to exchange news with relatives and friends. The position of telegrapher was one of the first skilled jobs for women.

———

THE PROGRESS OF THE RAILWAY across the prairies symbolized the beginning of a new era. The new settlers from afar arrived en masse at the same time as the buffalo disappeared. The famine, disease and social dislocation became a catalyst for severe social discontent among the prairie's original inhabitants. The Métis and several of their Indigenous allies—particularly the Cree and the Saulteaux (Plains Ojibwe)—dreamed of regaining control over their land and their lives, and over a world that was changing before their eyes into something alien, unreliable and hostile. The treaties so recently negotiated were already being dishonoured morally and legally, and people began to gather and talk of solutions for the future.

Eastern politicians were treating the land as their own Crown colony. Rather than viewing Indigenous peoples as full participants in the federation, absentee and often corrupt patronage-appointment officials made life-and-death decisions for people against their wishes and without their consent. The officials' priorities did not correlate with those of the original inhabitants; many were just morally righteous plunderers. The intensity of the anger and outrage, the poverty, starvation and tuberculosis—and the failure of the government to meaningfully address these problems—was the foundation of the discontent that fuelled two partly related uprisings, one of primarily Métis and their leader, Louis Riel, and the other of a faction of the Cree and their allies associated with the respected diplomat and leader Big Bear.

These challenges to the new order have become known collectively as the North-West Rebellion, the North-West Resistance or the Saskatchewan Rebellion. The underlying causes of the uprising were seething fury toward the government and anxiety about the future. The proximate cause, the spark that ignited the conflagration, was technically the survey of land lots that went against the customs of local Métis farmers along the South Saskatchewan River. It was the beginning of a tradition that has echoed down the ages, a tradition whereby Canadians are governed, at least in certain aspects, by what can only be described as an ineptocracy.

The events of 1885 are an oft-told story. The basic outline of what occurred is indisputable and had a direct and profound influence on the completion of the CPR, snatching it from the jaws of certain financial collapse, a collapse that would have had severe implications not just for the burgeoning Canadian financial sector but for the future settlement, political stability and development of the nation as an independent entity distinct from the United States.

In the fifteen years after the first uprising involving Riel, many Métis had migrated west from central Manitoba and settled in the region around the forks of the North and South Saskatchewan Rivers. They continued with their semi-nomadic lives, but by the 1880s their economy was less centred around the buffalo hunt and more on farming as the means of survival. As they had been earlier, their land plots were laid out in the old seigneurial style, narrow strips of land extending away from the river. And, as earlier, it was the government land surveyors who stirred dissent.

Back in 1883, the agents of the Dominion Land Survey began to divide the land into sections of one square mile, ignoring the existing Métis plots, claiming that the Métis did not hold clear title. With the buffalo disappearing, this was an existential threat. Coupled with the realization that they were no longer free from encroaching civilization, it was also a political awakening—there was no land farther west to which they could retreat. The endless grasslands now had an end, and many people didn't want to witness it.

Gaining recognition for their prior claims to the land was key to their survival. It was painfully obvious to the Métis, most of whom had ties to various Indigenous peoples who shared the land, that starvation, disease and suffering were crushing all those societies that had been dependent upon the buffalo for so many aspects of their existence. They

feared complete displacement and descent into the horrors now afflict-
ing the Plains peoples who had signed treaties and selected reserve
lands, but who were nevertheless in dire straits since the government
had refused to honour its commitments. Rations were being curtailed,
and the only logical reason for that, apart from gross mismanagement
and incompetence, was to hasten starvation. Yet one prominent chief,
Big Bear (Mistahimaskwa) of the Cree along the North Saskatchewan,
although reluctantly a signatory to Treaty 6, had refused to select a
reserve. In June 1884, Big Bear persuaded nearly two thousand Cree to
congregate at Poundmaker's reserve near Battleford. Poundmaker
(Pitikwahanapiwiyin) was another prominent Cree leader who was
rallying for better treatment of his people. Most of the Indigenous
grievances were substantially different from those of the Métis. They
just happened to occur at the same time.

The government in Ottawa was, as usual, oblivious to the goings-on
in the distant land; it just wanted a railway and the settlers and taxes
it would bring. The minister of the interior, David Macpherson, for
example, hadn't ever bothered to travel to the interior. The largest settlement and the capital of the administrative district, formed in 1882,
was Prince Albert, with about eight hundred people, with a secondary
settlement at Battleford having around five hundred people; perhaps
ten thousand lived in the entire region of central Saskatchewan,
including Métis, English and French settlers and Indigenous people.

Protest meetings were becoming regular along the north and south
branches of the Saskatchewan River. Across the land, people were meeting to discuss their options and ways to proceed in the chaotic new
world. Grievances were aired, and they were soon radicalized by the
dismissive and arrogant attitude of superiority from the eastern officials.
The rising discontent wasn't directed explicitly at the railway, but the
railway was a symbol of the upheaval as well as its harbinger. Ottawa
could have managed the situation properly, but it didn't, not for the

Métis with their anxiety over land title and their future, and not for the Indigenous peoples suffering malnutrition and disease on their reserves. The suspicion grew that the eastern government had no intention to treat the Métis as a self-governing entity, and might not even be inclined to recognize their prior land rights and customs.

Previously respected for their role in stamping out the illegal whiskey trade from Fort Benton, the NWMP now found themselves deployed to stamp out labour unrest in CPR work camps and intimidate Indigenous peoples chafing under the authoritarian mandates of the government regarding food distribution and haphazard application of treaty rights. In 1884, the Métis decided to send a delegation south, to find Riel and persuade him to return and become their spokesman, to deal with the government that sought dominion over them but that casually disregarded their interests and complaints.

THE DISTANCE WAS FAR, as Riel was now a schoolteacher at a Jesuit mission in Montana. The small party rode over one thousand kilometres southwest to discover him living in near poverty in a remote outpost. And this Riel was not the man he had been in 1869, when he emerged as a potent leader in the Red River Settlement whose actions resulted in the creation of the province of Manitoba. After being exiled in 1875, never being allowed to claim the honour and respect that his people had bestowed upon him, owing to government intransigence and eastern politics, compelled to skulk about back and forth across the border, he had become unmoored from reality. Believing himself a prophet and under the sway of hallucinations and delusions, he had spent nearly two years in asylums in Quebec. Afterward, Riel had made his way west with admonitions to avoid excitement, married a young Métis, Marguerite Monet, and had two children. Basically, he had found a peaceful, if dull, life. His fragile state of mind, soothed by his remote surroundings, was disturbed by the arrival of the delegation, and his old grievances resurfaced. He agreed to return, believing it his destiny.

Riel now occasionally raved about theology and other tangential ideas that had little to do with the bread-and-butter problems that were fuelling the discontent. Later, his erratic and seemingly nonsensical behaviour became even more concerning. He wanted to rename the days of the week to avoid any pagan influences and proclaimed Bishop Ignace Bourget of Montreal to be the new Pope. Believing himself a conduit to the divine, Riel regaled followers with his visions and his conversations with God and other disturbing claims, all of which were politely ignored.

One of the four delegates sent to find Riel was a prominent and respected leader named Gabriel Dumont, who would emerge as the chief strategist and military leader in the coming year. Dumont, now aged forty-seven, was a larger-than-life character in his community around Batoche, where he had settled with his wife, Madeleine Wilkie, whom he had married in 1858, and their two adopted children. Descended from a prominent voyageur and buffalo-hunting family in Red River, Dumont was a renowned hunter, community organizer and leader of the hunt when buffalo still roamed. He was also a renowned drinker and gambler and a naturally charismatic leader respected throughout the region. He was fluent in six or seven languages and dialects, including all of the local languages such as Michif, Siksiká, Sioux, Cree and Crow, as well as French, yet he spoke only a few phrases in English. He was also illiterate. Although Dumont was an obvious choice to spearhead Métis grievances, having in the past been a negotiator for Métis interests and having secured a peace treaty with the Niisitapi (Blackfoot) people, who were traditional enemies, he had no experience dealing with easterners and their customs. Laconic and practical, he was not suited to diplomacy, giving speeches, writing legal documents or issuing political ultimatums to foreigners.

Although Dumont was instrumental in developing a self-governing council in the Batoche region, his influence was mostly limited to one faction of the dispersed Métis people. Sam Steele praised his virtues, writing, "One might travel the plains from one end to the other and talk to the Métis hunters and never hear an unkind word said of Dumont. . . . When in trouble the cry of all was for Gabriel." It was thought that, when partnered with Riel, they would be a potent force. And they were. While Riel fell down the rabbit hole of delusion, believing that he was a new prophet, hectoring, beseeching and gesticulating while propounding his theological musings, Dumont devoted himself to the practical business of defeating the Dominion forces to liberate his people from what he believed was the yoke of oppression. He was a man of action rather than of letters. Their partnership was somewhat odd, considering Dumont had little patience for the church.

Riel at first presented a reasonable façade, convening meetings at farms around the forks of the Saskatchewan where he delivered speeches and formulated a plan. He listened to and wrote down the grievances and forwarded them on to Ottawa in late 1884, while the CPR was flirting with insolvency. Some of the demands included a responsible government in which citizens had a vote in the affairs of their land; more respectful treatment of the Indigenous peoples, who were in a destitute state; a reduction in grain transport tariffs; and the issuance of land scrip, such as had been given to other Métis years earlier around Red River. Riel was far more moderate in his tactics than Dumont later claimed to have urged: attacking forts, police outposts and settlers who weren't part of their cause, and destroying railway tracks in the south. Riel hoped the government would respond as it had in 1869–70.

While the requests were reasonable, the response from Ottawa was not. Riel was essentially ignored. Yet the signs of discontent were all around. A priest in the region became concerned and wrote letters to Edgar Dewdney, the lieutenant-governor of the North-West Territories warning of a possible uprising and relaying his fears that the discontent could spread to include the Cree and perhaps even the Niisitapi farther west—that the entire region could rise up against the ill treatment. He too was ignored. Others reported similarly, including Major L.N.F. Crozier of the NWMP detachment at Battleford, the mutton-chopped newly appointed superintendent and commander of northwestern Saskatchewan's force. The government agreed only to convene a commission to collect information and study the issue, a time-honoured delaying tactic. This angered the Métis even more, as their concerns were essentially being fobbed off as insignificant or irrelevant. There was even the suggestion that Riel could be bribed to depart again with his family, but whether true or not, he was certainly rebuffed—a fatal error that was to cost a great deal of money and end dozens of lives.

After all of Riel's appeals to Ottawa fell on deaf ears, in March he, Dumont and William Henry (Honoré) Jackson—a University of Toronto–educated Methodist who had moved west in 1881 and eventually became a sympathizer of the Métis cause and served as Riel's secretary—wrote up the Métis's grievances and set up what they called the Provisional Government of Saskatchewan, hoping that events would unfold as they had in 1869, with the mere threat of violence causing the government to buckle and negotiate. They sent riders out to cut the new telegraph line, captured some prisoners, plundered a few farms and generally began to make their discontent and intentions known.

The NWMP sent around a hundred police north in anticipation of further trouble. Crozier was holed up in Fort Carlton, an erstwhile fur trade outpost turned police headquarters near Duck Lake, when Riel demanded his surrender—he wanted the fortified post as his own capital. "We want blood! blood! If Carlton is not surrendered it will be a war of extermination; I must have an answer by 12 o'clock or we will attack and take the fort." Crozier, being proud, refused. He steeled himself and dispatched a detachment of nearly twenty to gather supplies from a nearby trading fort at Duck Lake. The contingent was intercepted by Dumont and a band of armed Métis and Cree, who prodded them in the chests with guns and jeered at them until they retreated back to Fort Carlton.

Crozier was apoplectic, his pride trampled and the honour of the police besmirched. Rather than await reinforcements from Prince Albert, he organized a retributory force that would reassert authority over the rebels. This force included fifty-three NWMP non-commissioned officers and forty-one men of the Prince Albert Volunteers, hauling a seven-pounder cannon. They ventured forth to set things right. Perhaps underlying Crozier's decision was a fear that the uprising would quickly spread from the Métis and spiral into a larger uprising of all the Indigenous peoples, which would be impossible for any local constabulary or militia to handle. They met Dumont and his Métis on the snow-blanketed prairie of late spring near Duck Lake, about ninety kilometres north of Saskatoon. The men on each side sought defensive positions, Dumont's in the small nearby cabins, Crozier's by overturning their sleds on the trampled ground that passed as a road.

Dumont sent his brother Isidore and an old, partially blind Cree chief named Assiwiyin forward, holding a pole with a white flag for a parley. Crozier strode forth along with an English Métis interpreter, Joe McKay. They talked about nothing in particular until Crozier ascertained that Métis men were sneaking into position, possibly to surround him. Apparently he spied Isidore and Assiwiyin on horseback drawing their guns and ordered McKay to fire, which he did, killing both men before they could do anything. As they dropped from their horses, events moved fast. Dumont's men began encircling the militia, levelling shots at them meanwhile. Riel himself then appeared, galloping across the snowy plain, giant white crucifix in his hand, accompanied by 150 mounted and armed charging Métis. Within a half-hour, Crozier had lost a quarter of his force and was routed. He retreated to Fort Carlton with twelve dead and eleven severely injured.

The familiar sequence of events followed over the next few months, with attacks and counterattacks involving Métis, NWMP and primarily Cree warriors. Easterners became suddenly familiar with western place names such as Batoche, Battleford, Frog Lake, Duck Lake and Lac La Biche, which were all west and north of Winnipeg and Red River, north even of the new towns springing up along the railway route. The easterners learned the formerly unfamiliar names of people such as Dumont, Jackson, Wandering Spirit, Big Bear and Poundmaker. They already knew the name Riel and had already formulated their opinions, which correlated with their allegiances and identity.

Soon there was a separate uprising by the nearby Cree, not directly related to Riel's uprising. This tertiary revolt was described in the eastern press not as a natural response to starvation, fear and anger at being left to die by the people who so recently had promised them aid, education and tools in exchange for their lands, but rather as another prong of a deadly rebellion that needed to be repressed. At Duck Lake and Frog Lake, the destitute people killed the local Indian agent and nine others, including two priests, and plundered supplies at the nearby Hudson's Bay Company outpost to alleviate their hunger and assuage their anger and sense of betrayal. Many of the killers were motivated by revenge, stemming from acts of cruelty such as withholding food and abuse of local women.

Despite the specific local grievances, however, the great fear was that these actions might inspire a general destabilizing uprising throughout the region and perhaps provide an excuse for the U.S. to move in—the usual fear of the Canadian ruling class. In a panic, in the early weeks of the uprising, the NWMP and officials sent emissaries to the Siksiká-speaking peoples to persuade them to stay neutral and not join with the Cree. While the Catholic priest Albert Lacombe worked to obtain assurances from Crowfoot (Isapo-Muxika) that his Niisitapi (Blackfoot) warriors would not participate in a rebellion, Jerry Potts did the same, riding from camp to camp, meeting and talking and spreading rumours of Cree defeats, up-playing the enmity between the Niisitapi and the Cree and urging caution and peace. Potts knew the North-West conflict in 1885 was a losing battle in a changing land, and he sought to keep his people out of it.

All of which was true. Potts was right. Riel was a deeply flawed leader unable to inspire a general uprising, and the outcome was not good for the participants. Not that their underlying discontent was unjustified; they just lacked the force, leadership, ammunition and manpower to effect real change. Riel's claim that God had commanded him to return to Canada as a prophet ruffled the Catholic priests, who soon offered only tepid support for the uprising because of Riel's heresy. His strongly religious pronouncements also alienated almost all of the Indigenous peoples and most of the Métis.

Crowfoot counselled his people against joining the uprising, despite his distrust of the agents of the recently created Department of Indian Affairs who were so lackadaisically tending to their obligations, not because he didn't think the uprising was justified, but because he didn't think it would be successful. Nevertheless, he was later praised for his loyalty, taken on tours of the East and given a lifetime pass to ride the CPR. In his later years, many of his children died, leaving him only a blind son and three daughters. His people were spiritually wounded and materially impoverished, and it would take generations to begin to claw back their dignity. A philosophical, introspective man, near the end of his life he looked back on the turbulence, heartbreak and betrayal of his years under the prairie sun. "A little while and I will be gone from among you," he mused, "whither I cannot tell. From nowhere we came, into nowhere we go. What is life? It is a flash of a firefly in the night. It is a breath of a buffalo in the winter time. It is as the little shadow that runs across the grass and loses itself in the sunset." Crowfoot died in the spring of 1890, aged sixty, at Blackfoot Crossing.

WITH NUMEROUS REPORTS being sent back from correspondents, the eastern media now focused its attention upon the districts of the North-West Territories, a land that had previously failed to interest them. It was only "sort of" part of the Dominion, a psychologically distant appendage safely tucked away in the remote corners of most people's imaginations, not a factor in anyone's political calculations (apart from the CPR's periodic demands for more loans). But from March 27 onward, it featured in the news, as did the railway—still to be completed—that would connect this region and its disparate people to the imperial heartland. On April 2, news of a massacre of priests and settlers at Frog Lake hardened eastern opinions against the protesters and their "unlawful" challenge to legitimate authority—that legitimate authority being themselves, since there was no responsible government in the region. Ostensibly the Cree chief Big Bear had been in charge, but in fact he had lost authority over his band by this point. Soon, Poundmaker was leading other Cree to assault settlers and police officers. It was believed a great general uprising could threaten all the new communities. Macdonald knew he had to do something or perhaps lose the entire North-West he had fought so long to obtain for Canada.

Van Horne recognized an opportunity when it presented itself. He was already in Ottawa, along with Stephen and Smith, and he made a bold promise to transport Canadian militia west to the scene of the uprising within twelve days. (During the previous Riel uprising it had taken ninety-six days of hard travel to get Colonel Wolseley's mostly volunteer troops from Toronto to Red River.) Two days later, trains were chuffing into Toronto, Kingston, Montreal and Ottawa as a general mobilization of volunteer reserve militia hastily gathered troops for the great action: more than three thousand soldiers and their ammunition, artillery, horses, food and supplies, commanded by Sir Frederick Middleton. New battalions were hastily formed and old, dusty equipment was unpacked and handed to young men, many of whom had incomplete uniforms. As usual, Van Horne knew that much would be overlooked in terms of efficiency and quality if there was plenty of good, hot food. The image of the railway was at stake, after all, since many had never yet ridden on it through these lands. Steak, roast turkey and coffee were eagerly consumed, when they were available. The journey wouldn't actually be that easy, since the railway wasn't complete and operational in many places.

At the time of its greatest triumph, as the conglomerate somehow came up with a million dollars to ship the troops west to pacify the upstart westerners, the CPR was mere weeks from financial ruin, unable to pay the bond interest that was due in June or even its employees' wages. There was worker unrest along the line, hardship and hunger for men with no credit and now no wages for months on end. Van Horne, of course, knew that long sections of track along Lake Superior were still little more than partially blasted tunnels and rockfaces interspersed with flat graded sections that weren't connected to anything. There were four major gaps, totalling nearly 140 kilometres, on which a locomotive could not be run. Van Horne went into action, spinning the wheels of logistics to get temporary track opened, a series of shuttling trains working between the incomplete sections. In a different season, the journey could have been relatively easy, but a winter cold snap made the long, arduous trek a dangerous undertaking. In freezing temperatures, men stood waiting for delayed trains or trudged across frozen lakes to connect with intermittent portions of track, only to lie on open flatbed cars. But once past Lake Superior, they rode in relative comfort west. It took them only seven days to reach Winnipeg, and two more days to be in the Qu'Appelle Valley, south of the main conflict.

Although many of Middleton's force were raw recruits, they greatly outnumbered Dumont's militia, by as much as five to one. Yet Dumont's creative guerrilla-style tactics allowed his men to drive off the imperial forces, and the Métis, numbering barely two hundred, retreated to Batoche. Once the Canadian soldiers reached Batoche, Dumont defended the community for four days, holding a vastly outnumbering force at bay until he ran low on ammunition and was routed. The Métis surrender and defeat were really a foregone conclusion, inevitable given the broader technological and demographic factors and political issues at play. The situation was radically different from fifteen years earlier, even if this was unknown or unappreciated by the rebels.

The speed with which the rebellion was defeated opened eastern eyes to the value of the railway for a whole different purpose: national defence. Empires can't exist without the force to sweep away opposition. Or perhaps, more cynically, law is about order, not right or wrong. Once the ugly duckling of the investment world, with fleeing directors, despondent financiers and an agitated, hand-wringing government nervously awaiting the falling axe, the CPR now leapt from its corporate grave, clawing toward the sun phoenix-like, to bask in the rarefied atmosphere of public acclaim. The CPR was suddenly a great patriotic enterprise, a necessity for the Dominion to project strength and stability, the foundation of the nation's future prospects. It now had a specific purpose: defending the empire's newly acquired lands from perfidious rebels and American encroachment. Macdonald seized upon the fortuitous turn of events, using the desired political cover to back the Bank of Montreal to guarantee the company's bonds and to advance a further loan, enough for the line to be completed. Lord Revelstoke of Barings Bank in London underwrote a further sale of stock, and the pressure was off; B.C. now has a scenic town and a national park named after him.

When Van Horne, Stephen, Smith and the others received the news, the months-long strain and stress dissipated and they let loose. Van Horne wrote, "We tossed up chairs to the ceiling; we tramped on desks; I believe we danced on tables. I do not fancy that any of us knows what occurred, and no one who was there can ever remember anything except loud yells of joy and the sound of things breaking!"

FOR THE LEADERS OF THE GENERAL UPRISING, however, there was no tossing chairs to the ceiling in celebration. They surrendered or were soon captured. There being no buffalo, and therefore insufficient food, there was nowhere to run.

Although he didn't directly participate in the 1885 uprising by Riel and Dumont, Big Bear was tracked down by Steele and a contingent of mounted police in early June. Near starvation and out of ammunition, he was captured and charged, along with fourteen others from his band. Convicted of treason, despite not personally participating in any violent activity, he served nearly two years in jail before being released into a world leached of its colour and vitality. A photo after his release shows him shorn of his hair, bent over and garbed in a ragged prison uniform, his powerful visage exuding defeat and regret. He died soon after, in 1888, on the Little Pine Reserve, where he had retired to live with his daughter.

Riel surrendered to NWMP constables on May 15 and was taken south in custody to Moose Jaw, the nearest CPR stop. An image from the time shows his eyes drooping in resignation over the formless bulk of his future: inert, sad, immutable. The plan had been to transport him to Winnipeg for trial, but without warning, on Macdonald's orders, the train headed instead to Regina, where there was no requirement to provide a trial in French, as was the law in Manitoba, which might have placed some sympathetic Métis on the jury. Riel's third child, a son, was born and died on the same day, about a month before his father was hanged.

The same political disputes erupted in Ontario and Quebec as they had the previous time Riel was defeated: Catholic Quebec stridently demanded leniency, while Protestant Ontario demanded blood. Riel refused to plead insanity and made speeches defending himself and pleading for the rights and future of the Métis people. The six-man jury of English Protestants found him guilty, but recommended leniency. Then Macdonald, so proud and pleased with himself for finally seeing his life's work about to be accomplished, a great transportation link that would unify the nation, famously refused to grant leniency to Riel, thereby hammering a stake into the nation's heart that disrupted unity for generations to come. It was a folly just as profound as Riel's own great error fifteen years earlier, when he ordered a firing squad to unleash its volley at Thomas Scott.

Stuck between unpalatable options, Macdonald brooded and calculated and then reputedly, and famously, exclaimed: "He shall hang though every dog in Quebec bark in his favour." There is little evidence he actually made such a statement; it was probably made up after the fact to satisfy a narrative. Macdonald wanted Riel found guilty and wanted him publicly hanged, as a message to others who might imagine acting upon similar anti-government sentiment.

Gabriel Dumont fled to the U.S. Joined by his wife, they considered settling in North Dakota, but when she died of tuberculosis in 1886 he agreed to join Buffalo Bill's Wild West show as a rebel and sharpshooter. After several years of wandering and giving speeches about his time at the heart of the uprising, he returned to his farm in Batoche to live out his life. He died of heart failure in 1906, at the age of sixty-eight.

Honoré Jackson, Riel's secretary, was captured in the Battle of Batoche and sent to a mental institution in Winnipeg. He escaped a few months later, fled to Chicago and joined the labour movement. He later returned to Canada for a couple of years and began interviewing participants in the rebellion and recording their reminiscences. After washing up in

New York City, he began organizing all the documents relating to the people and times of the 1880s, including newspaper clippings, pamphlets, eyewitness accounts and his own considerable notes. But in 1951, in poverty and extreme old age, he was evicted from his apartment, and the city workers, not knowing that his large collection of papers was essentially an archive of the history of the Métis people, sold it as waste paper. The history of the Métis nation, those who most powerfully challenged the Canadian government in all the years of its existence, boxes of documents of inestimable value to understanding the nuances of individual personalities and reasons for the pivotal events of 1885, were tossed out as trash on the gritty sidewalk of a foreign city thousands of kilometres away.

If it was not evident before, after the 1885 uprising it was no longer possible to overlook the reality that great swaths of land had been and were being handed off to politically connected members of the eastern establishment who would soon benefit from the influx of immigrant settlers brought by the railway. For whose benefit was this new empire being constructed? many asked. Of course, the federal government caused the uprising in the first place, with its callously arrogant and disdainful policies imposed from afar, and barely held on to its empire just as it was being born. The government did quickly smarten up in one respect, though, and resurveyed the Métis river lots in accordance with their wishes (although many of the deeds were then snapped up cheaply by speculators). All the Indigenous peoples on the prairies were now living on reserves, where their welfare could be monitored and attended to by the federal government, with the predictable results that plague them and the nation to this day.

THE LAST SPIKE WAS HAMMERED in at Craigellachie, just west of today's town of Revelstoke, on November 7, 1885, a mere nine days before

Riel was hanged in Regina. The first all-Canadian locomotive passenger train chuffed its way west on the 4,670 kilometres of track from Montreal to Vancouver in a handful of days instead of months, departing Montreal on June 28, 1886, and arriving in Vancouver on July 4. It was the start of regularly scheduled cross-country rail service. The primitive, smoke-belching contraption screeched to a stop for water, coal and supplies at the new and growing towns along the route, as the prairies filled up with new people. From a population of barely one thousand clustered around a sawmill operation in 1881, Vancouver grew to over twenty thousand by the early twentieth century; a decade later it had mushroomed to nearly a hundred thousand. The land would never be the same.

IMPERIAL TO EMPYREAL

———

Once the railway was completed, immigration was slow but steady on the prairies, and by the end of the century hundreds of thousands of people had made the journey west in crowded colonist cars, a stream that rapidly became a river after Wilfrid Laurier became prime minister in 1896 and aggressively promoted settlement. Hundreds of towns sprung up along the railway line and adjacent to the many spur lines that were established along its route, primarily grain shipment hubs or coal mining outposts. Many families became grain farmers, living in rudimentary sod huts, uninsulated tarpaper shacks or crude log cabins. Others worked in logging, in mining or on the railway in various capacities.

Many of these newcomers were from eastern and central Europe, from countries like Russia, Poland, Germany, Austria, Hungary, Sweden, Latvia and Ukraine, hoping to make a better life for themselves and their families. Southern or Mediterranean Europeans were frowned upon, as were Blacks from the U.S. The Laurier government believed that turning an empire into a nation involved increasing and promoting cultural and genetic homogeneity. After several thousand Blacks had migrated north to settle on the prairies, forming distinctive towns such as Amber Valley in Alberta, the government sought to stunt their arrival, and in 1911 Cabinet approved an order-in-council that prohibited "any immigrants belonging to the Negro race, which race is deemed unsuitable to the climate and requirements of Canada." The government sent agents to the U.S. to dissuade such people from coming north and instructed border agents to deny them papers certifying they were farmers, which made them ineligible for the subsidized train fare. These tactics were so successful that the order-in-council became no longer necessary and was repealed. In 1908, Laurier also limited the immigration of Japanese males to four hundred per year. He had earlier increased the Chinese head tax to restrict Chinese immigration.

These newcomers weren't squinting to the horizon searching for evidence of a bison herd or wild horses or migrating birds on the wing. These newcomers had a different vision for the future, of a land waiting to be tamed and manipulated. In their mind's eye they envisioned vast forests awaiting the axe, which would reveal rocky hills with rich veins of coal or copper; rivers and streams on their way to the ocean patiently awaiting a dam or waterwheel to grind the grain to be grown on the drained marshes and plowed-over grasslands. Meanwhile, the eastern government likewise dreamed of the bounty it would gather from these peasant farmers and labourers, who would pay taxes, consume the outputs of eastern industry and ship the products of their labour back east, at higher freight rates than the preferential shipping rates charged for manufactured goods being sent west on the new railway. Fortunes would soon be made supplying this new captive market.

The CPR also developed a passenger business through the clever marketing scheme of creating national parks to bring in tourists, starting as early as 1885, when Macdonald created the first small park around

Banff. Since its earliest days, the financial viability of the CPR was inextricably linked to tourism. Beginning in 1886, under Van Horne's direction, the CPR built a series of hotels and then expanded them into elaborate, architecturally fanciful châteaux in beautiful and striking locations, to induce wealthy European and American travellers to pay to ride the railway across the continent and stay in the luxury hotels: Château Frontenac in Quebec, Windsor Station in Montreal and, in the West, the Banff Springs Hotel, Chateau Lake Louise, Glacier House, Mount Stephen House and the Empress in Victoria. These hotels were for those travelling in luxury rail and dining cars to resorts to hobnob with others like themselves, in establishments complete with tennis courts and spas in the middle of what had previously been wilderness. They generated revenue for the railway and founded the tourism economy.

The CPR then established fleets of vessels on both the Pacific and Atlantic Oceans, laying the foundation for a transportation network that allowed subjects of the British Empire to travel around the world and facilitating the transfer of commodities from the interior to the coast—which in turn spurred further settlement. After the completion of the CPR, it was possible to travel and send messages from one coast to another with relative ease, which had an enormous influence on the development of the country. In the 1880s, for the first time, goods from China and Japan could sail to Vancouver, be loaded onto trains and end up in Toronto and Montreal. The British Empire had a new link in its globe-girdling network.

But far from being a boon to regional economies, other than resource extraction, the railway stifled the development of local manufacturing by flooding the western regions with cheap manufactured goods from eastern Canada, similar to the way in which a great influx of Chinese goods stunted the North American manufacturing industry in the early twenty-first century. But regardless of the relative balance of prosperity, the railway radically changed the country, enabling Canada to develop a national economy, which led to political stability and a national identity.

For the Indigenous and Métis, however, the picture was not so rosy. After the 1885 rebellion, a pass system was implemented that essentially imprisoned Plains people on their reserves unless they could obtain permission to leave from a government official, and these were often corrupt and self-serving. The objective was to keep the official "Indians" pacified and hidden away while the land was flooded with foreigners and irrevocably changed around them. For generations there existed a general meanness and condescending attempts to crush Indigenous spirits and culture, rather than to provide a bridge for them to flourish while adapting to changing economic realities.

Throughout the line of late nineteenth- and early twentieth-century prime ministers after Confederation—Macdonald, Mackenzie, Macdonald again, John Abbott and Laurier—the federal policy toward Indigenous people remained roughly the same. The goal was to assimilate them into Canadian society (not that there was much similarity at the time among non-Indigenous peoples, who, although mostly European in origin, came from different language, ethnic, cultural, historical and religious groups). Macdonald disallowed the Chinese the vote in 1885, yet introduced voting rights for Indigenous males, though these were soon taken away by Laurier, not to be universally regained until 1960. The objective remained the same: to shape a culturally similar demographic that would be loyal to the federation and the cultural and political institutions of the British Crown.

It is important to understand the decisions of historical figures within the context of their lives and times. What's right and what's wrong doesn't just depend on who you are but when and where you are as well. Everything is changing all the time, including ourselves, including society. At some level in history there is no good or evil, just what happened. It's up to us to do what we want with knowledge of past events.

The purpose of modern professional history is to produce a verifiable narrative that is based, as much as possible, on facts to prevent demagogues and tyrants from creating false past narratives for their own political or social agendas. History isn't about good or bad but about what happened and, just as importantly, how and why. Cause and effect. How some actions led to other actions. And ultimately, how the world was changed over time by people and their decisions.

John A. Macdonald is a central character in the development of Canada as a nation, as well as the main railway promoter. Was he a monster? No, but he set in motion some monstrous policies that were expanded and nurtured by others after his death in 1891. Macdonald should primarily be remembered for his overriding ambition, an ambition that swept aside all other considerations as subservient to the dream of a new political dominion that operated free from the United States. In trying to steer the future away from one outcome he found abhorrent— American political domination over North America—he ignored other cruel outcomes that were deemed necessary to achieve it. Was Macdonald a racist colonial persecutor or a man with limited power and knowledge trying to navigate the Scylla and Charybdis of his day? If he were alive today, the case for his infamy would be irrefutable; but we have the advantage of a century and half of technological and political evolution, and far more knowledge and power to effect change and influence society and the world. And what of Laurier, who amplified and expanded some of Macdonald's most odious policies? It seems an odd and meaningless analysis to judge people by criteria they were unaware of during their lives. People live within their time and era, and to measure anyone against another or a later culture and era is pointless.

Bad things happened, there is no doubt, and no point in trying to obscure it. People must have the courage to contend with the good, the bad and the ugly of everything to make sense of the world and plan for a better future. The question is not how such things could have happened or argue over whether certain historical decisions and actions were good or bad. Of course they were bad, or at least their outcome was. Rather, the question is: were these bad things done by evil people who should just be banished? Or were these actions the mostly banal behaviours of people who believed they were working toward a greater good, convinced that their decisions would result in a better world? This second, more likely scenario should be the cause of a lot more concern and self-reflection—that a great deal of evil in the world was and is caused by average people believing they are doing good, utterly convinced of the righteousness of their cause and blinded to the possibility of unintended consequences. Much harm is done by those who lack the humility to admit their power is an illusion.

An empire is often understood to be an aggregate of subject states, subdued by force and exploited for their resources to the aggrandizement of the heartland. It's hard to dispute that this was Canada's origin. But empire can also be construed as meaning to build, to connect or to unify. The older, now archaic word *empyreal* was used to denote something pertaining to the sky or heavens, something inspiring of awe. In a practical sense, relating to a political entity, the inspiration of awe could flow from the seemingly invincible power to control and direct and exploit; yet it could also flow from a string of grand or noble universal achievements. For many people these days, it's unclear from which tributary of history we have sprung, in which world we now live. It shouldn't be unclear to which world we should aspire.

A NOTE ON TERMINOLOGY

———

One of the challenges in writing this book was selecting the correct names for Indigenous Peoples. Some of the older, more familiar terms, such as Iroquois, Peigan, Shuswap, etc., are anglicizations of the names the peoples of the day used to describe themselves, which had been phonetically transcribed from their oral pronunciation into the earliest written historical records of the fur traders. Some were coinages based on superficial observations. These older terms have a historical pedigree; they are familiar to people today and are enshrined in place names, roads, historical sites, etc., thus are meaningful references as a result. The terms newer to the English language do not exist in historical records, and I was concerned that by using the new words alone, the references to and understanding of past stories might be lost. Respect should be accorded to evolving preferences in language and terminology, and care should also be taken to ensure the newer terminology accurately correlates to the Peoples who lived more than a century ago in very different times, and sometimes different places.

To bridge the gap between past and present, and to acknowledge previous usage while respecting evolving preferences, I have opted to use the newer terms, alongside the older ones parenthetically. Sometimes there are multiple possible spellings for the older and newer words, so I have generally based my choices on Gregory Younging's *The Elements of Indigenous Style*, as well as the Canadian Association of University Teachers guide on acknowledging Traditional Territories (https://www.caut.ca/content/guide-acknowledging-first-peoples-traditional-territory). Any errors or omissions will be respectfully rectified in future editions.

NOTES

CHAPTER ONE

"A rush to newly discovered gold fields brings in view every trait of human character": Mifflin Wistar Gibbs, *Shadow and Light*, 1st paragraph of chapter 5.

"who could, if necessary, truss a murderer up and hang him from the nearest tree": Quoted in Roy St. George Stubbs, "Sir Matthew Baillie Begbie," *MHS Transactions*, Series 3, no. 25 (1968–69).

"My idea is that if a man insists on behaving like a brute": Quoted in Sydney G. Pettit, "Judge Begbie in Action: The Establishment of Law and Preservation of Order in British Columbia," *British Columbia Historical Quarterly* 11, no. 2 (April 1947): 143.

"The notorious Ned McGowan, of Californian celebrity": Willard E. Ireland, ed., "First Impressions: Letter of Colonel Richard Clement Moody, R.E., to Arthur Blackwood, February 1, 1859," *British Columbia Historical Quarterly* 15 (January–April 1951): 95.

"a Salute, firing off their loaded Revolvers over my head—Pleasant": Ibid., 97.

CHAPTER TWO

"up to their ankles in filth": Robert Whyte, *Robert Whyte's 1847 Famine Ship Diary: The Journey of an Irish Coffin Ship*, 65.

"hundreds . . . literally flung on the beach": Ibid.

"After a voyage of two months' duration": Ibid., 64.

"Untutored, degraded, famished and plaguestricken": Ibid., 101.

"in silence, every one bearing his trouble like a Briton": Mark Sweeten Wade, *The Overlanders of '62*, 42.

"in such dense clouds as to almost darken the air and inflicting such torment": Ibid., 62.

"an attractive country, pleasantly diversified by hills and valleys": Ibid., 58.

"*Where the wild rose, and pea in abundance*": Ibid.

"It is a nice place. I think I could live here contented if I could get provision": Ibid., 75.

"nasty low wet country": Ibid., 91.

"lofty snow-clad peaks, standing out in bold relief against the blue sky beyond": Ibid., 93–94.

"Great sympathy was manifested for the brave and devoted mother": Thomas McMicking, *Overland from Canada to British Columbia*, xxvi.

"so delicate and rare that it might have tempted the palate of Epicurus himself": Mark Sweeten Wade, *The Overlanders of '62*, 98.

"few *men* would have the courage to undertake": Ibid., 117.

CHAPTER THREE

"utterly unworthy of the name": "The Bute Inlet Route," *British Columbian*, June 1, 1864, from "Nobody Knows Him: Lhatŝ'aŝʔin and the Chilcotin War," Great Unsolved Mysteries in Canadian History, https://www.canadianmysteries.ca/sites/klatsassin/archives/newspaperormagazine article/274en.html.

"so stinted in their provisions that they were led to starve the Indians": Ibid.

"There was no mistaking him": Robert Christopher Lundin Brown, *Klatsassan, and Other Reminiscences of Missionary Life in British Columbia*, 98.

"The Indians have I believe been most injudiciously treated": Matthew Begbie to the Governor of British Columbia Including Notes Taken by the Court at the Trial of 6 Indians, from "Nobody Knows Him: Lhatŝ'aŝʔin and the Chilcotin War," Great Unsolved Mysteries in Canadian History, https://www.canadianmysteries.ca/sites/klatsassin/archives/colonial correspondence/208en.html.

"You hold as payment for work," he announced, "a large amount of road scrip": "The Bute Inlet Route," *British Columbian*, June 1, 1864, from "Nobody Knows Him: Lhatŝ'aŝʔin and the Chilcotin War," Great Unsolved Mysteries in Canadian History, https://www.canadianmysteries.ca/sites/klatsassin/archives/newspaperormagazinearticle/274en.html.

CHAPTER FOUR

"Few cities in the province have been more free from professional beggars": See the City of Ottawa Archives web page "A Virtual Exhibit: Ottawa Becomes the Capital." This is an interesting collection of photographs and newspaper articles from 1867. https://documents.ottawa.ca/sites/documents/files/ott_capital_en.pdf. The following newspaper excerpts are from the same source.

the Indigenous population in Canada had declined to 102,358, according to the 1871 census: Statistics Canada, "Aboriginal Peoples," Censuses of Canada 1665 to 1871, https://www150.statcan.gc.ca/n1/pub/98-187-x/4151278-eng.htm.

CHAPTER FIVE

"His eyes lively and his look pleasant": Quoted in Richard Gwyn, *Nation Maker: Sir John A. Macdonald*, 8.

"British Columbia offered and gave protection": Mifflin Wistar Gibbs, *Shadow and Light*, 63.

"bought homes and other property, and by industry and character vastly improved their condition": Ibid.

"The journey from San Francisco by railway opened our eyes": Sebastian Helmcken, *The Reminiscences of Doctor John Sebastian Helmcken*, 259, 261.

"It is just as well that the Dominion Government should know that there are very many people in this Colony": British Columbia, Legislative Council, *Debate on the Subject of Confederation with Canada*, 52.

CHAPTER SIX

"My guide and I got on the front platform of one of these air engines, and were shot into the tunnel": Samuel H.M. Byers, *Twenty Years in Europe: A Consul-General's Memories of Noted People*, 155.

CHAPTER SEVEN

"races struggling to emerge into civilization": Earl of Carnarvon, quoted in C.C. Eldridge, *The Imperial Experience: From Carlyle to Forster*, 22.

"took a friendly interest in the 'indentured young gentlemen'": Beckles Willson, *The Life of Lord Strathcona and Mount Royal*, 50.

"in a highly pitched treble" that he would not tolerate "any upstart": Ibid.

"as Mrs. Smith had some shopping to do, we all went into the city together.": Ibid., 140.

CHAPTER EIGHT

"take them into your Council. This man Riel . . . is a clever fellow": Joseph Pope, *Memoirs of the Right Honourable Sir John Alexander Macdonald*, vol. 2, 53.

"If, however, it [the proclamation] were disobeyed, your weakness and inability . . . would be painfully exhibited": Ibid., 54.

"has ingeniously contrived to humiliate himself and Canada": Ibid, 60.

"If the revolutionists of Red River are encouraged and sustained": Ignatius Donnelly, quoted in Joseph Kinsey Howard, *Strange Empire*, 137.

"The Red River revolution," proclaimed Joseph Wheelock . . . "is a trump card in the hands of American diplomacy": See also Alvin C. Gluek Jr., *Minnesota and the Manifest Destiny of the Canadian Northwest*, chapter 9.

"I would be quite willing . . . to leave the whole country a wilderness": John A. Macdonald, quoted in Douglas Hill, *The Opening of the Canadian West*, 58.

"The United States Government are resolved . . . to get possession of the western territory": Macdonald to C.J. Brydges, January 28, 1870, in Pope, *Memoirs*, 162.

"Gentlemen," Smith proclaimed, "Canada is prepared to respect the people of this country": Donald Smith, quoted in Beckles Willson, *Lord Strathcona: The Story of His Life*, 80.

"wild scene of drunkenness and debauchery": William Francis Butler, *The Great Lone Land: A Narrative of Travel and Adventure in the North-West of America*, 192.

"As far as the eye can see," he rhapsodized, "there is stretched out before you an ocean of grass": Garnet Wolseley, "Narrative of the Red River Expedition by an Officer of the Expeditionary Force," *Blackwood's Edinburgh Magazine*, 178.

CHAPTER NINE

"From our isolated position and want of unison and unanimity": Roderick MacKenzie to Roderick MacFarlane, quoted in Beckles Willson, *The Life of Lord Strathcona and Mount Royal*, 281.

"It is all very well for Donald A. Smith . . . to puff the new arrangements": Chief Trader J. Lockhart, quoted in ibid., 338.

"into trackless, inhospitable regions, obliged to carry their provisions on their backs": George Monro Grant, *Ocean to Ocean: Sandford Fleming's Expedition through Canada in 1872*, 7.

"As a matter of curiosity I had a hind-leg of the skunk for breakfast": James Carnegie, *Saskatchewan and the Rocky Mountains*, 175.

"Let me here . . . deprecate censure from fastidious readers": Ibid., 175, note.

"'to ascertain whether any practicable pass or passes . . . existed across the Rocky Mountains'": Grant, *Ocean to Ocean*, 2.

"The knowledge of the country . . . would never lead me to advise": Ibid., 3.

"By uniting together," he claimed, "the British Provinces had declared": Ibid., 7–8.

"Travel a thousand miles up a great river; . . . and you have travelled . . . through Canada": Ibid., 1.

"No white man is known to have crossed from the Upper Ottawa to Lake Superior": Ibid., 6.

"In a word, the country between Old Canada and Red River was utterly unknown": Ibid., 6–7.

"It will be sufficient for our purpose . . . to begin at Toronto": Ibid., 11–12.

"a gentleman, out for his holidays on a botanical excursion to Thunder Bay": Ibid., 21.

"the mosquitoes are not more vicious than in the woods": Ibid., 31.

"How many cottars, small farmers, and plough boys in Britain": Ibid.

"The road was heavy": Ibid.

"broad, handsome": Ibid., 40.

"These Iroquois, and most of the Ojibbeways we have met, are men above the medium size": Ibid., 33.

"the terms on which they would allow free passage through . . . the country": Ibid., 47.

"Poor creatures! not much use have they ever made of the land": Ibid., 33–34.

"Whatever the benefits that have been conferred on them": Ibid., 40–49.

"She was dirty, joyless-looking and prematurely old": Ibid., 38.

"The Indians grow on us day by day": Ibid., 41.

"Thirty-two new species already; it's a perfect floral garden": Ibid., 62.

"in the dirtiest, most desolate-looking, mosquito-haunted of all our camping grounds": Ibid., 58.

"a flat country, much of it marshy, with a dense forest": Ibid., 58–59.

"Great was the astonishment of our teamsters": Ibid., 59.

"sea of green sprinkled with yellow, red, lilac, and white": Ibid., 62.

"The wealth of vegetation and the size of the root crops astonished us": Ibid., 76.

"If Canada is to open up her North-west . . . , there must be a road for troops": Ibid., 64.

"The men had straight delicate features": Ibid., 121.

"The characteristic of the Blackfeet braves . . . is daring": Ibid., 146.

"they were handsome fellows, with well cut, refined Italian features": Ibid., 155.

"the farming is on a very limited scale": Ibid., 163.

"Souzie mounted his horse and waited patiently at the gate of the Fort": Ibid., 182.

"the luxuries of white-fish, fresh eggs, cream, butter and young pig bountifully served up": Ibid., 188.

"The simple fact is that the coal deposits of the North-west are so enormous in quantity": Ibid., 195.

"He might have been sitting there for centuries": Ibid., 196.

"There is a wonderful combination of beauty about these mountains": Ibid., 233.

"delicious Java coffee, sweetened with sugar from the Sandwich Islands": Ibid., 242.

"A walk through the streets showed the little capital to be a small polyglot copy of the world": Ibid., 340–41.

CHAPTER TEN

"The act will provide for building a north shore road to Fort Garry": Jay
Cooke to H.C. Fahnestock, January 16, 1872, quoted in Leonard B. Irwin,
Pacific Railways and Nationalism in the Canadian-American Northwest,
1845–1873, 171–72.

"If we had the same means possessed by hon. gentlemen opposite":
Canada, House of Commons Debates, 2nd Parl., 2nd Sess., Vol. 7, 136–44.
Library of Parliament, Canadian Parliamentary Historical Resources,
https://parl.canadiana.ca/view/oop.debates_HOC0202_01.

he would be most willing to vote confidence in the Government: See also
Roy MacLaren, *Commissions High: Canada in London, 1870–1971,* 20.

CHAPTER ELEVEN

"The Indians are evidently decreasing": George Monro Grant, *Ocean to*
Ocean, 190.

"Pure whites & British & French Half Breeds": Philip Goldring, "The
First Contingent: The North-West Mounted Police, 1873–74," *Canadian*
Historic Sites: Occasional Papers in Archaeology and History No. 21, http://
parkscanadahistory.com/series/chs/21/chs21-1c.htm.

"If the people of Canada could were to see us now": James Finlayson,
"Jottings on the March from Fort Garry to Rocky Mountains," September
27, 1874, https://glenbow.ucalgary.ca/wp-content/uploads/2019/06/m-9836
-83-transcript.pdf.

"He won the confidence of all ranks the first day out": Sam Steele, *Forty*
Years in Canada: Reminiscences of the Great North-West, 76.

"It will at once be seen that the liberty of our fellow citizens": *Fort Benton*
Record, October 16, 1875.

"There it is. Sacrificing the liberty of American citizens": Ibid., July 16,
1875.

"is quite a young man and looks as if he might or might not be a murderer":
Ibid., October 16, 1875.

"the arrests were made to perfect a stroke of policy": Ibid., July 16, 1875.

CHAPTER TWELVE

"Jerry was about the most decent specimen I ever met with": W.S. Stocking,
quoted in Rodger Touchie, *Bear Child: The Life and Times of Jerry Potts*, 85.

"you could fire with your eyes shut and be sure to kill a Cree": *Lethbridge
News*, April 30, 1890. See also Hugh Dempsey, *The Vengeful Wife and Other
Blackfoot Stories*.

"The fiery water flowed as freely . . . as the streams running from the Rocky
Mountains": Alexander Morris, *The Treaties of Canada, with the Indians
of Manitoba and the North-West Territories*, 248.

"Ten years ago," the Methodist missionary George McDougall wrote,
"the Blackfeet were rich in horses": John McDougall, *George Millward
McDougall, The Pioneer, Patriot and Missionary*, 198.

"He was the man who had trained the best scouts in the force": Sam Steele,
Forty Years in Canada, 276–77.

"The first cannot be put more clearly or baldly than it was in a letter":
George Monro Grant, *Ocean to Ocean*, 93–94.

The second commonly discussed way, Grant wrote, "is to insist that there
is no Indian question": Ibid., 94–95.

"terrible deeds have been wrought out in that western land": William
Francis Butler, *The Great Lone Land*, 241.

"The third way, called, sometimes, the paternal, is to . . . explain that,
whether they wish it or not, immigrants will come into the country":
Grant, *Ocean to Ocean*, 95–96.

"We are few in numbers compared to former times": Chief Mistawasis, quoted
in Peter Erasmus, *Buffalo Days and Nights*, 249; see also James Daschuck,

Clearing the Plains: Disease, Politics of Starvation, and the Loss of Indigenous Life, 98.

"We want none of the Queen's presents": Quoted in Morris, *The Treaties of Canada with the Indians*, 174.

CHAPTER THIRTEEN

"We all see that the day is coming when the buffalo will all be killed": Chief Crowfoot, quoted in Canada, Secretary of State, Indian Branch, *Report of the Secretary of State of Canada for the Year Ending on the 30th June, 1869*, 22; see also Hugh Dempsey, *The Great Blackfoot Treaties*, 157.

"The North-American Indians are indeed no ordinary race of savages": Duncan George Forbes Macdonald, *British Columbia and Vancouver's Island*, 131.

"The lovely valley in which warriors stand forth in their triumphant glory": Ibid., 133.

"the lowest phase of humanity": Ibid., 141.

"Early the next morning there was quite a stir in the Indian camp": William Parker, quoted in Hugh Dempsey, ed., *William Parker, Mounted Policeman*, 40.

"All formerly warring elements of a great region were present": Frank Oliver, "The Blackfeet Indian Treaty," *Maclean's Magazine*, March 15, 1931, 8.

"The chief difficulty about his interpretations": Quoted in Dempsey, *The Great Blackfoot Treaties*, 93. See also R.G. Matthews, "Life in the Mounted Police," *Scarlet and Gold*, 18.

"He was a striking . . . figure": Oliver, "The Blackfeet Indian Treaty," 28.

"While I speak, be kind and patient": Alexander Morris, *The Treaties of Canada with the Indians*, 272; see also Dempsey, *The Great Blackfoot Treaties*, 108.

"five or six hundred mounted warriors": Cecil Edward Denny, *The Riders of the Plains: A Reminiscence of the Early and Exciting Days in the North West*, 100.

CHAPTER FOURTEEN

"The reader would scarcely be interested in a dry account of the culverts and bridges": George Monro Grant, *Ocean to Ocean*, 11.

"the Mackenzie Government . . . had greedy mercenaries hanging upon its skirts": Sir John Willison, *Reminiscences, Political and Personal*, 36. In *The National Dream: The Great Railway*, Pierre Berton gives a more detailed listing of the politicians and businesses involved in these fraudulent schemes, in his chapter "The Stonemason's Friends," 239–48.

"The fault of the Liberal party was voluble virtue": Willison, *Reminiscences*, 36–37.

"Was that work less or more expensive than it would have been to a private company": Canada, *Report of the Canadian Pacific Railway Royal Commission*, vol. 2, 1314.

"I generally felt that those persons employed through political influence": Ibid., 1315.

"I wish to get your opinion on this point": Ibid., 1317.

"We felt the cold very severely during the night": R.M. Rylatt, *Surveying the Canadian Pacific: Memoir of a Railroad Pioneer*, 14.

"The night was very cold, and as I watched and shivered": Ibid., 37.

"Poor deluded fools": Ibid., 23.

"Mighty mountains, towering upwards," wrote Rylatt, . . . "their peaks almost in the blue of the sky": Ibid., 16–17.

"In solitude I watched the sun guild the tops of the lofty mountains": Ibid., 30.

CHAPTER FIFTEEN

"People were ready to buy anything," he wrote. "The hotels did a roaring trade": Sam Steele, *Forty Years in Canada*, 164.

"the demand for marriageable females was perfectly wild": Charles Napier Bell, *Winnipeg Daily Sun*, March and April 1887, http://www.mhs.mb.ca/docs/mb_history/53/greatwinnipegboom.shtml.

"One young and promising youth who had been started out of Toronto by a considerate father": Ibid.

"the effect on the real estate market was sudden and far reaching": Ibid.

"Real estate advertisements quietly disappeared": Ibid.

CHAPTER SIXTEEN

"seemed to look and see through everything at once": Tom Wilson, *Trail Blazer*, 14.

"He had no mercy on horses or men": Ibid., 17.

"Give Rogers six plugs of chewing tobacco and five bacon rinds": Ibid., 14.

"We must take no chances on this season's work": William Van Horne to A.B. Rogers, February 6, 1883, "Van Horne Letter Book No. 1: 1882–1883," 279; http://www.okthepk.ca/dataCprSiding/articles/201708/monthoo.htm. See also Pierre Berton, *The Last Spike: The Great Railway*, 168–69.

"Very serious reports have been made to the Government . . . about the inadequacy of the supplies": Ibid.

"There has been a good deal of feeling among some of the Canadian Engineers": William Van Horne to Jno. [John] W. Sterling, January 30, 1883, "Van Horne Letter Book No. 1," 234. See also Berton, *The Last Spike*, 168–69.

"Very few men ever learned to understand him": Tom Wilson, *Trail Blazer*, 17.

"trying to find out how far an Indian can travel between suns": Albert Rogers, "Major A.B. Rogers' First Expedition Up the Illecillewaet Valley, in 1881," in A.O. Wheeler, *The Selkirk Range*, 418.

"ten strapping Indians on rather an ironclad contract": Ibid.

"2 rifles, 200 rounds ammunition, 8 pairs blankets, 2 axes, 50 feet ⅜-inch rope": Ibid.

"a strict ration," which "caused much discontent among the Indians": Ibid., 419.

"picking our way over mudflats": Ibid.

"crush[ed] the timber into match wood for several hundred feet": Ibid.

"The terrible travelling with our heavy loads . . . had begun to show on all our faces": Ibid., 420.

"We crawled along the ledges," Albert recalled, "getting a toe-hole here and a finger-hole there": Ibid.

"They fell some thirty feet straight down": Ibid.

"Such a view! Never to be forgotten!": Ibid., 421.

"The grandeur of the view . . . crowded out all thoughts of our discomforts": Ibid.

"The British flag was flying to-day": See also Wilson, *Trail Blazer*, 9.

"Blackfeet, Peigans and Bloods . . . worried us somewhat": Wilson, *Trail Blazer*, 11.

"the chief was in an ugly mood": Ibid., 24.

"thick timber where we could not see a yard ahead": Ibid., 19.

"tea, bannock and boiled salt pork": Ibid.

"He was plainly choked with emotion: Ibid., 20.

"For some time," Wilson recalled, "we sat and smoked": Ibid., 30.

"You'll never leave these mountains again as long as you live": Ibid.

"Blue Jesus!" Rogers erupted . . . "We won't get through here to the Columbia in two weeks": Ibid., 31.

"was even more difficult than the Kicking Horse": Ibid., 33.

"If that boy don't show up what in hell will I do?": Ibid., 36.

"down and up gorges, hundreds of feet deep, amongst rocky masses": Quoted in Wheeler, *The Selkirk Range*, 161.

"the rain continue[d] falling incessantly": Ibid., 167.

"The walking is dreadful, we climb over and creep under fallen trees of good size": Ibid., 166.

CHAPTER SEVENTEEN

"was something more than just the point to which track had been laid":
P. Turner Bone, *When the Steel Went Through: Reminiscences of a Railroad Pioneer*, 43.

"We had planned to do some office work on the way": Ibid., 47.

"It had been a very dry season": Charles Aeneas Shaw, *Tales of a Pioneer Surveyor*, 147–48.

"I wish you could have seen those men": J. Burgon Bickersteth, *The Land of Open Doors: Being Letters from Western Canada 1911–13*, 194.

"There must have been 200 of us and more [crammed in the cookhouse]": Ibid.

"I suppose, dear reader," wrote an early twentieth-century prairie homesteader": A. Woods, "Digging the Ditch in '08," *Western Producer*, C2.

"So there we left him [on the bank of the Athabasca River]": Bickersteth, *The Land of Open Doors*, 152.

"We were a strange gathering at night-time": Morley Roberts, *The Western Avernus*, 86.

"No such mountain work had ever been attempted in Canada before": Noel Robinson, interview with Henry J. Cambie, "Blazing Trails in B.C.," *Maclean's Magazine*, January 1, 1924, 40.

"The difficulty of keeping this road open": Ibid.

"We, who hold cleanliness so high and propriety so dear": Dukesang Wong, *The Diary of Dukesang Wong*, 53.

"The poor labourers sit on deck and sing": Ibid., 36.

"It has been said that the land to which I am now headed is wild and uncivilized": Ibid., 35.

"The misery I see daily disturbs my thoughts": Ibid., 54.

"degrading treatment of the white people in the town": Ibid., 55.

"Our people would talk through differences and hear each other": Ibid.

"I must continually remember only him": Ibid., 15.

"venture to that country they call 'the Land of the Golden Mountains'":
Ibid., 34.

"English is hard to speak": Ibid., 58.

"village language," which he also found "hard to understand": Ibid.

"The people working with me are good, strong men": Ibid., 57.

CHAPTER EIGHTEEN

"If you wish to have the railway finished within any reasonable time":
Canada, *Official Debates of the House of Commons*, May 12, 1882, 1477. See
also David Chuenyan Lai, *Chinatowns: Towns within Cities in Canada*, 33.

"an alien race in every sense": Canada, *Official Debates*.

"My soul cries out. I wish I had never experienced such bad days":
Dukesang Wong, *The Diary of Dukesang Wong*, 59.

"spending their days in the opium shacks, with little food and even less
strength": Ibid., 61.

"There is some fresh food for us and enough fish to fill our stomachs":
Ibid., 62.

"Today Hsin Wun Ming resisted a young white man's attempt to rob him":
Ibid., 64.

"It is not enough for us to allow Chinamen to come to our shores": George
Monro Grant, *Ocean to Ocean*, p. 347.

"The leaders of the white people demand money": Wong, *The Diary of
Dukesang Wong*, 60.

"There is much work to be done and not enough people to labour at it": Ibid., 61.

"These mighty lands are great to gaze upon": Ibid.

"I do not see how people would get on here at all without Chinamen":
Canada, *Report of the Royal Commission on Chinese Immigration*, 75.

"We have been burying some of the people who died over the hard, foodless
days": Wong, *The Diary of Dukesang Wong*, 60.

"I have pondered this fresh new land," he wrote, "yet it is a land already full of sadness": Ibid., 63.

"I desire material things sufficient for my living": Ibid., 64.

"It is still the feast of the full moon": Ibid., 106.

CHAPTER NINETEEN

"I will give you great power in war": Hugh Dempsey, *The Vengeful Wife and Other Blackfoot Stories*, 156. Dempsey's book recounts many tales from the Siksiká-speaking peoples in the nineteenth century and is a fascinating introduction to this dramatic period.

"Be all brave and do your best": Ibid.

"I am a woman. Men don't know how to sew": Ibid., 157.

"Of buffalo we saw millions, and very near the same number of antelope": *Abbeville Banner*, April 1, 1858. See also https://allaboutbison.com/bison-in -history/1800s/1851-1860/.

"Let them kill, skin, and sell until the buffaloes are exterminated": General Philip Sheridan, quoted in Mari Sandoz, *The Buffalo Hunters: The Story of the Hide Men*, 173. See also John R. Cook, *The Border and the Buffalo*, 80.

"I have never seen anything like it since my long residence in this country": James Stewart, quoted in James W. Daschuk, *Clearing the Plains*, 110.

"Thousands . . . had perished on the great sandy plains": William Francis Butler, *The Great Lone Land*, 202.

"Everyone here knows that almost all of the Indians in the district suffer from scrofula and dyspepsia": Quoted in Daschuk, *Clearing the Plains*, 151.

CHAPTER TWENTY

"two hundred miles of engineering impossibilities": William Van Horne, quoted in Valerie Knowles, *From Telegrapher to Titan: The Life of William C. Van Horne*, 148.

"I saw the primaeval forest torn down": Morley Roberts, *The Western Avernus*, 61.

"Glaciers which had never left their rocky beds above the clouds": Sam Steele, *Forty Years in Canada*, 195–96.

"You will have to loan them the money": John Henry Pope, quoted in P.B. Waite, "Pope, John Henry," in *Dictionary of Canadian Biography*, http://www.biographi.ca/en/bio/pope_john_henry_11E.html.

CHAPTER TWENTY-ONE

"One might travel the plains from one end to the other": Sam Steele, *Forty Years in Canada*, 93.

"We want blood!": Report of North-West Mounted Police Assistant Commissioner L.N.F. Crozier, 1885, quoted in Keith D. Smith, ed., *Strange Visitors: Documents in Indigenous–Settler Relations in Canada from 1876*, 65.

"What is life? It is a flash of a firefly in the night": Chief Crowfoot, quoted in Susan Ratcliffe, ed., *Oxford Essential Quotations*. See also the Blackfoot Crossing Historical Park website for additional information: https://blackfootcrossing.ca/wordpress/our-culture-2/.

"We tossed up chairs to the ceiling": William Van Horne, quoted in "Sir William Van Horne," *Cornhill Magazine*, 245.

SELECTED BIBLIOGRAPHY

———

Artibise, Alan. *Winnipeg: An Illustrated History.* Toronto: James Lorimer and National Museum of Man, 1977.

Berton, Pierre. *The Last Spike.* Toronto: McClelland & Stewart, 1971.

Berton, Pierre. *The National Dream.* Toronto: McClelland & Stewart, 1970.

Bickersteth, J. Burgon. *The Land of Open Doors: Being Letters from Western Canada.* London: Wells Gardner, Darton, 1914.

Black, Conrad. *Rise to Greatness: The History of Canada from the Vikings to the Present.* Toronto: McClelland & Stewart, 2014.

Bone, P. Turner. *When the Steel Went Through: Reminiscences of a Railroad Pioneer.* Toronto: Macmillan, 1947.

Borrows, John, and Michael Coyle, eds. *The Right Relationship: Reimagining the Implementation of Historical Treaties.* Toronto: University of Toronto Press, 2017.

Bourrie, Mark. *Canada's Parliament Buildings.* Toronto: Hounslow Press, 1996.

Bown, Stephen R. *The Company: The Rise and Fall of the Hudson's Bay Empire.* Toronto: Doubleday Canada, 2020.

British Columbia. Legislative Council. *Debate on the Subject of Confederation with Canada: Reprinted from the Government Gazette Extraordinary of March, 1870.* Victoria, 1912.

Brown, G.I. *The Big Bang: A History of Explosives.* Stroud, U.K.: Sutton, 1998.

Brown, Robert Christopher Lundin. *Klatsassan, and Other Reminiscences of Missionary Life in British Columbia.* London: Gilbert and Rivington, 1873.

Burney, Shehla. *Coming to Gum San: The Story of Chinese Canadians.* Toronto: D.C. Heath for the Multicultural History Society of Ontario, 1995.

Butler, William Francis. *The Great Lone Land: A Narrative of Travel and Adventure in the North-West of America.* London: Sampson Low, Marsten, Low & Searle, 1872

Byers, Samuel H.M. *Twenty Years in Europe: A Consul-General's Memories of Noted People, with Letters from General W.T. Sherman.* Chicago: Rand, McNally, 1900.

Canada. *House of Commons Debates.* 2nd Parl., 2nd sess., vol. 7. Ottawa, 1873. https://parl.canadiana.ca/view/oop.debates_HOC0202_01/1.

Canada. *Official Debates of the House of Commons of the Dominion of Canada.* 4th Parl., 4th sess., vol. 12. Ottawa, 1882.

Canada. Department of the Secretary of State, Indian Branch. *Report of the Secretary of State for Canada for the Year Ending on the 30th June, 1869.* Ottawa, 1870.

Canada. Royal Commission on Chinese Immigration. *Report and Evidence.* Ottawa, 1885. www.canadiana.ca/view/oocihm.14563/3?r=1.

Canada. Royal Commission to Inquire into Matters Connected with the Canadian Pacific Railway. *Report of the Canadian Pacific Railway Royal Commission.* 2 vols. Ottawa, 1882.

Carlson, Keith Thor, ed. *You Are Asked to Witness: The Stó:lō in Canada's Pacific Coast History.* Chilliwack, B.C.: Stó:lō Heritage Trust, 1997.

Carnegie, James (9th Earl of Southesk). *Saskatchewan and the Rocky Mountains: A Diary and Narrative of Travel, Sport, and Adventure, during*

a Journey through the Hudson's Bay Company's Territories, in 1859 and 1860.
Edinburgh: Edmonston and Douglas, 1875.

City of Ottawa Archives. *A Virtual Exhibit: Ottawa Becomes the Capital.*
https://documents.ottawa.ca/sites/documents/files/ott_capital_en.pdf.

Cook, John R. *The Border and the Buffalo: A Story of Mountain and Plain.*
Topeka, Kans.: Crane, 1907.

Daschuk, James. *Clearing the Plains: Disease, Politics of Starvation, and the
Loss of Indigenous Life.* Regina: University of Regina Press, 2019.

Davis, Chuck, ed. *The Greater Vancouver Book: An Urban Encyclopaedia.* Surrey,
B.C.: Linkman Press, 1997.

Dempsey, Hugh. *The Amazing Death of Calf Shirt and Other Blackfoot Stories:
Three Hundred Years of Blackfoot History.* Saskatoon: Fifth House, 1994.

Dempsey, Hugh. *Big Bear: The End of Freedom.* Vancouver: Douglas &
McIntyre, 1984.

Dempsey, Hugh. *Crowfoot: Chief of the Blackfeet.* Edmonton: Hurtig, 1976.

Dempsey, Hugh. *Firewater: The Impact of the Whiskey Trade on the Blackfoot
Nation.* Calgary: Fifth House, 2002.

Dempsey, Hugh. *The Great Blackfoot Treaties.* Victoria: Heritage House, 2015.

Dempsey, Hugh. *Jerry Potts: Plainsman.* Calgary: Glenbow Alberta Institute,
1966.

Dempsey, Hugh. *The Vengeful Wife and Other Blackfoot Stories.* Norman:
University of Oklahoma Press, 2006.

Dempsey, Hugh, ed. *William Parker, Mounted Policeman.* Edmonton: Hurtig,
1973.

Denney, Cecil Edward. *The Riders of the Plains: A Reminiscence of the Early
and Exciting Days in the North West.* Calgary: Herald, 1905.

den Otter, A.A. *The Philosophy of Railways: The Transcontinental Railway
Idea in British North America.* Toronto: University of Toronto Press, 1997.

Eldridge, C.C. *The Imperial Experience: From Carlyle to Forster.* London:
Macmillan, 1996.

Erasmus, Peter. *Buffalo Days and Nights*. Calgary: Fifth House, 1999.

Finlayson, James. "Jottings on the March from Fort Garry to Rocky Mountains." 1874. https://glenbow.ucalgary.ca/wp-content/uploads /2019/06/m-9836-83-transcript.pdf.

Fisher, Robin. *Contact and Conflict: Indian-European Relations in British Columbia, 1774–1890*. 2nd ed. Vancouver: UBC Press, 2011.

Fisher, Robin. "Joseph Trutch and Indian Land Policy." *BC Studies* 12 (Winter 1971–72).

Friesen, Gerald. *The Canadian Prairies: A History*. Toronto: University of Toronto Press, 1984.

Gibbs, Mifflin Wistar. *Shadow and Light: An Autobiography with Reminiscences of the Last and Present Century*. Lincoln: University of Nebraska Press, 1995.

Gluek, Alvin C., Jr. *Minnesota and the Manifest Destiny of the Canadian Northwest: A Study in Canadian-American Relations*. Toronto: University of Toronto Press, 1965.

Grant, George Monro. *England and Canada, a Summer Tour between Old and New Westminster, with Historical Notes*. Montreal: Dawson Brothers, 1884.

Grant, George Monro. *Ocean to Ocean: Sandford Fleming's Expedition through Canada in 1872: Being a Diary Kept during a Journey from the Atlantic to the Pacific with the Expedition of the Engineer-in-Chief of the Canadian Pacific and Intercolonial Railways*. London: Sampson Low, Marston, Low & Searle, 1873.

Gwyn, Richard. *Nation Maker; Sir John A. Macdonald: His Life, Our Times*. Toronto: Doubleday, 2011.

Hamon, M. Max. *The Audacity of His Enterprise: Louis Riel and the Métis Nation That Canada Never Was, 1840–1875*. Montreal and Kingston: McGill-Queen's University Press, 2020.

Hauka, Donald J. *McGowan's War*. Vancouver: New Star, 2000.

Helmcken, Sebastian. *The Reminiscences of Doctor John Sebastian Helmcken*. Edited by Dorothy Blakey Smith. Vancouver: UBC Press, 1975.

Higgitt, W.L. Introduction to *Opening Up the West: Being the Official Reports to Parliament of the Activities of the Royal North-West Mounted Police from 1874-1881*. Facsimile reprint. 4 vols. Toronto: Coles, 1973.

Hill, Douglas. *The Opening of the Canadian West*. London: Heinemann, 1967.

Howard, Joseph Kinsey. *Strange Empire: A Narrative of the Northwest*. New York: William Morrow, 1952.

Hubbard, Freeman H. *Encyclopedia of North American Railroading: 150 Years of Railroading in the United States and Canada*. Toronto: McGraw-Hill, 1981.

Ireland, Willard E., ed. "First Impressions: Letter of Colonel Richard Clement Moody, R.E., to Arthur Blackwood, February 1, 1859." *British Columbia Historical Quarterly* 15 (January–April 1951).

Irwin, Leonard B. *Pacific Railways and Nationalism in the Canadian-American Northwest, 1845–1873*. Philadelphia: University of Pennsylvania Press, 1939.

Knowles, Valerie. *From Telegrapher to Titan: The Life of William C. Van Horne*. Toronto: Dundurn, 2004.

Lai, David Chuenyan. *Chinatowns: Towns within Cities in Canada*. Vancouver: UBC Press, 1988.

Lamb, W. Kaye. *History of the Canadian Pacific Railway*. New York: Macmillan, 1977.

Macdonald, Duncan George Forbes. *British Columbia and Vancouver's Island: Comprising a Description of These Dependencies*. London: Longman, Greene, Longman, Roberts and Green, 1862.

MacLaren, Roy. *Commissions High: Canada in London, 1870–1971*. Montreal and Kingston: McGill-Queen's University Press, 2006.

Macleod, Rod. *Sam Steele: A Biography*. Edmonton: University of Alberta Press, 2018.

Macnaughtan, S. "Lord Strathcona: A Sketch." *Cornhill Magazine*, March 1914.

Matthews, R.G. "Life in the Mounted Police." *Scarlet and Gold*, 3rd annual, 1921.

McDonald, Donna. *Lord Strathcona: A Biography of Donald Alexander Smith.* Toronto: Dundurn, 2002.

McDougall, John. *George Millward McDougall: The Pioneer, Patriot and Missionary.* Toronto: William Briggs, 1888.

McKee, Bill, and Georgeen Klassen. *Trail of Iron: The CPR and the Birth of the West.* Vancouver: Douglas & McIntyre, 1983.

McMicking, Thomas. *Overland from Canada to British Columbia.* Edited by Joanne Leduc. Vancouver: UBC Press, 1981.

Moberly, Walter. *The Rocks and Rivers of British Columbia.* London: H. Blacklock, 1885.

Mole, Rich. *The Chilcotin War: A Tale of Death and Reprisal.* Victoria: Heritage House, 2009.

Moore, Christopher. *1867: How the Fathers Made a Deal.* Toronto: McClelland & Stewart, 1998.

Morris, Alexander. *The Treaties of Canada with the Indians of Manitoba and the North-West Territories, including the Negotiations on Which They Were Based, and Other Information Relating Thereto.* Toronto: Belfords, Clarke, 1880; Willing & Williamson, 1880.

Morton, James. *In the Sea of Sterile Mountains: The Chinese in British Columbia.* Vancouver: J.J. Douglas, 1976.

"Nobody Knows Him: Lhatŝ'aŝʔin and the Chilcotin War." Great Unsolved Mysteries in Canadian History. 2016. https://www.canadianmysteries.ca/sites/klatsassin/home/indexen.html. A collection of all the primary documents related to the Chilcotin affair.

Oliver, Frank. "The Blackfeet Indian Treaty." *Maclean's Magazine*, March 15, 1931.

Ormsby, Margaret. *British Columbia: A History.* Vancouver: Macmillan, 1958.

Pettit, Sydney G. "Judge Begbie in Action: The Establishment of Law and Preservation of Order in British Columbia." *British Columbia Historical Quarterly* 11, no. 2 (April 1947).

Pope, Joseph. *Memoirs of the Right Honourable Sir John Alexander Macdonald*. Vol. 2. London: Edward Arnold, 1894.

Ray, Arthur J. *I Have Lived Here Since the World Began: An Illustrated History of Canada's Native People*. Toronto: Key Porter, 1996.

Roberts, Morley. *The Western Avernus: or, Toil and Travel in Further North America*. London: Smith, Elder, 1887.

Robinson, Noel. "Blazing Trails in B.C." *Maclean's Magazine*, January 1, 1924.

Rosen, William. *The Most Powerful Idea in the World: A Story of Steam, Industry, and Invention*. New York: Random House, 2010.

Ross, J. Andrew, and Andrew D. Smith, eds. *Canada's Entrepreneurs: From the Fur Trade to the 1929 Stock Market Crash*. Toronto: University of Toronto Press, 2011.

Rylatt, R.M. *Surveying the Canadian Pacific: Memoir of a Railroad Pioneer*. With a foreword by William Kittredge. Salt Lake City: University of Utah Press, 1991.

Sandoz, Mari. *The Buffalo Hunters: The Story of the Hide Men*. Lincoln: University of Nebraska Press, 1978.

Sandström, Gosta E. *The History of Tunnelling: Underground Workings through the Ages*. London: Barrie and Rockliff, 1963.

Shaw, Charles Aeneas. *Tales of a Pioneer Surveyor*. Edited by Raymond Hull. Toronto: Longman, 1970.

Smith, Keith D., ed. *Strange Visitors: Documents in Indigenous–Settler Relations in Canada from 1876*. Toronto: University of Toronto Press, 2014.

Steele, Samuel Benfield. *Forty Years in Canada: Reminiscences of the Great North-West with Some Account of His Service in South Africa*. New York: Dodd, Mead & Company, 1915.

Stewart, Robert. *Sam Steele: Lion of the Frontier*. Regina: Centax, 1999.

Stonechild, Blair, and Bill Waiser. *Loyal till Death: Indians and the North-West Rebellion.* Calgary: Fifth House, 1997.

Stubbs, Roy St. George. "Sir Matthew Baillie Begbie." *Manitoba Historical Society Transactions*, ser. 3, no. 25 (1968–69). https://www.mhs.mb.ca/docs/transactions/3/begbie_mb.shtml.

Teillet, Jean. *The North-West Is Our Mother: The Story of Louis Riel's People, the Métis Nation.* Toronto: HarperCollins, 2019.

Touchie, Rodger D. *Bear Child: The Life and Times of Jerry Potts.* Victoria: Heritage House, 2008.

Van Horne, William. "Sir William Van Horne." *Cornhill Magazine*, January–June 1916.

Van Horne, William C. *Van Horne Letter Book.* No. 1: *1882–1883.* South Yarra, Australia: Leopold Classic Library, 2015.

Wade, Mark Sweeten. *The Overlanders of '62.* Edited by John Hosie. Victoria: Charles F. Banfield, 1931.

Waite, P.B. "Pope, John Henry." In *Dictionary of Canadian Biography*, vol. 11. Toronto: University of Toronto, 1982.

Wheeler, A.O. *The Selkirk Range.* Vol. 1. Ottawa, 1905.

Whyte, Robert. *Whyte's 1847 Famine Ship Diary: The Journey of an Irish Coffin Ship.* Edited by James J. Mangan. Cork, Ireland: Mercier Press, 1994.

Wickberg, Edgar, et al. *From China to Canada: A History of the Chinese Communities in Canada.* Toronto: McClelland and Stewart, 1982.

Willison, John. *Reminiscences, Political and Personal.* Toronto: McClelland and Stewart, 1919.

Willson, Beckles. *The Life of Lord Strathcona and Mount Royal.* Toronto: Cassell, 1915.

Willson, Beckles. *Lord Strathcona: The Story of His Life.* London: Methuen, 1902.

Wilson, Thomas E. *Trail Blazer of the Canadian Rockies.* Edited by Hugh A. Dempsey. Calgary: Glenbow-Alberta Institute, 1972.

Wolseley, Garnet. "Narrative of the Red River Expedition by an Officer of
the Expeditionary Force." *Blackwood's Edinburgh Magazine* 108 (December
1870) and 109 (February 1871).

Wong, Dukesang. *The Diary of Dukesang Wong: A Voice from Gold Mountain.*
Edited by David McIlwraith. Translated by Wanda Joy Hoe. Vancouver:
Talonbooks, 2020.

Woodcock, George. *Gabriel Dumont: The Métis Chief and His Lost World.*
Edmonton: Hurtig, 1975.

Woods, A. "Digging the Ditch in '08." *Western Producer*, March 1, 1973.

Young, Carolyn Ann. *The Glory of Ottawa: Canada's First Parliament
Buildings.* Montreal and Kingston: McGill-Queen's University Press, 1995.

FURTHER READING

———

Archive.org and Google Books, among other sites associated with universities, have digitized many old books, as well as historical newspaper archives and modern reprints. The wealth of information available is astonishing and easy to access, although a subscription is sometimes required. For historical newspaper articles go to the Library of Congress at https://chroniclingamerica.loc.gov/; Historic Newspapers at https://www.historic-newspapers.com; or Newspaper Archive at https://newspaperarchive.com.

For a general-interest overview of the Canadian Pacific Railway that is much more focused on the details of the railway negotiations, arguments and finances, see *History of the Canadian Pacific Railway* by W. Kaye Lamb (Macmillan, 1977). A good illustrated account of the railway's creation is *Trail of Iron* by Bill McKee and Georgeen Klassen (Douglas & McIntyre, 1983). For a great collection of articles and documents related to the CPR over the years, see "Canadian Pacific Railway" at http://www.okthepk.ca/dataCprSiding/articles/articles.htm.

For a general-interest economic history from an Indigenous perspective, see *I Have Lived Here Since the World Began* by Arthur Ray (Key Porter, 1996).

For an overview of the culture and history of Indigenous peoples across northern North America, see Olive Patricia Dickason's *Canada's First Nations: A History of Founding Peoples from Earliest Times* (Oxford University Press, 2008).

For an entertaining yet thorough biography of John A. Macdonald during the railway years, see Richard Gwyn's *Nation Maker; Sir John A. Macdonald: His Life, Our Times* (Doubleday, 2011).

For a chilling chronology of the diseases, mismanagement and general mistreatment of Indigenous Plains people during the railway era, see James Daschuk's *Clearing the Plains: Disease, Politics of Starvation, and the Loss of Indigenous Life* (University of Regina Press, 2019). This is an important if narrowly focused book, not to be passed over, despite its disturbing topic.

For a more detailed window into Dukesang Wong's life, see *The Diary of Dukesang Wong*, edited by David McIlwraith; it is the only first-hand account by a Chinese railway worker. See also the Foundation to Commemorate the Chinese Railroad Workers in Canada's website, The Ties That Bind, www.mhso.ca/tiesthatbind.

For more information on the enigmatic Van Horne, see Valerie Knowles, *From Telegrapher to Titan: The Life of William C. Van Horne* (Toronto: Dundurn, 2004).

For more information on Louis Riel and the North-West Rebellion, see Jean Teillet's *The North-West Is Our Mother: The Story of Louis Riel's People, the Métis Nation* (Toronto: HarperCollins, 2019).

For more information on Crowfoot, see Hugh Dempsey's *Crowfoot: Chief of the Blackfeet* (Edmonton: Hurtig, 1976).

For information on the history of Black immigration in the West, visit the BC Black History Awareness Society at https://bcblackhistory.ca.

For more information on steam power and the Industrial Revolution, see William Rosen's *The Most Powerful Idea in the World: A Story of Steam, Industry, and Invention* (New York: Random House, 2010).

ACKNOWLEDGEMENTS

———

For a variety of reasons, *Dominion* was a challenging and difficult project. Owing to the sheer quantity of research material I had to wade through to discover my narrative of early Canada and the sensitive nature of some of the topics and events in this time period, I wasn't even sure I wanted to tackle such a project at this point in time. John Pearce convinced me that this sequel-of-sorts to *The Company* needed to be written. There are times when I cursed him for doing so, but now that the manuscript is complete, I'm glad he did. Many thanks to him and Chris Casuccio at Westwood Creative Artists for their ongoing support. Thanks also to the Canada Council for the Arts for a project grant. And thanks too to Bryan White of Bow Media in Banff (www.bowmedia.ca) for updating my author photo.

Once again, I was pleased to work with the excellent team at Doubleday Canada, who dedicated their skills and insight into transforming my manuscript into another beautiful book. It all started and finished with Doubleday Canada senior editor Tim Rostron, who was enthusiastic about the project from the outset. Copyeditor Shaun Oakey again deftly applied his encyclopedic historical knowledge and eye for nipping repetition in the bud to the manuscript as a whole, as well as his unerring ability to catch minor dyslexic discrepancies in my version of historical quotes and the real thing. Proofreader Gillian Watts gave the manuscript yet another thorough and thoughtful review, raised some further questions and caught additional repetitions missed by the eyes that preceded hers. Andrew Roberts designed the dramatic cover and clear and helpful maps, and correlated the design to match that of *The Company*. Angela Sahi helped track down historical images of high enough resolution to put into print. Meanwhile, managing editor Maria Golikova kept us all on track, coordinating everyone's input with her schedules and deadline reminders, and turning her eye to the challenging area of new and old Indigenous names.

Last but certainly not least, a big shout-out to my wife, Nicky Brink—I couldn't have finished this project without her. Her keen editorial eye helped restructure some particularly difficult sections in the first few chapters. She also cracked the whip, spurring me into action during the final phases of the project when my energy and enthusiasm were flagging, and ensuring I answered all my emails instead of going on a mountain bike ride.

INDEX

———

© Bow Media

STEPHEN R. BOWN is the author of eleven books on the history of exploration, science and ideas, including the medical mystery of scurvy, the Treaty of Tordesillas and the lives of Captain George Vancouver and Roald Amundsen. His books have been published in many English-speaking territories and translated into nine languages. He has won the BC Book Prize, the Alberta Book Award and the William Mills Prize for Non-Fiction Polar Books. His previous book, *The Company: The Rise and Fall of the Hudson's Bay Empire*, was a national bestseller and winner of the 2021 National Business Book Award and the J.W. Dafoe Book Prize. Born in Ottawa, Bown now lives near Banff in the Canadian Rockies.